Owning Performance
        Performing Ownership

OWNING PERFORMANCE |
PERFORMING OWNERSHIP

Literary Property and the
Eighteenth-Century
British Stage

Jane Wessel

University of Michigan Press   ANN ARBOR

For questions or permissions, please contact um.press.
perms@umich.edu

Published in the United States of America by
the University of Michigan Press
Manufactured in the United States of America
Printed on acid-free paper

First published July 2022

A CIP catalog record for this book is available from the
British Library.

ISBN 978-0-472-13307-9 (hardcover : alk. paper)
ISBN 978-0-472-22025-0 (ebook)

Acknowledgments

I am exceptionally grateful for the support I have received while researching and writing this book. I would not have been able to start or finish without guidance and support from mentors, colleagues, and friends. My mentors at the University of Delaware saw this project through its earliest iterations. First and foremost is Matt Kinservik, who oversaw the project's development. Matt pushed and encouraged me at the some of the hardest moments and shared in my excitement at archival finds. I would not have come to take such joy in theater history without him. Siobhan Carroll and Julian Yates were generous mentors and smart readers, always guiding my thinking forward. Numerous other faculty at Delaware supported me, whether by offering suggestions for the project or by helping me into a career that has enabled me to continue research and writing: thank you to Melissa Ianetta, Miranda Wilson, Ed Larkin, Joan DelFattore, John Ernest, Iain Crawford, Tim Spaulding, and the late Charlie Robinson and Don Mell. Certainly not least, friendship and writing groups with fellow graduate students—especially Kyle Meikle, Jordan Howell, Petra Clark, Rachael Green-Howard, and Matt Rinkevich—were sustaining.

I have been grateful in the years since to have found academic community in the American Society for Eighteenth Century Studies, and especially the Theatre and Performance Studies Caucus. Chelsea Phillips, Mattie Burkert, and Leah Benedict have been stalwart academic companions and friends, as we've exchanged drafts, turned to each other for advice, and shared many a conference dinner. Leslie Ritchie read the earliest version of the manuscript in its entirety and helped me envision how to turn it into a book. At Austin Peay State University, friendship and writing exchanges with Mercy Cannon helped me stay connected to my research while carrying a heavy teaching load. At my current institution, the United States Naval Academy, I have been grateful to find a supportive and energetic community in the English department, leaving me with more names than I can list here; in particular, though, conversations with Nancy Mace and Jason Shaffer have helped me think through this project as well as future research directions. I am also grateful for feedback, advice, and camaraderie from Tonya Moutray, Amelia Dale, Doug Murray, Julia Fawcett, Fiona Ritchie, Diana Solomon, Emily

Friedman, and Tita Chico. Many more colleagues have inspired me through their work, cited throughout these pages.

Research for this book has been supported by numerous universities, libraries, and organizations. At Austin Peay State University, the College of Arts and Letters provided research travel support, helping me to spend a month at the Chawton House Library. The United States Naval Academy has generously provided funding that has made writing, revisions, and image permissions possible through Junior Naval Academy Research Council grants and a Volgenau Faculty Fellowship. The archival research so central to this project has been supported through fellowships from Yale University's Lewis Walpole Library; the Folger Shakespeare Library; the Houghton Library at Harvard University; and the Chawton House Library. The American Society for Eighteenth-Century Studies awarded me an Aubrey L. Williams Research Travel Fellowship, enabling me to conduct research in York and London. Thank you to the librarians at each of these places, as well as at the British Library, the Victoria & Albert Museum, and especially the York Minster Library. Additional thanks go to the libraries that have allowed me to reproduce images from their collections: the Yale Center for British Art, the Lewis Walpole Library, the York Minster Library, the Metropolitan Museum of Art, and the National Art Library at the Victoria & Albert Museum. Portions of two chapters were previously published as articles. Part of chapter 1 appeared in *Theatre Survey* and is reprinted with permission of Cambridge University Press. Part of chapter 2 appeared in *The Eighteenth Century: Theory and Interpretation* and is reprinted with permission of the University of Pennsylvania Press (*The Eighteenth Century*, Vol. 60, No. 1 Copyright 2019 University of Pennsylvania Press. All rights reserved). I am grateful to both journals for allowing me to reproduce this material here.

My sincere thanks go to my editor, LeAnn Fields, for supporting this project, and to Flannery Wise, Marcia LaBrenz, Richard Isomaki, Paula Newcomb, and the staff at the University of Michigan Press for seeing it through from manuscript to book. Thank you, in particular, to the two anonymous reviewers for taking the time to read the manuscript so carefully. Their feedback was detailed, incisive, and generous, undoubtedly making the book much stronger.

Finally, to the friends and family who have never doubted that I could do this, and who have always provided joy that transcends the work we do: thank you to Maryanne Felter and Kris Willumsen; Jan Wessel and Colleen Farley; Jack and Abby Wessel; Elizabeth Downs; Julia Pompetti; Kate Hunt and Mike Gruszczynski; and, of course, Feste.

Contents

Digital materials related to this title can be found on the Fulcrum platform via the following citable URL: https://doi.org/10.3998/mpub.12124390

Introduction

Eighteenth-century actor-playwright Charles Macklin was tenacious about controlling the performance of his 1759 farce, *Love à la Mode*. When he caught wind that provincial managers were preparing to stage the unprinted farce, he confronted them by writing threatening letters, assuring them that he would "put the Law against every offender of it respecting my property, in full force."[1] Knowing Macklin's reputation for litigation and even violence, managers often called off their performances. Yet on one occasion, Macklin received an unexpectedly audacious response from a country manager: "*Your* 'Love à-la-mode,' Sir! I'm not going to play *your* Love à-la-mode; I'll play my *own* Love à-la-mode: I have twenty Love à-la-modes. I could write a Love à-la-mode every day in the week, I could write three hundred and sixty-*six* Love à-la-modes in *a* year."[2] The manager's response is shocking, since anyone remotely connected to the theater world in eighteenth-century England knew how protective Macklin was of the farce. The response is all the more shocking for its flippant attitude toward originality, creative labor, and textual production. The manager's mocking response—both playful and caustic—raises serious questions about textual authenticity, authorship, and ownership. If the manager had seen Macklin's farce performed and then created his own version from memory, was it a new work? Or perhaps the manager had surreptitiously obtained a manuscript copy of the farce and was suggesting that the performance itself made the work his own? The manager's claims about the ease of writing a farce like *Love à la Mode*—a sentiment mirrored by his excessive repetition of the farce's title—diminishes the stature of the dramatic "author" and suggests the tenuousness of ownership within the realm of theater. He treats the popular farce as a sort of common property, free for modification and performance. And indeed, there was some truth to his belief. While authors enjoyed the right to own their works for the first time following the passage of the 1710 Copyright Act, this law protected only print, offering no protection for the medium of performance. This anecdote points to one of the major challenges facing eighteenth-century playwrights: without legal protection for the performance of plays, dramatists were unable to assert ownership of their works in the same way that print-based authors could. During an era when authorship was increasingly tied to ownership, this limitation in literary property law seriously affected the nature of dramatic authorship.

Eighteenth-century dramatists were preoccupied by literary property. Macklin was certainly the most tenacious in this respect, but one would be hard pressed to find a dramatist in the second half of the century who was not thinking about his or her ownership of plays in one way or another. Elizabeth Inchbald, for instance, was concerned about the effect of unauthorized performances on her authorial reputation. When she suspected that Yorkshire manager Tate Wilkinson had reconstructed a version (or a "jumble") of *Such Things Are* (1787) from memory, she apparently wrote to him to say that "she would advertise [his] production as a flimsy, disgraceful imposture."[3] Richard Brinsley Sheridan, meanwhile, followed Macklin's example in keeping his plays out of print "in order to preserve his language from mutilation, and prevent the play being produced at any theatre where the proper attention could not be paid to its 'getting up.'"[4] Indeed, the opening anecdote about Macklin is nestled into the playwright John O'Keeffe's 1826 autobiography, *Recollections of the Life of John O'Keeffe*. As he discusses the unauthorized performances of his own plays, O'Keeffe deploys stories about Macklin intentionally to draw readers' attention to the economic and legal situation of dramatic authors. Although O'Keeffe was not particularly assertive when it came to his own plays, he was aware of how the limitations of literary property affected not only his profit, but also his artistic control, and he uses his *Recollections* to distance himself from the error-laden derivatives of his works that appeared both in print and in performance:

> In justice to myself, it may not be amiss to take some little notice of the great injury done to the reputation of a dramatic author, (and none other can be injured in the same way,) by the circulation of spurious printed copies of his plays through the world. My five Haymarket-pieces locked up in MS. have been repeatedly printed and published surreptitiously, (as well as those of other authors,) and are full of the most glaring errors.[5]

In this dense passage, O'Keeffe gestures to a complex chain of events resulting from literary property law. Theater managers who wished to be the
exclusive suppliers of particular plays bought the right to print the works
alongside the right to first performance; they often kept these plays out of
print to deny other theaters access to them. As a result, many plays, including five of O'Keeffe's plays that Haymarket manager George Colman the
Elder had bought, were being "locked up" in manuscript form, forcing other
theater managers and publishers to obtain or recreate the texts by surrepti-
tious means. The result of this situation, O'Keeffe argues, was piratical print-
ings and performances "full of the most glaring errors." Especially striking
in this passage is O'Keeffe's statement that "none other can be injured in
the same way." In a deceptively casual but incredibly important parenthetical aside, O'Keeffe clearly asserts what nearly all modern scholarship on
eighteenth-century authorship has yet failed to recognize: dramatic authorship was different.

Dramatists were working in a vastly different economy than their print-
based contemporaries. They were also navigating a different legal landscape.
Evolving literary property laws did not protect the primary medium in
which dramatists published their works: performance. The first law to grant
dramatists control and profit from the repeated performance of their works
was not passed until 1833, more than a century after the Copyright Act.[6] And
in the many studies of proprietary authorship, in which scholars have recognized that this was a period when authorship was increasingly being defined
in terms of ownership, no one has yet asked what happens to the idea of the
"author" when dramatists' ability to "own" performance trailed far behind
novelists' and poets' ability to own their printed books.

This study asks what happened to the medium of performance, and to
those authors who published their works primarily through this medium,
during a period when the legal systems that rewarded and regulated literary production were solidifying around print. I focus on the years between
the passage of the 1710 Copyright Act and the 1833 Dramatic Literary Property Act—a period during which performance was a culturally dominant
mode and highly valued within the entertainment market, but was valued
differently by the law. During a period that offered authors the right to own
their printed works, we might expect that dramatists would embrace print
publication. Yet, as my work reveals, dramatists responded to the lack of
legal protection for performance by turning away from print and embracing
the affordances of performance—especially its unfixity and ephemerality. In
order to compensate for their lack of legal protection, dramatists made their

works less accessible and less easily reproducible. One of the most effective ways to do this was by keeping plays out of print, making it more difficult for theaters to obtain and produce the play without the author's involvement. Macklin was the first major playwright to make this move, and he made a show of doing so. Macklin set a precedent, with playwrights, and managers, including Samuel Foote, Colman, and Sheridan, following suit. But as the opening anecdote illustrates, theaters found ways to obtain or recreate popular texts. As a result, some playwrights, most notably Foote, went further, making their own bodies integral to the production of their works. In a move that anticipated current debates surrounding the recreation of performance art, Foote commodified his physical presence, making his relationship with the audience a crucial part of his productions.[7] In doing so, he, and others like him, relied on the singularity of their bodies and their celebrity to ensure that only they could reperform their works. These authorial strategies signify a larger cultural shift: playwrights, and especially actor-playwrights, turned away from print, the medium that enabled their productions to circulate independently of the author. Instead, the theatrical community embraced performance, the medium that bound the production to the producer, guaranteeing some degree of control or "ownership" of performance.

Dramatists performed the ownership they lacked in law. Some, like Macklin, did this by asserting their property rights as loudly and as widely as they could, creating a customary respect for theatrical property and setting precedents that would eventually become law. Others "performed ownership" by literally performing their own plays, physically tying the works to their bodies. Taken together, these strategies created a culture of ephemerality that sharply contrasts with the increased value put on the printing of plays during the Restoration era immediately preceding it. Although the concept of ephemerality is controversial in performance studies, it is also useful, for it was the performance event's inability to be reproduced en masse (in contrast to print) that playwrights found empowering. This project joins Diana Taylor and Rebecca Schneider in resisting the idea that performance is "that which 'vanishes,'" instead focusing on the ways that theater professionals strategically embraced the medium—including its features, like ephemerality, that are often spoken of in terms of loss.[8] I define a "culture of ephemerality" as a theatrical culture that resisted the march toward print and instead existed primarily in performance. We need to understand the eighteenth century in this way, or we risk making arguments about the decline of drama, in terms of both literary quality and cultural value.[9] It was in playwrights', and especially actor-playwrights', proprietary interest to insist on the primacy of performance and assert drama's difference from the printed book.

Owning Performance examines the ways that dramatists celebrated and manipulated the affordances of performance, its embodiment and its existence in time, to define their authorship and achieve proprietary control over their works. To understand the conditions that created this culture of ephemerality, this introduction outlines the development of legal systems for rewarding and regulating literary production, focusing on their print-centric nature. The failure of property law to account for the medium of performance meant that other, sometimes conflicting, modes of ownership within the theaters governed what happened to a play in production and in print. Thus, I continue by tracing the life cycle of a play in performance and print, focusing on the various modes of ownership that shaped this life cycle. Finally, I introduce the strategies playwrights developed to "perform ownership" that they lacked in law. In examining the relationship between literary property and performance, this book answers three central questions: How did literary property and the economics of the theater affect the practice and perception of dramatic authorship? How did the theater intervene in the legal and conceptual development of intellectual property? And how did a shift away from print impact the ways eighteenth-century drama has been preserved and studied? Looking at theatrical culture as one of strategic ephemerality asks us to open up our archive, expand our methodologies, and understand theatrical culture during the period in a new way—a way that resists narratives about the cultural supremacy of print.

THE SUPREMACY OF PRINT:
LEGAL SYSTEMS AND LITERARY CULTURE

The eighteenth century has long been studied as "the period in which print was becoming the dominant, conventional mode of transmitting what we consider literary and academic writings."[10] While scholarship in the last few decades has challenged the dominance of print culture, focusing especially on manuscript culture's continued importance throughout the century, less has been written about the medium of performance, which persisted as a powerful and profitable mode of publication.[11] I use the term "publication" in its broadest sense of making ideas public, rather than narrowly equating publication with print. Performance functioned as a way of producing knowledge and circulating literature. Yet performance and publication had a complicated legal relationship in the late seventeenth and eighteenth centuries, because while performance undoubtedly disseminated ideas (sometimes including seditious or obscene ideas), it lacked the tangibility and fixity of print publication. As print increasingly became tied to state power and legal institutions, the unfixity of performance made it difficult to regulate and reward.[12] Thus when Parliament passed the Stage Licensing Act in 1737, it created a law that regulated dramatic performance not through the performance itself, but through the preperformance review of dramatic manuscripts and the regulation of actors' bodies.[13] They approached performance, in other words, through ancillary media. Regulation was one realm in which the intangible nature of performance eluded the state's efforts at control. Rewarding authors with property rights was another.[14]

When Parliament passed the world's first copyright act in 1710, An Act for the Encouragement of Learning, members were thinking only about the physical reproduction of printed books. This is unsurprising, for the idea for the act had been brought to Parliament by the Stationers' Company, the London guild regulating the book trade. The company, whose power and monopoly over the book trade grew more tenuous as the print market multiplied, sought legal reinforcement of its long-standing privileges, particularly as Scottish and Irish booksellers were reprinting works registered to stationers.[15] The Copyright Act was motivated by booksellers as an extension of the rights granted by the Stationers' Company. From its inception, then, it was designed to protect print reproduction; it was not about a broad formulation of literary or intellectual property in the way we think about these concepts today. The act directed that

> the Author of any Book or books already printed who hath not transferred to any other the copy or copies of such Book or Books share or shares thereof or the Bookseller or Booksellers printer or printers or other person or persons who hath or have purchased or acquired the copy or copies of any Book or Books in order to print or reprint the same shall have the sole right and liberty of printing such Book and Books.[16]

Its language focused exclusively on books, booksellers, and printers and did not provide protection for other media like manuscript, visual arts, or performance.

I should pause here to explain how I am using terms, particularly given the disconnect between legal rights that existed at the time and the discourse surrounding them. While "copyright" refers to the actual legal right to reproduce a work afforded to authors and publishers, the phrase "literary property," while not technically a term of law, was regularly used during the period. As Meredith McGill succinctly puts it, "Literary property could refer to rights claims and violations that fell outside the formal copyright system . . . ; to rights that advocates hoped would ultimately be embraced by the statutes and defended by the courts (such as rights of translation or dramatic performance); or to the general and controversial concept of property in ideas."[17] Throughout this book, I echo eighteenth-century uses of "literary property" in instances where I am referring to the more capacious concept rather than the formal copyright system.

For as narrow as the Copyright Act was, the discourses that developed over the century to strengthen and extend copyright protection were much more capacious, invoking the inherent and perpetual rights of the author. Booksellers were dissatisfied with the temporal limits established by the Copyright Act, and after their copyrights expired, they began to argue for a perpetual common-law copyright. In doing so, they focused their rhetoric on authors' rights instead of booksellers' rights. These rights, they argued, derived from an author's property in his own person, personality, and original invention.[18] Deploying metaphors of landownership and drawing on Lockean theories of property, they developed the idea of proprietary authorship, leading to a strong cultural connection between authorship and ownership.[19] As eighteenth-century playwright and copyright lawyer Arthur Murphy pointed out, booksellers' language was disingenuous. In his notes for *Millar v. Taylor* (1769), Murphy mocks booksellers' celebration of "authorial genius":

> He [the bookseller] begins to talk of a Common Law right, and says, he has bought a perpetual property. After having made a hard bargain, his language then is, "pray be tender of the Author, the man of genius and invention. Let the work of the mind be protected."—And thus, while his own self-interest is working at the bottom, the Author is held forth ostensibly: encouragement is craved for learning, that the bookseller may reap the profit.[20]

The image of the author was being manipulated for ends that did not always serve the author.[21] Nevertheless, the rhetoric was extraordinarily powerful. By 1759, Edward Young declared in his *Conjectures on Original Composition* that "property alone can confer the noble title of an *Author*."[22] Within the public imagination, "ownership" was becoming a defining feature of authorship. As Mark Rose writes, "a representation of authorship based on notions of property, originality, and personality" developed, contributing to the Romantic image of the solitary genius.[23] Once the idea of author-as-owner was established as a cultural norm, there was no reason for these authors to think of their ownership rights as being limited to print reproduction.

The rhetoric surrounding the Copyright Act was more capacious than the act itself, leading authors and artists publishing their work in other media to feel excluded from the protection that their original productions seemed to warrant. The disconnect between broad cultural ideals about proprietary authorship and the practical limits of the law left those publishing their works in nonprint media in a vulnerable position, without the full rewards of their authorship. In the art world, William Hogarth responded to pirated reproductions of his popular paintings and engravings by leading a group of artists to petition Parliament for the Engravers' Act (1735). This was the first piece of legislation after the Copyright Act that granted protection to something other than printed books. As Ronan Deazley has argued, the artists' petition located the value of an artistic work not in the physical page it was printed on, but in the labor and artistic conception of the piece.[24] Such thinking would, in the long term, contribute to modern ideas about intellectual property. In the theaters, too, playwrights fought for control over the reproduction and circulation of their works in performance. Unlike booksellers' and artists' arguments for copyright protection, playwrights' struggles for such rights happened most often outside of the law courts, although there were some significant legal cases and injunctions against unauthorized performances. Playwrights controlled their works through the clever manipulation of print publication and their own performing bodies.

It is curious, given interest in literary cultures that existed alongside print culture, that scholarship on England's earliest literary property law pays little attention to other media. In spite of the fact that the medium of performance continues to be a determining and challenging factor in intellectual property law today, scholarship on England's earliest literary property laws tends to pay it little attention.[25] Histories of copyright focus almost exclusively on the printed word.[26] Works that specifically address the development of "performance copyright," or an author's right to control and profit from the production of his or her works onstage, meanwhile, typically focus on the nineteenth century, paying little attention to the groundwork laid by eighteenth-century dramatists and managers.[27] In her essay on the Dramatic Literary Property Act (1833), Isabella Alexander mentions a few cases in the late eighteenth century but quickly moves into the nineteenth century.[28] Deazley briefly mentions performance in *Rethinking Copyright*, arguing that the "origins" of "the exclusive right to perform a work in public . . . lie in the mid-nineteenth century," with the 1833 act.[29] Even Jessica Litman's essay on the history of performance copyright in the *Berkeley Technology Law Journal* speeds through the eighteenth century, dedicating only three paragraphs to the years between 1710 and 1833.[30] The most significant recent investigation into the relationship between copyright and performance—Derek Miller's *Copyright and the Value of Performance, 1770–1911*—considers the case of

Macklin, but moves from there into the nineteenth century.[31] It is certainly true that very few court cases took up the issue of performance copyright during the eighteenth century. Yet, as McGill has argued about literary property, "The law often lags behind business practices, and legal discourse is often at a considerable remove from ordinary citizens' assumptions about the world they inhabit."[32] By beginning in the nineteenth century with concrete legal changes, current scholarship misses nearly a century of shifting discourse.

This book reconsiders proprietary authorship with a focus on the medium of performance. Drawing on the type of work that Margaret Ezell has done for manuscript culture, I ask how dramatists played "the 'game' of authorship" during a period when performance was a highly profitable, but legally unprotected mode of publication.[33] In thinking about this game of authorship—or how authors sold and circulated their works, targeted specific audiences, and developed professional personae—it is imperative to broaden our study, approaching dramatists as professionals who had to maneuver between print and performance, two media that sometimes supported and sometimes undermined each other. Printing a work gave dramatists copyright protection and thus the sort of ownership that novelists and poets enjoyed. But printing their plays also made them susceptible to unauthorized performances. The Copyright Act, by protecting one medium that playwrights worked in but not the other, created a rift between the two media, prompting dramatists to turn away from print and thus unintentionally exclude themselves from literary recognition and literary authorship. During a period when authorship and ownership were intertwined, the effect of the act's print focus was to yoke not only ownership to print, but also authorship to print, edging other media out of literary culture.

THE LIFE OF A PLAY:
FROM PERFORMANCE TO PRINT AND BACK

The print-centric nature of legal systems and their failure to account for performance greatly affected the media forms through which a play was published. Indeed, ownership—whether based on laws or on customs of the theater—affected all stages of a play's life cycle. What was the relationship between print and performance in a play's public life? What was the playwright's relationship to his or her play? And how did this differ between London and provincial theaters? The answers to these questions change over the eighteenth century and depend not just on literary property law, but also on changing customs and practices within the theaters. Let's begin at the point at which the dramatist has had a play accepted to be performed in one of the patent theaters. London only had two legally sanctioned theaters: the patents that Charles II had granted Thomas Killigrew and William Davenant during the Restoration era gave two theaters exclusive rights to perform legitimate, spoken drama, and this duopoly was reinforced in 1737 with the Stage Licensing Act. In a city with only two legally sanctioned theaters, in which much of the repertory was made up of stock plays or (as new playwrights lamented) plays and adaptations by the managers, having a play accepted for performance was itself a great feat.[34] Unlike early modern playwrights, who would likely be attached to a particular company, nearly all eighteenth-century playwrights were freelancers. Once the play was accepted, the playwright would earn an author's benefit on the third, sixth, and ninth nights.[35] If the play closed after only a few nights, the author might earn close to nothing. If it succeeded, the reward could be phenomenal.[36] A successful play might live on in the repertory of one or more theaters for decades, generating an immense amount of revenue for the theaters for years to come. The playwright's remuneration, by contrast, stopped with the initial run. There were neither additional payments for subsequent runs nor royalties when a new theater—metropolitan or provincial—picked up the play. There were no permissions needed or authorial oversight required. The playwright's role in the play's stage life was, in most cases, over.

Beginning in the Restoration period, the dramatist could make an additional sum of money by printing his or her play. As Paulina Kewes and Judith Milhous and Robert Hume have argued, this was a major innovation, and it enabled playwrights not only to earn additional profit (a typical payment from the publisher was anywhere from £15 or £20 early in the century to £100 later on), but also to develop a literary reputation and assert greater aesthetic control over the play text.[37] And indeed, 89 percent of new plays staged between 1660 and 1700 were published, increasing drama's status not just as a seen genre, but as a read one.[38] More fundamentally, it gave playwrights a choice of whether or not to print their plays. This is a choice they never fully lost, although, as I will argue, by the end of the eighteenth century, many playwrights felt pressured into selling their print rights to theater managers.

What became of the play text after the first run? What were the conditions that affected its subsequent performances, its circulation in London and provincial theaters, and its existence or nonexistence in a printed edition? The story that our scholarship has told up to this point can be (reductively) summarized as such: a popular play would typically be printed within a month of its premiere, allowing the play to complete its full run before entering print circulation.[39] While during the Restoration period, the play would be exclusive "property" of a single theater, to be performed only on that stage, by the middle of the eighteenth century, plays were generally considered to be in the public domain for performance as soon as they were printed. Thus, a popular midcentury play would likely exist in printed form (possibly multiple editions) and could be found playing in one or both of the London theaters, as well as in provincial theaters. This narrative produces an image of access, suggesting the free circulation of drama. By this logic, it follows that the popularity of a play and the roles it provided for London's most popular actors would be primary factors in its place in the repertory, in how often it was performed, and in the number of print editions it went through.

Why is it, then, that publication rates began to drop in the latter half of the century? Why was Richard Brinsley Sheridan's *The School for Scandal* (1777), one of the most popular plays of its time and most enduring works of the period, never legally printed during the author's lifetime? Why, when John O'Keeffe decided to print his dramatic works in 1798, did he leave out five of his most well-known pieces? Why did Charles Macklin literally put his *Love à la Mode* manuscript in his coat at the end of each night, refusing to allow the theater to keep a complete copy? And why did the Yorkshire theater manager Tate Wilkinson complain of play manuscripts being kept "under lock and key"?[40] The common answer to these questions has to do with performance rights. In the absence of any legal protections treating performance as a form of property, playwrights and managers attempted to control performances by controlling and limiting theaters' access to play texts. By the second half of the eighteenth century, some playwrights began forgoing print publication for the simple reason that a play in print was widely available for use by theaters in London and around the country. Such widespread print accessibility removed any control they had over its performances and continuing remuneration for their labors.

The urgency for playwrights and managers of creating legal protections for performance—or in their absence, of controlling performance by controlling access to the text—became clear only as other forms of theatrical ownership weakened or outright disappeared over the course of the century. These modes of ownership, which I discuss at greater length in chapter 1, were the division of the repertory (theater companies' royally granted rights to exclusive performance of their repertory of plays) and the custom of part possession (an actor's informal right to exclusive possession of his or her dramatic parts). Each of these forms of ownership, neither of which existed in law, was respected in the Restoration era and into the early eighteenth century. But for reasons I will discuss, each slowly weakened until it eventually no longer existed. Part possession, repertory, and performance copyright affected one another, for this was a theatrical culture in which there was great overlap between actors, playwrights, and managers. In particular, a large number of actor-playwrights during the period wrote plays to provide themselves with dramatic parts. As I argue in the first two chapters, actor-playwrights' desire to be the sole performers of parts they had written for themselves motivated much of their concern about when and where their plays could be performed. These customary forms of ownership—the division of the repertory and the custom of part possession—had made legal language about performance rights unnecessary in the Restoration and early eighteenth century. But their decline left behind a hole: from the middle of the century onward, the use of plays in performance was very much an unregulated territory, causing consternation to those playwrights, managers, and actors who had a stake in performance.

The problems surrounding performance rights in the London theaters were amplified by the steady increase in the number and influence of provincial theaters over the course of the century. Charles Beecher Hogan calculates that by 1800, there were 150 provincial theaters in Britain, 17 of which had royal patents. "Taken in the aggregate," he argues, these theaters "can be considered almost as important as the three great London playhouses."[41] Provincial theaters were quick to perform works from the London repertory and were rarely concerned with what right they had to do so. To understand changing discourses surrounding performance rights, it is necessary to study provincial theaters seriously alongside their London counterparts. Doing so is especially important when considering property and performance rights: given their geographic remove from London, provincial managers were often willing to perform even those works that playwrights and managers were most avidly trying to protect. Moreover, as I will discuss in chapter 4, some of the most forward-looking attitudes toward performance rights developed out of the push and pull between London and the provinces. In paying attention to the relationship between London and provincial stages, this project builds on calls by scholars including Jane Moody and Michael Ragussis to decenter our study of British theater.[42]

The ability of multiple theaters in and out of London to reperform a play after the first run with no fees or permissions needed might seem to be less a loss to authors than to the theaters that had originally staged the works, since authors did not profit from anything after the first run of a new play. And in practical terms, that is true. But these changes occurred alongside changing ideals of proprietary authorship. If multiple theaters were going to profit from the play, why wasn't the author entitled to part of these profits?

This was not a concern raised immediately or by the majority of playwrights. As Hume points out, since there was such a limited market for new plays, dramatists were essentially in a "take it or leave it" position when it came to the payment system.[43] But as the examples above show, by the middle of the century, playwrights from Macklin to Sheridan began leveraging the relative inaccessibility of manuscript (as opposed to print reproduction) to assert control over performance. They were claiming an active and ongoing role in the stage and print lives of their plays. Moreover, many of these figures did so to support multiple proprietary interests, whether their exclusive possession of dramatic parts (as actors) or a monopoly on the performance of particular plays within their theaters (as managers). By the second half of the century, it was no longer a given for playwrights to assume that their wisest move was to sell their print rights to a publisher.

By the end of the eighteenth century, many popular plays existed only in performance and in manuscript circulation. And this presents an important new story about theatrical culture. The story of how eighteenth-century playwrights, managers, and performers dealt with the lack of protection for the repeat performance of dramatic works is one that has not yet been told. These are the stories of this book.

PERFORMING OWNERSHIP: THE UNTOLD STORIES

Understanding the struggle for performance copyright during the eighteenth century requires looking closely at individual dramatists' career choices. For unlike in later centuries, during which negotiations and ownership battles were played out in court cases, these issues early on were played out within the theatrical community. Playwrights negotiated with theater managers, limited print access to their plays, and leveraged their celebrity to gain control over the circulation of their works. They made their strategies known within the theater community, setting precedents and attempting to change managerial attitudes toward use.

For this reason, I take a biographical approach to the subject. Each chapter explores a strategy that playwrights developed to control the use of their works, or a response to these strategies by theater managers, taking a single figure or group of figures as a case study. This approach provides a closer look at how these figures shaped their careers and responded to changing laws and customs within the theaters. It also charts a progression in ideas about the fair use of plays, following the push and pull of playwrights, actors, and managers vying for control over popular plays and dramatic parts. Thus, one chapter builds on another, and though each chapter has a main case study, all are intertwined, for all of the figures in this study worked with or were influenced by one another. In this way, the chapter divisions are organized around professional biographies, but are situated within broader legal and cultural frameworks of the period. This approach sets the book apart from more economically oriented works on the subject, including Julie Stone Peters's *Theatre of the Book*, John Russell Stephens's *The Profession of the Playwright*, and Milhous and Hume's *The Publication of Plays*, which collectively reach many of the same conclusions about trends in play publication and performance agreements, but which do not capture the working life of individual playwrights in the eighteenth-century theaters.[44]

This is a story about playwrights and authorship; but it is equally one about performers and celebrity. For in focusing on the medium of performance as a primary and valuable mode of publishing plays, it is necessary to consider the actors whose bodies were the vehicles for publication. Moreover, as I have suggested above, the proprietary interests of playwrights, actors, and managers were intertwined. This book highlights the interplay of authorship, performance, and celebrity, building on work by Julia Fawcett, Joseph Roach, Emily Hodgson Anderson, Nora Nachumi, and Ellen Donkin.[45] I pay particular attention to the relationship between the creative labor of writing and performing and to the strategic self-fashioning of actors and actresses. Those who were able to conceive of and sell their own celebrity identity as a "tradeable public commodity" gained a great deal of power over their acting careers and public images.[46] Yet actors also traded on their celebrity to further other ends: their writing careers. Calling the period "the age of the actor," prior scholarship has often used the development of celebrity to dismiss the literary productions of the theater.[47] But it was not an either-or game. Actor-playwrights abounded, as theatrical professionals came to realize that their success as an actor might be aided by their own pen, and vice versa. The actor's celebrity and the playwright's aspirations were intertwined. And both roles were tied up with actors' and dramatists' attempts to "own" performance.

To understand these figures' professional lives and the development of new ideas about literary property and performance, I turn not just to plays and thespian biographies, but also to the archival traces of performance and the material remnants of the relationships among theater stakeholders. These include playbills, advertisements, reviews, promptbooks, letters, and contracts. While some of these are digitized, many remain unpublished, residing in archives including the Folger Shakespeare Library, the Lewis Walpole Library, the Harvard Theatre Collection, the York Minster Library, the British Library, and the Victoria & Albert Museum's National Art Library and

Theatre and Performance Collection. In turning to these documents, I treat them as more than sources of historical information. Building on the methodological approach championed by Christopher Balme, Jacky Bratton, and Mark Vareschi and Mattie Burkert, I approach them as documents that both communicated and produced changing ideas about the use of plays in performance.[48] For instance, Tate Wilkinson's personal archive of playbills, held in the York Minster Library, forms the foundation for chapter 4, and I study these bills as "central point[s] of articulation" between the manager and his theatrical publics.[49] What I have found is that from the start to the end of his career, Wilkinson used his playbills to tout his ability to provide provincial audiences with access to unprinted plays. Yet while his early bills celebrate his unauthorized appropriation of plays, dramatic parts, and even performance styles, his later bills literally call particular plays "private property" and advertise the permission he has received from the authors to perform the works. This shift reflects the provincial manager's increasing respect for emergent ideas about performance copyright. As paratheatrical texts, the playbills communicate these ideas to audiences and work to establish them as norms within the theatrical community. This approach to the materials reveals how discourses about theatrical property develop in the interactions between theater professionals and theatrical publics.

The leading characters in this book are Charles Macklin, Samuel Foote, Tate Wilkinson, Elizabeth Inchbald, John O'Keeffe, and, to a lesser extent, Richard Brinsley Sheridan, George Colman the Elder, and Thomas Harris. They are chosen because of their active engagement with property issues. Changing legal systems, managerial policies, and ideas of authorship affected a wealth of playwrights to varying degrees. However, these, more than others, were aware of the effects of property law and theatrical custom on their control over the performance of their works, and they sought to reshape custom through their professional choices.[50] They are not the playwrights who are best remembered today—though this is, perhaps, a by-product of their authorial strategies. But they were among the most famous playwrights and theatrical celebrities of the middle and late eighteenth century. Moreover, they are all figures who held multiple roles in the theaters: Macklin was both actor and playwright; Foote an actor, playwright, and manager; Wilkinson an actor and manager; Inchbald an actress and playwright; O'Keeffe (briefly) an actor and playwright; Sheridan a playwright and manager; and Colman a playwright and manager. This book focuses primarily, though not exclusively, on the second half of the century, when these figures were active. Yet, because their choices were tied to changing legal systems and theatrical customs, including the division of the repertory during the

Restoration, the 1710 Copyright Act, and the 1737 Stage Licensing Act, this project is also about the long eighteenth century in its entirety, beginning with the reopening of the theaters in 1660 and culminating in the Dramatic Literary Property Act of 1833.

The book's structure follows a recognizable pattern in histories of intellectual property. I begin with the artistic creators—playwrights and actors—who developed new strategies for controlling the performance of their work. I shift in the second half of the book to examine the appropriation of these strategies by the figures most poised to benefit from performance rights: theater managers. Chapter 1, "Charles Macklin and the Turn Away from Print," charts the changing modes of theatrical ownership in eighteenth-century England. At the same time that the author's right to own his work was being held up as a crucial incentive for creativity, the actor's customary "right" to permanently possess a set of dramatic parts was quickly waning. Tracing the complex relationships between these modes of ownership, I demonstrate why it was so important for dramatists, and particularly actor-playwrights, whose plays provided them performance vehicles, to be able to own not just the printed publication of their works, but also the performance. This stake in performance prompted Macklin to keep his popular farce, *Love à la Mode* (1759), out of print, setting a precedent that would impact play publication for over half a century. Rather than focus solely on his attempt to control the production of *Love à la Mode*, and his legal case against the magazine publishers who printed the first half of the farce, I argue that his ideas about property developed through his work as both an actor and playwright. Thus, I examine his career more broadly, situating the start of his ownership concerns not with the farce, but rather with his watershed performance of Shylock in the 1741 staging of *The Merchant of Venice* at Drury Lane.

Macklin did not simply withhold *Love à la Mode* from print: he "performed ownership" by publicizing his decision, threatening managers who performed the work without his consent, creating a vengeful and litigious persona, and intentionally eliding his public persona with his most famous part: Shylock. Macklin is remarkable for being the earliest performer not only to recognize performance as an artistic medium requiring legal protection, but to publicly claim the sole right to perform his works. Macklin's nonpublication of *Love à la Mode* set an important precedent, and, following his decision, play publication began to decline. Yet the play text was a valuable commodity, both for the theatrical public and for rival theaters wishing to perform popular new works. Pirates went to great lengths to recreate unprinted plays, sending shorthand writers into the theaters to create manuscript copies, bribing prompters for copies, and even piecing together complete texts from individual actors' parts. Macklin and his successors discovered that nonpublication alone would not ensure the dramatist's control over the performance of his plays. As a result, some actor-playwrights went much further, using their bodies to compose elements of the work onstage.

Following on the story of Macklin, the second chapter, "Samuel Foote's Strategic Ephemerality," also focuses on an actor-playwright who wrote parts for himself and thus had a double stake in the performance of his works. Foote's print publication choices reflect Macklin's influence. Yet rather than tenaciously monitoring and stopping unauthorized performances, as Macklin did, Foote took a different approach. He deployed his celebrity as an actor to make his physical presence integral to the production of his works. For many of Foote's early works, there was no stable text. Instead, like a stand-up comedian, he composed elements of his works during performance, through improvisation, mimicry, and bodily humor. He varied and updated the humor regularly, drawing audiences who were eager to see what Foote might satirize or whom he might impersonate. Unlike Restoration dramatists, who saw print publication as their greatest tool for exercising authorial control over the play text, Foote embraced the affordances of performance— especially its ephemerality—to control his works. The evolving nature of his works, and their dependence on his body, made them difficult to reproduce. Audiences who went to see Foote's plays were often going specifically to see Foote. During the era that saw the emergence of modern "celebrity," Foote made his presence integral to the performance of his work—so much so that after he lost a leg in a horseback-riding accident, he began writing one-legged characters that only he could perform. Foote relied on the singularity of his celebrity to "own" the works he wrote and physically embodied. Yet in doing so, he also discovered that his celebrity was, perhaps, not as singular as he hoped. Fellow mimics, especially Foote's protégé Tate Wilkinson, reproduced Foote's body and performance style in order to reperform his unpublished works. Mimicry became a new mode of piracy.

While the first two chapters focus on strategies playwrights used to control the circulation of their work, the second half of the book explores how the theater community reacted to these cultural shifts. A brief interlude chapter, "Managerial Interventions: George Colman, Thomas Harris, R. B. Sheridan, and the Practice of Buying Copyrights," acts as a hinge between the book's two halves. In it, I show how nonpublication, once a strategy for dramatists, was soon co-opted by theater managers, who increasingly bought the right to print directly from playwrights to ensure exclusive performance at their venues. The practice of "buying copyrights" came to be the norm, and many playwrights were no longer given the option to publish.

This chapter examines the shift from an authorial strategy to a managerial one, showing the effects of property issues on play publication in the second half of the century. The practice of buying copyrights, I argue, became a power struggle between managers and playwrights. Such power struggles were constant throughout the century as freelancing playwrights were generally at the mercy of theater managers. But this particular iteration was new, for it was chipping away at a foundational right that playwrights had acquired during the Restoration period: the right to print their works.

Chapter 4, "Tate Wilkinson's Reperformances: Mimicry as Piracy and Preservation," follows the career of one theater manager more closely, asking how the turn away from print and toward performance affected the creation of a national theatrical culture and the preservation of eighteenth-century drama. How did unprinted works circulate beyond London? This issue, I argue, was addressed most fully through the practice of mimicry—an art form that at once challenged the performer's "property" in his celebrity persona and afforded Britons around the nation greater access to theatrical culture. This chapter builds on chapter 2 by examining mimic and Yorkshire theater manager Tate Wilkinson's celebrity reenactments of Foote and other popular performers. If mimicry challenged Foote's attempts to "own" his performances, it also offered a solution to the seeming limitations of the medium—specifically its existence in a particular place and time. Wilkinson actively participated in the preservation of English performance by reperforming works of art that could, to quote Diana Taylor, "be passed on only through bodies."[51] Building on work by Taylor, Schneider, and Emily Hodgson Anderson, this chapter reassesses the narratives of ephemerality and loss that accompany discussions of performance. As Wilkinson reperformed unprinted works in provincial theaters, reproducing not only the texts themselves, but also celebrity performances through his mimicry, he drew the theater into a project of preserving national memory and identity. His celebrity imitations went far beyond reproducing Foote: Wilkinson created entire shows out of imitations of England's most popular actors in their most famous roles. He adapted generic conventions, developing performance-based equivalents to printed genres like literary anthologies. Rather than staging a conventional main piece and afterpiece combination, Wilkinson pieced together key scenes from the most popular plays of the day. Wilkinson's "anthologies of performance," which were supported by his mimicry, enabled him to circulate the most popular segments of unprinted plays beyond London and, in doing so, nationalize a London-based theatrical culture.

My final chapter, "Printing and Performing Drama in the Final Quarter of the Century: Elizabeth Inchbald and John O'Keeffe," considers the effects of property law on dramatists' professional success and posthumous reputations after managers had begun buying copyrights. I focus on the careers of two of the period's most commercially successful, popular, and prolific dramatists: Elizabeth Inchbald and John O'Keeffe. Inchbald and O'Keeffe experienced and reacted to the new theatrical trend of buying copyrights in vastly different ways and with tellingly different outcomes. Inchbald developed literary celebrity through both print and performance, using her reputation and name to negotiate lucrative performance and publishing contracts, and parlaying a print reputation into an editorial career that vested her with critical authority and further established her reputation in the literary world. She was able to do this, I argue, because she largely rejected the practice of selling her copyright to the theaters, choosing instead to print her popular works. O'Keeffe, by contrast, began selling his copyrights to the theaters early in his career—a choice that left him powerless to control the circulation of some of his most popular works and less able to fashion his own literary celebrity. Decades after his works premiered, they were still "locked up" in manuscript form, as he lamented in his *Recollections*, zealously protected by theater manager George Colman the Younger, leaving O'Keeffe unable to include five of his most popular plays in his *Dramatic Works*. Yet O'Keeffe's failure to control the circulation of his plays is as significant as Inchbald's success, for while the dramatists I consider earlier in this book performed ownership, O'Keeffe performed his exploitation. He publicly took on the role of exploited author to make a point about the limits of copyright law. As nonpublication became a managerial strategy, printing plays became an act of defiance and self-empowerment for dramatists in a theatrical culture that was increasingly defined by exclusivity of performance and inaccessibility of play texts.

The epilogue looks ahead to the parliamentary debates leading up to the passage of the 1833 Dramatic Literary Property Act—the first law to give dramatists exclusive rights over the representation of their plays in performance. I argue that the discursive work of eighteenth-century dramatists, their performances of ownership, was crucial to the legal debates of the nineteenth century. The hearings of the Select Committee on Dramatic Literature frequently drew on a rich tradition of theatrical anecdote developed around figures from Macklin to O'Keeffe. A close look at these hearings reveals that the legal development of performance copyright, so often seen as a nineteenth-century phenomenon, was dependent, for its language, examples, and conceptual frameworks, upon the property debates played out in the eighteenth-century theaters.

Taken together, these chapters describe a theatrical community that embraced the ephemerality of performance and the power and control over their works that ephemerality afforded them. This community, of course, simultaneously lamented that very same quality of performance, worrying about the loss of the actor's art.[52] It is the latter effect of ephemerality that is most often commented on. *Owning Performance* asks us to see performance's seeming ephemerality not as loss, for as Taylor and Schneider argue, this very notion of ephemerality derives from a "logic of the archive" that privileges print culture.[53] And as I argue in chapter 4, actors and mimics preserved the art form through reperformance. Instead, the project approaches the medium's affordances—its ephemerality, its unfixity, its existence in a particular place and time—as empowering qualities. By turning away from print publication; by writing works that resisted the fixity of print, altering them from one performance to the next; and by performing the works themselves, making their physical presence integral to production, playwrights asserted their own rights—and the value of performance—within a developing legal system of literary property that privileged print publication. They performed ownership. Playwrights, managers, and actors negotiated for and among themselves how to control the use of plays in performance.

Questions about ownership were regularly played out in the eighteenth-century theaters. We see it in the push and pull between playwrights and managers, in angry letters about unauthorized performance, and in negotiations as performance or print rights were bought and sold. We see evidence of this on playbills, through which theaters communicated information about property, ownership, and authenticity with their publics in astonishing ways. We see it in newspaper notices, in letters between playwrights and actors, and in theater account books. And we see it in the evidence left behind about actors' performing bodies. These are my archives. Hume writes that "drama historians usually seem to have little idea how drastically the staging of plays is affected by property issues."[54] Taking that claim as an invitation, this book seeks to better understand the effects of developing literary property law on the theaters before such laws addressed this realm.

Chapter 1

Charles Macklin and the Turn Away from Print

On February 14, 1741, Charles Macklin walked onto the Drury Lane stage, wearing a red hat, a black gown, and a "piqued beard." He slowly and deliberately spoke the words "three thousand ducats," which, according to one observer, he "lisp[ed] as lickerishly as if he were savoring the ducats and all that they would buy."[1] He was performing Shylock in Shakespeare's *The Merchant of Venice*, a role that would come to define both his career and his public persona. Macklin's performance shocked and entranced audiences, for not only was it the first time in forty years that they were seeing Shakespeare's original play instead of George Granville's 1701 adaptation, *The Jew of Venice*, but Macklin had transformed the character from a comic villain to a frighteningly dark one. His performance was a complete innovation, changing the way the play and the character would be performed for the rest of the century and contributing to a broader shift in acting styles. Macklin would continue to perform Shylock for the next forty-eight years, considering the character to be a sort of theatrical property—a character that he alone could perform. He would also embrace the association that often arose between character and actor on the eighteenth-century stage, allowing Shylock's vengefulness to permeate his own professional reputation. The character's insistence on his bond and adherence to the law proved useful to Macklin years later in his quest to obtain exclusive rights to the performance of his plays. He adopted Shylock's vengeful persona as a means of scaring theater managers away from performing his popular comic afterpiece, *Love à la Mode* (1759), without his permission.

Macklin's desire to possess the character of Shylock exclusively and to own the performance rights in *Love à la Mode* were intertwined in multiple ways. When Macklin debuted his afterpiece at Drury Lane in December 1759, performing the part of the Scotsman Sir Archy MacSarcasm and marking his return to the stage after a six-year absence, he paired it with the play that had provided his most successful role: *The Merchant of Venice.*[2] He would continue to pair *The Merchant of Venice* and *Love à la Mode* over the next few decades, especially for his own and his daughter's actor benefit nights—the night each season when an actor would take home all the profits beyond the theater's running costs. The two plays were natural companions not just because of Macklin's popularity in both roles, but also because the afterpiece echoes the casket scene in Shakespeare's play. In both, a series of suitors from various countries attempt to win the hand of the heroine, and in both, the suitors face a test. Offstage, Macklin deployed Shylock—a character he felt a sense of ownership over—to try to gain property in an afterpiece that was derivative of *The Merchant*, which was itself a play dealing with the circulation of money and property. The character of Shylock sits at the nexus of the ownership issues that define Macklin's theatrical career.

Macklin's long career brings together the many issues involving "ownership" within the theaters. I use the term "ownership" carefully, for the various ways in which theaters, actors, and authors "owned" plays, parts, or performance rights were governed primarily by custom rather than law. As both an actor and a playwright, Macklin had various stakes in theatrical property. As an actor, he wished to possess his cast of characters permanently and exclusively. As a playwright, he wished to have control over the repeated performance of his works and to profit from those performances beyond the first run.[3] These two goals, moreover, were closely linked, for like many actors throughout the century, he wrote plays to create performance vehicles for himself. And if these actor-playwrights had no control over subsequent productions of their plays, they also could not guarantee that they would be hired to act the parts they had specifically written for themselves. It is for this reason, I argue, that the earliest arguments for dramatic literary property came not just from a playwright, but from an actor-playwright. The complex and fluid relationship between acting and writing, between an actor's ability to possess a part and an author's ability to own his or her literary works, prompted the first major attempt by a playwright to control not only the print publication but also the performance of his works. Macklin was determined to control the circulation of his plays so that he could perform certain parts exclusively. As early as 1759, after the huge success of his farce *Love à la Mode*, he began withholding his plays from print, an unusual move at a time when nearly all popular plays appeared in print shortly after the first run.[4] Not only did he withhold his most popular plays from print, but he made that decision and the reasons behind it public through initiating lawsuits, writing threatening letters to managers who were performing his work without permission, and cultivating a discourse of property within the theatrical community. As a result, managers and theatrical publics knew exactly why Macklin's work remained unprinted, and they understood that if they performed the work without consent, he would seek retribution. Macklin performed ownership. His innovative strategies for controlling the production of his farce in an era when major questions concerning copyright and literary property were still up in the air set a precedent for later-century playwrights and managers, who learned from Macklin the power of leveraging print for securing exclusive performance rights. This chapter traces the changing modes of theatrical ownership, from the divided repertory to the custom of part possession to the role of literary property law in the printing of plays. It is because of these informal, but often powerful modes of "ownership" that ideas about literary property develop differently in the theaters than in the print world. Macklin, as a figure with a precarious position in the theaters and therefore a material investment in the ownership of his plays and parts, was the first playwright to publicly acknowledge the need for a law relating to dramatic literary property.

Macklin was determined to possess his dramatic parts permanently as a form of job security, for both his personality and happenstance often left him in a precarious professional state. A talented actor who was known in his own time to have revolutionized acting methods and trained some of the century's greatest actors, he was also an argumentative man who could be a difficult collaborator and employee. When he attained a position of power and security, acting as Charles Fleetwood's stage manager at Drury Lane from 1734 to 1743, he made an enemy of the proprietor by walking out with the rest of the actors in 1743.[5] In Fleetwood's eyes, Macklin's walkout was unforgiveable because he was not just an actor but a trusted lieutenant in the management of the theater. From that time on, Macklin moved among various theaters in multiple cities, negotiating temporary contracts and occasionally quarreling with other actors and managers. And he knew that simply writing himself a character would not be enough to secure his employment. After all, what if he was fired after one season and another, more tractable actor took over his parts? Monopolizing a part, as Macklin sought to do, was no easy task, given that an actor could not legally own a part. Part possession, which had been a theatrical custom during the late seventeenth and early eighteenth centuries, was quickly waning by the time of Macklin's acting career. As a result, he needed to find a new way to possess his parts exclusively. In his arguments for why he should be able to earn and possess parts he had not written himself, Macklin emphasized the creative labor of his interpretation, adopting much of the same language that authors used to argue for literary property. This strategy would prove particularly successful for his famous characterization of Shylock, yet it depended on public support rather than law. And later in his career, when he tried to "earn" the character of Macbeth through the same method, he ran into serious opposition.

The second way that Macklin turned to literary property as a strategy for possessing a part was by writing his own plays, keeping them out of print, and protecting the unique manuscripts so that theaters could not produce them without his consent. Macklin's quest to possess parts revealed the limitations of literary property law for protecting drama. Because performance was not legally considered publication, it was not protected under England's first copyright act, An Act for the Encouragement of Learning, by Vesting the Copies of Printed Books in the Authors or Purchasers of Such Copies, during the Times Therein Mentioned (1710), also called the Statute of Anne or the Copyright Act.[6] This was a serious shortcoming, given how profitable performance could be. Macklin was aware of the limits of copyright as articulated in the Statute of Anne. He was also aware of the debates that continued throughout the century over the relationship between statute law and a perpetual common-law copyright. He theorized that as long as he kept his works out of print, he continued to hold a perpetual common-law property right in them, allowing him to dictate their use in performance. An unprinted play, Macklin argued, had not been made a gift to the public for free use and performance. This belief, strengthened by the 1769 *Millar v. Taylor* ruling that determined that common-law property existed independently of the Statute of Anne, shaped Macklin's interactions with theater managers, emboldening him to claim "literary property" in the performance of his plays.

Scholars have traditionally situated the fight for performance copyright in the early nineteenth century and have taken for granted that the movement must have been motivated by dramatists' aspirations for control and profit. A careful evaluation of Macklin's career, however, reveals that dramatic literary property was a pressing concern in the eighteenth century and was bound up with the possession of parts, the repertory, and the proprietary privileges of not only authors but also actors and managers. Before the Dramatic Literary Property Act of 1833 endowed authors with performance copyright, a range of theater professionals found innovative ways to control and profit repeatedly from the performance of dramatic literature. Macklin successfully manipulated the rhetoric of literary property to protect the performance of his plays. His vocal insistence that he should be able to control performance raised concerns in the theatrical community about the ways drama circulated. His very public decision to keep *Love à la Mode* out of print initiated a shift in theatrical culture away from print and toward performance that would affect the way audiences throughout Great Britain experienced drama for the remainder of the century.

POSSESSING PARTS

In the late seventeenth and early eighteenth centuries, even before the Statute of Anne began to grant authors property rights, various forms of "ownership" operated in the London theaters that granted companies, managers, and actors proprietary privileges. One such privilege, which was established by the division of the repertory, made particular plays the exclusive property of specific companies. Another customary "right" was an actor's right to exclusively perform his or her personal repertory of parts. An extreme example, in which the Lord Chamberlain intervened in casting decisions, illustrates just how powerful the idea of a personal repertory could be. In 1667, the Lord Chamberlain ordered the King's Company to rehire actress Anne Quin after she had left the theater two years earlier. Moreover, he commanded that the theater give her all of her former roles: "that you assign her all her owne parts which she formerly had & that none other be permitted to act any of her parts without her consent."[7] Restoration actors and theatergoers held a strong belief that an actor had the sole right to his or her parts. There are a number of possible reasons why this practice developed in the Restoration period. David Brewer suggests that it was an "offshoot of the division of the repertory at the Restoration."[8] That is, if a play belonged to a single company, it made sense that a single actor within that company would hold a particular part.[9] Peter Holland connects part possession to continuity of performance, or handing down the same interpretation of a character from one actor to the next.[10] New plays lent themselves to part possession, as authors often wrote characters with particular actors in mind. Judith Milhous and Robert D. Hume point out that the theater companies were so small during the Restoration period that few actors were available who could challenge an actor's claim to a part.[11] Moreover, because actors had to act parts in quick succession due to a quick turnover of plays, maintaining a steady repertory of parts benefited actors in terms of workload. During the Restoration period, then, the system of part possession seemed logical and natural.

However, changes in theatrical culture and management over the course of the eighteenth century threatened the custom of part possession. By 1695, the repertory was no longer neatly divided. When Thomas Betterton, Elizabeth Barry, and Anne Bracegirdle left Drury Lane to set up at Lincoln's Inn Fields that year, they disregarded Drury Lane's claim to exclusive rights in the repertory of old plays. For a period, the two London theaters respected each other's rights to new plays during the initial season of performance. But after 1728, when the Little Theatre in the Haymarket put on *The Beggar's Opera* almost immediately after it closed at Lincoln's Inn Fields, the theaters no longer considered new plays to be exclusively their property.[12] As a result, actors at multiple London theaters might simultaneously possess a part, occasionally even performing them on the same night. Such was the case in 1750 when Drury Lane and Covent Garden famously staged competing performances of *Romeo and Juliet*.[13] Critics reveled in comparing the two representations of the play, and as the public was made the judge of competing actors, they came to celebrate multiple interpretations of a role. Part possession across companies had never been a legal, or even a customary, right. What is important is that increased variety of interpretation *across* companies threatened the custom *within* companies by fostering a public desire for novelty. The tradition of passing down an interpretation from one actor to the next was no longer the exclusive, or even dominant, mode of performance. A growing belief that a part could be performed well in a variety of ways weakened actors' claims that their success in a part should ensure their perpetual possession of it.

As the custom of part possession declined over the eighteenth century, actors eager to maintain principal roles had to mount a case for their right to a personal repertory. Proponents of part possession relied on two central arguments: (1) that if an actor had won public approval in a part, he or she had earned a right to keep that part; and (2) that part possession was a well-established custom in the theaters. Such were the arguments of Kitty Clive and her supporters in the much-publicized "Polly War" between Clive and Susannah Cibber. When Theophilus Cibber suggested to Drury Lane manager Charles Fleetwood in 1736 that his wife, Susannah, play Polly in *The Beggar's Opera*, Clive, who had played the role at Drury Lane in 1732, fought back. In a letter to the *London Daily Post* on November 19, Clive insisted that the "design" to take away her part was "contrary to a receiv'd Maxim in the Theatre, *That no Actor or Actress shall be depriv'd of a Part in which they have been well receiv'd, until they are render'd incapable of performing it either by Age or Sickness.*"[14] Clive argued that she had previously succeeded in the part and that, as a result, it was hers for as long as she wanted it. She knew that because she did not have a legal right to the part, she would have to rely on public support for her case. To that end, she and her supporters repeatedly praised the public's discernment and endowed them with the power to dictate theatrical representation. The originator of the newspaper war, a writer calling himself "Spectator," reminded the town that they approved of Clive as Polly and argued that "she has a right to" the role "from the town's approbation of her."[15]

Advocates of part possession further suggested that this custom and actors' respect for it made acting a polite profession. They found examples of actors who had turned down parts that "belonged" to other actors and praised their sense of justice. When, for example, the patentees of the United Company tried to give Elizabeth Barry's "chief Parts" to the younger Anne Bracegirdle, Bracegirdle's "good Sense" prevented her from taking the parts "that properly belong'd to" Barry and "entring into any such rash, and invidious Competition."[16] David Garrick, too, deferred to the custom. His biographer Thomas Davies recalls that when he returned to Drury Lane from Dublin in 1743, he relinquished some of his former characters that had been taken by others in his absence. Davies speculates that he "did not wish either to offend, or risque a competition with, either [Henry] Woodward or Macklin, by acting characters to which they had a claim."[17]

Ultimately, though, both public approval and custom were weak arguments for part possession. Customs are not legally enforceable, and as times change, so do practices. A 1765 contributor to the *Universal Museum* called part possession an "injudicious custom," arguing that "continuing a number of characters to several of their performers" prevented the public from seeing actors of potentially greater merit.[18] Moreover, the public could approve multiple actors in a single character. In a case such as Garrick's return to Drury Lane, multiple actors had succeeded in the same set of roles at the same theater. By the logic that popular success in a role established ownership, Garrick, Woodward, and Macklin would all have had a right to the same parts at Drury Lane. Equally complicated situations arose when actors moved between the two London theaters. Relying on the public's applause to guarantee a role put actors in a precarious position. In fact, Clive succeeded in making her case not because of public enthusiasm about her performance but because of her successful manipulation of their sympathies. As Berta Joncus points out, Clive had not been particularly successful as Polly in 1732, a fact the public must not have remembered as she insisted in newspapers and onstage that she was being deprived of her rightful part.[19] In spite of Clive's victory, public support was not an approach upon which all actors could rely.

By the end of the century, most actors seemed to recognize that the practice of part possession was a thing of the past, though many still referred to it with a sense of hope. In an 1807 letter to the Haymarket manager George Colman the Younger, for instance, Charles Mathews writes that "I have long since discovered that there is no such phrase as <u>possession of parts</u> allowed in your Theatre." Despite this knowledge, Mathews complains that Colman has let another actor perform the parts "you once did me the favor to entrust me with."[20] The question of whether the custom was sustainable or beneficial to drama was addressed explicitly in 1800 when a group of actors lodged a series of complaints against the proprietors of Covent Garden Theatre. The Covent Garden actors were primarily upset about an increased charge for their benefit night. Among a series of lesser complaints, they included the decline in the practice of part possession. In *A Statement of the Differences Subsisting between the Proprietors and Performers of the Theatre-Royal, Covent-Garden* (1800), the actors observed that "the right to the possession of his cast of characters, a most important privilege which appertained to the Actor, has of late years been so constantly violated, that it can scarcely be said to exist."[21] In their shorter "Memorial" to the Lord Chamberlain, the actors summarized their grievances: "They do not seek any new and speculative Advantages, but . . . they simply beseech the Restoration of Privileges attached to their Profession by ancient and established Usage."[22] Their appeals relied entirely on tradition. Covent Garden proprietor Thomas Harris responded to the actors' demand by suggesting that for the good of the theater, the most talented and physically apt actors must fill each part: "Can any thing be more preposterous than a right to a Cast of Characters? Granting to the complainants their own estimation of their own Talents, is it *impossible* that Superior abilities may arise? Must the Romeos, the Young Belvilles &c be for life possessed by the present Actors though years should compleatly disqualify them?"[23] The tone of Harris's response was more dismissive than any of his responses to their other complaints, illustrating managerial opinions of this practice in 1800. The Lord Chamberlain supported Harris, arguing that it was "necessary for the good Management of the Theatre" that managers should be able to cast actors "in such Characters as the Proprietors shall think proper."[24] The actors were ultimately unsuccessful. A once well-respected theatrical privilege—part possession—could no longer be counted on. Yet as one form of theatrical "ownership" was declining, another form of property was becoming stronger. After the breakdown of the divided repertory and the custom of part possession, literary property was the one form of ownership that was still enforceable. As a result, theater professionals of all types, not just authors, began to look to it.

THE CREATIVE LABOR OF INTERPRETATION

Macklin's unusually long career in the theater as both an actor and a play-wright, and as a member of not only the London theaters but also strolling companies and the Dublin theaters, exposed him to theatrical politics and showed him the challenges inherent in both professions, particularly in rela-tion to property. From the time he began acting in the 1720s to his retirement in 1789, he was assertive (at times aggressive) about his working conditions, pay, and property. Indeed, this assertiveness sometimes got him in trouble and contributed to his reputation for litigiousness and volatility. His reputa-tion cannot be attributed wholly to professional assertiveness. His temper showed itself in more trivial situations as well. In 1735, he stabbed fellow actor Thomas Hallam in the eye with his cane and accidentally killed him after Hallam had used his favorite property wig. Yet the sensational nature of this episode often overshadows Macklin's serious dedication to ensuring fair working conditions. His quarrel with Fleetwood and Garrick after the actor rebellion of 1743 is one instance in which his determination to secure actor rights threatened his ability to work. Seven years later, in 1750, Thomas Sheridan fired him from Smock Alley after the two disagreed over benefit arrangements, management policies, and, most tellingly, parts.[25] Matthew J. Kinservik argues that by 1753, Macklin was forced into retirement as a result of his poor relations with three managers and his dwindling repertory of parts.[26] The success of his farce Love à la Mode in 1759 brought him back to the London stage, but his employment remained precarious. In 1770, George Colman refused to hire Macklin "on the same Footing on which other actors usually engage," instead offering a contract in which he would act one night a week.[27] Macklin's biographer William W. Appleton suggests that Colman proposed this arrangement because he did not want Macklin backstage every night.[28] Without steady employment or a personal repertory, Macklin articulated an explicit argument for earning dramatic parts on the basis of labor and original interpretation.

Late in his career, in 1773, Macklin began negotiating with Colman for employment at Covent Garden. As he had been three years earlier, Colman was hesitant to work with him. Macklin's contentiousness was not his only obstacle. The type of parts he excelled in—comic roles—were already filled. He wrote to Colman, "I am sensible that you can not make so extensive a use of me in the comic Parts that I used to perform in Drury Lane and Covent Garden Theatre; other People are in possession of them."[29] His unwilling-ness to challenge the current actors in their parts shows Macklin's profound respect for part possession. Thus, Macklin proposed that instead of pursuing his usual parts, he should act a set of tragic roles, specifically Richard III, Macbeth, and Lear, which were left open when William "Gentleman" Smith left Covent Garden to set up his own company.[30] Concerned to establish his "usefulness" in the theater, or, as he described it to Colman, "the utility that arises from ordinary service," Macklin did not wish to perform these parts only temporarily; he wanted to make them part of his personal repertory.[31] To ensure that Colman understood the value of his performance, Macklin emphasized the originality of his proposed interpretations of these characters. He wrote to Colman, "My worth then must consist in shere attraction . . . Theatrical Attraction has but one source,—which is novelty."[32] His performance of Macbeth later that year would show that he was willing to put significant work into creating new interpretations.[33] If his performances were popular with the audience, he argued, then his experiment in novelty would be "an Ingredient of Utility," or a way to make him indispensable to the company. Along with the novelty of his interpretations, Macklin offered Colman "novelty in Composition" in the form of a new play and two new farces. In the juxtaposition of his acting and writing, we see that Macklin viewed the two activities in much the same light. He understood that because originality in composition secured him property in his plays, originality in acting might secure him permanent possession of his parts.

Macklin had already succeeded once in maintaining possession of a part through his creative labor. In 1741, he introduced a radically new interpretation of Shylock in Shakespeare's *The Merchant of Venice*. Macklin's huge success in possessing the character for the next forty years probably resulted from the rhetoric that arose around his performance, which emphasized his labor, his understanding of Shakespeare, and his originality. Much of this language reflected Lockean ways of thinking about property, although neither Macklin nor his critics explicitly invoked Locke.[34] Descriptions of Macklin's Shylock so pointedly emphasize his creative process that we can take his successful possession of the part to reflect more than just the popularity of his interpretation. In descriptions of his performance, we see theater critics thinking through what it might mean to earn possession of a character through the same means that authors earned property in literary work.

Macklin's portrayal of Shylock struck audiences as exceptionally original because of both his textual and his performance choices. For the forty years before Macklin's debut, the London stage had seen only George Granville's adaptation of Shakespeare's play, *The Jew of Venice* (1701). Granville's adaptation cut a number of the characters, omitted roughly one thousand lines, and added a masque scene. A number of comic actors, including Thomas Doggett, played Shylock as a comic villain.[35] Macklin rejected this text, instead reintroducing Shakespeare's original text, or something close to it. Moreover, as reviews of his performance emphasized, he broke with the comic interpretation of Shylock, instead depicting the character as truly threatening. John Ireland observed: "I have been told, that previous to Mr. Macklin's performance of Shylock, it was looked upon as a part of little importance, and played with the buffoonery of a Jew pedlar; to the understanding of that venerable performer, we are obliged for the first true representation of the character."[36] Critics believed that Macklin's approach best reflected Shakespeare's intention. Such a belief is expressed in the famous couplet attributed to Alexander Pope: "This is the Jew, / That Shakespeare drew." While we have no evidence of how Shylock was played in the original production, we do know that Macklin's performance convinced audiences that they were seeing the character in his original form. Moreover, audiences equated Shakespeare with nature, so that by adhering to Shakespeare's text and intentions, Macklin was also imitating nature. Arthur Murphy, writing pseudonymously in the *Morning Chronicle* in 1773, remembered that "Macklin looked deeply into nature, and nature, from the hand of Shakespeare, requires great thinking."[37] Macklin had studied nature by studying Shakespeare, Murphy explained. He had also studied nature directly, as the writer of *The Present State of the Stage in Great-Britain and Ireland* (1753) observed: "The Actor should like the Author, search thro' Nature for the Constituents of the Character which he is to fill. This Rule Mr. *Macklin* generally observes, his Distinctions are critically right; and he draws from Nature the Heightning and Completion of his Characters."[38] According to limited and anecdotal evidence, he observed Jews in the Royal Exchange and nearby coffeehouses, "that by a frequent intercourse and conversation with 'the unforeskinn'd race,' he might habituate himself to their air and deportment."[39] He even dressed himself in the style of Italian Jews, describing his costume as "my red hat on my head, my piqued beard, loose black gown, &c."[40] Macklin's costume would have been particularly striking because it was not yet common practice for actors to wear period costumes. His costume, interpretation, and performance all gave his audience the impression that he was harnessing nature.

Following his debut as Shylock, Macklin came to have a reputation for the work he put into character development. "Labor" was a word frequently found in reviews of his performances, from an anonymous reviewer who called him a "laborious performer" to Thomas Davies's declaration that Macklin was the only actor who "made acting a science."[41] Even his severest critics recognized the work he put into a role: "It may be fairly said, that he has shewn no evidence of Genius as an Actor, or a Writer. As an Actor, all his merits were the mere result of labour."[42] These evaluations reflect his own statements about his creative process. His notes indicate that in addition to observing Jews in the Royal Exchange and studying the clothing of Italian Jews, he read about them in Josephus's *History of the Jews*.[43] He took notes in his commonplace book that briefly detailed key moments in Jewish history and advised himself to "go thro the history of it—act the great characters."[44] Macklin took character development and original interpretation seriously, and because of that, he expected some security in the possession of his parts.

Contemporary critics were explicit in their belief that Macklin's labor and originality endowed him with a right to perform Shylock. In *A General History of the Stage* (1749), William Chetwood wrote of Macklin: "The Science of Acting is not to be learn'd without great Labour and Study; and, not copying any Performer that went before him, he has at length shone out a finish'd Original." Macklin's success was well earned, "since with long laborious Pains" he had created his roles.[45] Chetwood's use of the word "pains" calls to mind Locke's chapter on property in the *Second Treatise of Government*, where he writes that he "who takes . . . pains about" removing something from nature has a right to property in that thing.[46] While Macklin could not claim to be drawing from nature directly, because the character of Shylock was written by Shakespeare and thus not in a state of nature, his choice to obtain specifically Shakespearean characters was important: Shakespeare and his texts were considered by many Britons in the eighteenth century to be part of the common stock of British literature. And if Shakespeare was the common property of Englishmen, his works could be appropriated and reworked by individuals. Describing Shylock specifically, Chetwood wrote, "*Shylock* the *Jew*, in the Merchant of *Venice*, is so inimitably counterfeited, that we cannot say more than what a Gentleman said *extempore* on seeing him perform the Part: '*This is the* Jew / *That* Shakespear *drew.*'"[47] His use of the word "counterfeited" is fascinating. In an era when charges of literary plagiarism and an overreliance on imitation were rampant, Chetwood used "counterfeited" in a surprisingly positive manner, praising Macklin for coming so close to the "original," or Shylock as Shakespeare drew him. Chetwood's word choice echoes Bassanio's reaction when he sees the portrait of Portia in the leaden casket: "What find I here? / Fair Portia's counterfeit! What demi-god / Hath come so near creation?"[48] While copying a previous performer would have decreased Macklin's success as Shylock, counterfeiting the original ensured it. Thus, Chetwood concluded by establishing Macklin's ownership of his parts: "*This* Jew, *this* Colonel, Lopez, Ben, *has shown, / He makes each various Character his own.*"[49]

Macklin's possession of Shylock was strengthened by the equation of the actor with the character. For eighteenth-century theatergoers, Macklin was Shylock. James Leigh, author of the *New Rosciad*, insisted that Shylock's death would accompany Macklin's: "In future times when *Shakspere* shall be read, / When *Shylock* is no more, when Macklin's dead, / Then shall posterity revere *thy* name, / And future *Shylocks* wish to match thy fame."[50] At the same time that he acknowledges that there will be future Shylocks, he insists that after Macklin, Shylock will be "no more." Macklin's biographer William Cooke judged Macklin's behavior in relation to Shylock's, describing his 1743 falling out with Garrick by writing that Macklin, "in imitation of Shylock, insisted upon the particulars of his bond with Garrick."[51] Audiences drew parallels between the courtroom scene and Macklin's own trials, including his trial for murdering Hallam. Critics constantly compared the physical likeness between the actor and character, often describing Macklin's appearance in terms of Shylock's. Georg Lichtenberg, a German visitor to the London theaters, for instance, described Macklin's appearance in the character in terms that mirrored his sinister interpretation of the part: "Imagine a rather stout man with a course yellow face and a nose generously fashioned in all three dimensions, and a long double chin, and a mouth so carved by nature that the knife appears to have slit him right up to the ears."[52] Emily Hodgson Anderson has argued that Macklin brought so much life and power to Shylock that the character began to overtake the actor. She argues that "Macklin's Shylock seems larger than life, or large enough at least to eclipse the life behind it."[53] This claim is further borne out through theatrical illustrations from the period. While prints abounded of actors in their parts, printed images of Macklin adapted this convention, showing caricatures of "Shylock turned Macbeth" and "Sir Archy McSarcasm in the Character of Macbeth." Macklin's association with his two most famous characters was so strong that audiences could not see him performing other roles without remembering him in those parts—a particularly powerful example of what Marvin Carlson has called "ghosting."[54] If Macklin's identity became subsumed in Shylock's, the actor would have had all the more reason for wanting property in the character.

Macklin's possession of Shylock was hugely successful and prompted him to view labor and novelty as more effective rhetorical strategies than custom or public approval. He performed Shylock from 1741 to 1789, when he was roughly ninety years old. Because actors could not legally own characters, his possession of Shylock was not entirely exclusive. John Gross counts at least a dozen other actors who performed Shylock during Macklin's tenure.[55] But very few of them succeeded in the part because audiences were convinced that only Macklin could truly embody Shylock. Macklin's hold on Shylock in

Fig. 1. Unknown artist, *Shylock turn'd Macbeth* . . . Hand-colored etching, 1773. Yale Center for British Art, Paul Mellon Fund, B1976.1.67.

the public imagination and within the theater companies was so strong that Kitty Clive refused to play Portia when Garrick cast Samuel Foote as Shylock in 1758.[56] Toward the end of Macklin's career John Henderson succeeded in the role, but even Henderson could not act the part without constantly being compared to Macklin, who was called "the veteran" because he had acted for so long. Macklin's performances of Shylock had inspired public interest in the process of character development and what that creative labor might mean for an actor's "right" to his characters.

Macklin surely had his successful possession of Shylock in mind when, in 1773, he offered Colman "novel" interpretations of a set of tragic parts at Covent Garden. In October of that year, he staged a new production of *Macbeth*, and his commitment to original interpretation this time extended well beyond his own part. Appleton writes that Macklin "anticipated the function of the director in the modern theatre"; he made choices not only about his own character but about staging, sets, and blocking.[57] Three pages of Macklin's detailed notes, held in the Harvard Theatre Collection and printed in facsimile by the *Harvard Library Bulletin*, illustrate Macklin's extensive decision-making. He went to great lengths to interpret his own role and introduced Scottish dress to *Macbeth*, outfitting himself "in russet, broadsword pistols at his girdle, dirk a cap imitating a bonnet, a ruff—hair tied behind but short."[58] Furthermore, he reinterpreted the title character: while Garrick's Macbeth had been led into evil by others, Macklin's was innately evil. Kinservik describes Macklin's "Shakespearean agenda," from Shylock to Macbeth, as primarily concerned with "a revisionist interpretation of dramatic character, the restoration of Shakespeare's text, and historical accuracy in costumes."[59] While these were ends in and of themselves, they were also means to a personal repertory and, with it, job security.

Macklin's performances of *Macbeth* failed, however, and this was in large part because the actor who had previously possessed the part at Covent Garden, William Smith, returned before the start of the season. Smith's return complicated Macklin's bid for a new role. Macklin had been trying to respect the system of part possession, knowing that his own livelihood depended upon his popularity in his long-held parts. But now, at the same moment he was trying to secure a part through creative labor, he was challenging Smith's exclusive right to his parts. Sensitive to the issue, Macklin proposed that the two actors should alternate nights in the parts.[60] But Smith's friends did not support this compromise, and they repeatedly came to the theater on the nights Macklin performed the part to hiss him. The disagreement escalated into riots that left Macklin unable to perform Macbeth.[61] Macklin's commercial failure as Macbeth was bound up in this issue of part possession.

Had theatrical politics not interfered, Macklin's approach to possessing Macbeth through creative labor could have succeeded, judging by the positive criticism. As Kinservik argues, the interpretation was a "commercial failure" but a "critical success."[62] Supportive critics applauded Macklin's concept and deliberate approach to the role and the play. A writer in the *Morning Chronicle* on October 25 observed that "few performers . . . have been so theoretically profound," adding that "he seemed to have studied the character with peculiar and profound attention."[63] The reviewer was one of many to recognize the labor and study Macklin put into his interpretation. He also acknowledges the originality of Macklin's approach. At the same time reviewers praised Macklin's concept, though, they found fault with his execution. The "veteran actor" was too old for the role; he was not expressive or agile enough. His long pauses between lines, critics speculated, were the result of his failing memory. A reviewer calling himself "Criticus" described the concept and execution with an extended birthing metaphor: "Though he may be *impregnated* with his own *ideas*, whatever he has *conceived* of Macbeth, his want of execution will render him unable to *bring it forth*. It is the *brat of his own brain*, that lives and dies in his own *imagination*. In short, it is an *unnatural labour*, or rather a *miscarriage*."[64] While the metaphor is critical of Macklin, it also endows him with creative power akin to an author's. Birthing metaphors were commonly applied to writers.[65] By applying a metaphor commonly used for writers to Macklin's acting, "Criticus" is suggesting (perhaps unintentionally) that Macklin's original interpretations of plays and characters are a form of creative labor akin to writing. If Macklin had been at the peak of his acting ability, and if he had not been trying to gain a part that Smith already possessed, his creative labor may very well have functioned as it had for Shylock.

Creative labor had succeeded in securing Shylock for Macklin and might have secured Macbeth for him under different circumstances. But originality as a means for possession was double-edged: while an original interpretation might be grounds for part possession, increasing public enthusiasm for originality also meant that critics and audiences might encourage many actors to try the same part—a trend that would imperil the system of part possession. Thus, some of Macklin's supporters in his bid for the part would not have supported an exclusive right to it. Murphy, for instance, did not "see any reason, why we should not have as many editions of Macbeth on the stage, as the critics have given us off the stage."[66] The *Morning Chronicle*, likewise, censures critics and audiences who are so "accustomed" to one actor in a role that they automatically dismiss any other attempt, calling Macklin's performance "a bold new endeavor." As Macklin employed creative labor to possess dramatic parts, he also contributed to a growing demand for originality and variety. His acting career had coincided with the many literary property debates that used concepts of originality and creative "genius" as grounds for owning literary productions. Macklin took advantage of this concurrence, making a point of emphasizing the originality of his interpretations and staking a claim to his characters. But while his use of creative labor for part possession could be wildly successful, as it was with Shylock, it was, like theatrical custom, not a strategy that could be relied on.

INTERPRETING LITERARY PROPERTY LAW

Although Macklin succeeded in possessing Shylock through his creative labor, at no point during the Restoration or eighteenth century could an actor legally own a role. What could be legally owned, however, was literary property. So Macklin used his playwriting and the rights with which he was endowed as an author to retain and control dramatic parts. In the first legally printed editions of Macklin's *Love à la Mode* and *Man of the World* (1793), his friend and editor, Arthur Murphy, explained that because Macklin had retired from acting, the farce was "of no further use to him."[67] The "use" Murphy referred to is the play's use in providing a performance vehicle for Macklin. Macklin very consciously kept the plays out of print so that he could exclusively perform the parts of Sir Archy MacSarcasm and Sir Pertinax MacSycophant and repeatedly profit as both the author and the lead actor. He exercised his rights as an author to further his career as an actor. In turn, and perhaps more importantly for literary history, his quest to further his acting career led him to see the limitations of literary property as it applied to the theater and to treat his plays in a way that anticipated the development of performance copyright in England. Macklin's thirty-year mission to control the production of *Love à la Mode* illuminated the complex and murky relationship between print and performance and revealed the need for literary property to account for the stage.

Although the meaning of the Statute of Anne was debated throughout the eighteenth century, it was clear on one point: it applied to the "book," or print publications. This point was reinforced almost a century later in 1793, when Chief Justice Lloyd Kenyon ruled that the Copyright Act "only extends to prohibit the publication of the book itself."[68] But what of publishers who worked in modes other than print? In the seventeenth and early eighteenth centuries, oral publication was still considered a form of publication, a fact that becomes particularly evident when looking at regulation and punishment. Surveyor of the Press Roger L'Estrange's 1663 treatise on press regulation, *Considerations and Proposals in Order to the Regulation of the Press*, included ballad singers among the usual "agents for publishing."[69] L'Estrange recognized the interworkings of print and orality and the ways that one enabled the other. Barbara A. Mowat highlights the complex relationship between print and performance during the early modern period and the "dual (legal) existence" of a genre that was published in two forms: "The printing and selling of plays for readers made the boundary between theater and literary culture increasingly porous."[70] To illustrate this point, she turns to a 1611 Star Chamber case in which a group of strolling players defended themselves against charges of sedition by arguing that they were reading from a printed book. They believed that because the book had already been licensed and published in one form, they were safe in publishing it in another mode: performance. As late as the early eighteenth century, performers could be punished as publishers, regardless of whether the play was already published in print. From 1700 to 1702, a series of prosecutions were brought against actors for speaking obscene language while performing plays that had already been printed.[71] In his famous speech on the 1737 Stage Licensing Act, Lord Chesterfield argued against preperformance censorship on the grounds that the government could always punish the publishers: one "can be under no difficulty to prove who is the publisher; the players themselves are the publishers."[72] In each of these instances, we see performance being imagined as an act of publication that was distinct from but related to a printed text. The porous relationship between print and performance complicated any effort to regulate performance in a consistent manner.

The legal status of performance as a mode of publication was further complicated by the collaborative nature of performance. As Gerald Eades Bentley has argued, "Every performance in the commercial theatres from 1590 to 1642 was itself . . . the joint accomplishment of dramatists, actors, musicians, costumers, prompters (who made alterations in the original manuscript) and . . . managers."[73] The same was true in eighteenth-century theaters. Because the playwright was not the sole creator of the performed work, it was more difficult to secure his or her proprietary right to profit by performance. Moreover, as W. B. Worthen writes, while both literature and theater claim drama as part of their domains, they value plays differently. The theater, interested in a play's use for the company, decentered the author, whereas a print- and manuscript-based literary culture increasingly celebrated authors as creators.[74] The centrality of the author was essential to discourses of property. Extrapolating from Locke, Mark Rose argues that an author's personality underwrote his literary property: "A work of literature belonged to an individual because it was, finally, an embodiment of that individual."[75] Thus, as vast strides were made in articulating proprietary rights within the author-centric realm of print throughout the eighteenth century, performance remained unaddressed and unprotected. Once a play was published in print, a theater could perform it free of charge, without having to so much as consult the author. As Milhous and Hume put it, print "publication essentially put a script into the public domain."[76]

Ironically, it was an early form of theatrical ownership during the Restoration period that had enabled playwrights to begin printing their works in the first place. The division of the repertory that followed the reopening of the theaters meant that a manager did not have to worry about the other theater purloining the script. As a result, managers allowed playwrights to supplement their incomes by publishing their plays. As the divided repertory fell apart, however, and playwrights continued to print their works, performance rights became an issue.[77] Julie Stone Peters argues that "in England more than anywhere else, play publishing practices were affected by the vicissitudes of performance copyright."[78] Although this proved true by the end of the century, when managers such as Harris, Colman, and Sheridan began buying copyrights to delay publication, for most of the eighteenth century, playwrights did not meddle with issues of performance copyright, instead simply taking what they could get from performance and print publication. Macklin was exceptional in his early challenge to remuneration systems and literary property law.

In order to keep *Love à la Mode* out of the public domain, Macklin intentionally withheld the play from print. He emphasized this fact in a suit against Robert Owenson, the manager of the City Theatre, Fishamble Street in Dublin, who had performed the farce without Macklin's permission. Macklin's lawyer, D. Hussey, argued that although Macklin could have profited substantially by selling the copyright to a publisher, he "refused large sums of money which were from time to time offered him for the copy or the copy right thereof by persons who intended to print or publish the same." Hussey explained that Macklin refused to print the play "from an imagination that property of an author in works of genius was as inviolable as any other property."[79] However, literary property rights did not extend to prohibit unauthorized performance, and merely keeping the play out of print was not enough to ensure that managers would not get hold of a copy. So in addition to withholding publication, Macklin carefully protected his unique manuscript copy.[80] His moves were quite unusual, and contemporary commentators described his eccentric strategies in colorful detail. John O'Keeffe documented Macklin's habit of taking his script home each night:

When he came to rehearsal, his method was to take his MS. from the breast of his great coat, where he had buttoned it up, put it into the hands of the prompter, and, rehearsal done, walk quietly over to him, saying, "Give me that,"—take it from the prompter's hand, button it up close again in the breast of his coat, and walk out of the house to his own lodgings.[81]

Macklin cited his own vigilance when he prosecuted pirates. Macklin and Hussey's bill against Owenson documents the lengths to which Macklin went to protect his script. The bill explains that during the first run of the farce, Drury Lane's transcriber was given a full script, so he could copy out parts for individual actors. But "such transcribers were always expressly forbidden to make any entire copys or transcripts of said entertainment or to suffer any to be made there from."[82] In forbidding theaters to keep copies of *Love à la Mode*, Macklin was more or less contracting for a single run of the show. He would earn authorial profits from the play for as long as it ran, and when it was over, he could take his script and peddle it elsewhere. This type of contract, which was hugely beneficial to the playwright, was, according to Milhous and Hume, "totally unprecedented in the eighteenth-century London theatre."[83]

Macklin's strategy of keeping the play out of the public domain was a smart move financially. He earned a phenomenal amount of money from *Love à la Mode*, particularly given that it was only an afterpiece. His contract with Drury Lane did not operate under the usual third-night benefit system used for mainpieces, in which authors earned all of the theater's profits minus operating costs on the third, sixth, and ninth nights of performance. Instead, Macklin's contract stipulated that he would receive a fifth of the profits from the first five nights at £63 charges (i.e., operating costs) plus a sixth-night benefit. Milhous and Hume estimate that he earned £370 at Drury Lane. Because Macklin was not a regular member of the Drury Lane company for the 1759–60 season, the remuneration was for both his writing and his acting.[84] The next season he contracted with Covent Garden on similar terms and earned an additional £340. This was a highly unusual move, for authors did not earn money from multiple theaters for the performance of the same play. These first two runs alone earned him significantly more than the average afterpiece earned for its author. Typically, authors who sold afterpieces on a benefit system might earn around £100 from the theater and an additional £30 or £40 for its publication.[85] Thus we can see that a successful play had much more profit potential for its author in the theaters than in print. Macklin's decision to keep the play out of print and guard his manuscript proved highly profitable.

Macklin's protection of *Love à la Mode* also ensured his employment as an actor. In contracting with theater managers, he used the play as a selling point. If theater managers wanted the popular afterpiece, they had to take Macklin as well. William Cooke remembers that as Macklin brought the piece to new theaters in London and Dublin, he "retained the character of Sir Archy M'Sarcasm for himself."[86] By Shirley Strum Kenny's count, Macklin played Sir Archy 135 times out of a total of 147 eighteenth-century performances of *Love à la Mode*.[87] With a few exceptions, then, only Macklin could play Sir Archy. When Garrick wrote to Tate Wilkinson in 1760 asking him to perform Sir Archy at Drury Lane, Wilkinson declined, purportedly out of respect for Macklin's right to the character, although he was also dissatisfied with the terms of the agreement.[88] At this point, Macklin had left Drury Lane and was performing at Covent Garden, where he would stage *Love à la Mode* that December. Wilkinson writes that Garrick intended to "hurt (if possible) Mr. Macklin's property in that excellent piece."[89] If Drury Lane staged *Love à la Mode* at the same time as Covent Garden, Macklin's authorial profit would have been lessened as the two theaters competed. Wilkinson situated the phrase "Macklin's property" in a section about his decision not to play Sir Archy, implying that Macklin had property in the role as well as in the text. Wilkinson added, as an afterthought, "Surely the labourer deserves his hire."[90] In referring to Macklin as "the labourer," Wilkinson did not differentiate between the actor and the playwright. Wilkinson's vague use of "property" and "labourer" is reasonable, as the acts of writing and acting were bound up with each other for Macklin. If Macklin's literary property in the piece were not respected, his hold on Sir Archy would not be guaranteed.

And in fact, Macklin's property in the popular farce was not wholly respected. *Love à la Mode* was both printed (in part) and performed without his consent. In April 1766, the *Court Miscellany* printed the first act of Macklin's farce with a promise to print the second act soon thereafter.[91] The magazine's owners, Richardson and Urquhart, had hired shorthand writer Joseph Gurney to go to the theater and copy down the play. Macklin sued the printers. The defendants claimed that because the farce had been performed, it had been published already, which "gave a right to any of the audience to carry away what they could, and make any use of it."[92] But the court held that performance was not a form of publication and that because Macklin had never printed the work himself, he held common-law property in the piece perpetually: "Where the author did not print or publish his work, it was never doubted that no other person had a right to print or publish it." When a work was published in print, it became a "gift to the public," enabling the public to make use of it in various ways, including reprinting small pieces in newspaper reviews and reciting it aloud. "Representation" onstage, however, "was no gift to the public."[93] Chancery delayed hearing Macklin's case until a ruling was reached in *Millar v. Taylor*. The *Millar* case determined that common-law property rights existed independently of statute law. By waiting for that ruling to come down, Macklin was able to claim perpetual rights in his unprinted play.

Macklin used this same logic—that he had perpetual rights in his unprinted play—to argue against unauthorized performances. While the Statute of Anne protected only print, Macklin reasoned that common law protected any publication, including performance. Indeed, he stated this explicitly in a letter to Tate Wilkinson just two days after the *Millar* ruling, explaining that performing the farce without permission was an "illegal act" and "a more offensive Invasion of Property than you perhaps may imagine, as the pirating Booksellers of Edinburgh proved two days ago in Westminster Hall, when the Court of King's Bench finally determined the writings of an Author to be his inherent and perpetual Right."[94] Macklin's letter is exceptional and proves how closely he was following the development of literary property law. In his assertions to Wilkinson, he applied his own interpretation of the ruling, extending common-law rights to protect performance. The *Millar* ruling did not explicitly apply to performance, and indeed it would be overturned within a few years. But Macklin nevertheless built on the case through appeals to managers and assertion of common-law property rights, creating a sort of de facto respect for performance rights. As I will discuss at greater length in chapter 4, Macklin's claims changed the practices of some provincial managers, including Wilkinson. As managers around the country continued to perform Macklin's farce, he continued to claim his rights, ultimately creating a discourse of property rights within the theaters.

In spite of the fact that *Love à la Mode* was not fully printed while Macklin was still performing it, provincial and Irish theaters found ways to recreate the script, enabling them to perform the farce without having to pay Macklin an author's benefit or hire him as an actor. Cobbling together an entire version of the script was tricky work, but it was worth the trouble for such a popular farce. Wilkinson, who in 1760 had declined Garrick's invitation to play Sir Archy at Drury Lane, decided in 1766 to put on the play at Newcastle. He explains, in his *Memoirs*, how he reconstructed the script by piecing together individual parts:

> The part of Sir Archy I had to prepare myself in; Mr. Garrick sent it to me at Winchester in the year 1760; Squire Groom from my friend Ned

Shuter; Mordecai from Mr. Creswick, who had acted the part at Covent Garden; the lady's part from Mrs. Burden's copy, who played it at the same theatre: So I had only to make the Irish character of Sir Callaghan, which by the frequency of seeing the farce, and the help of the first act being printed in a magazine, made it with a little trouble more than half ready to my hands; Sir Theodore, a part from remembrance; the rest of my own manufacture.[95]

While Macklin made a point of taking the full script home with him each night, he did not, apparently, take the actors' sides from them at the end of a run. A number of other theaters performed the play without Macklin's consent, perhaps using techniques similar to Wilkinson's to create a text. Based on Macklin's angry letters to managers, we know that James Whitley's strolling company performed it in 1771; Henry Mossop and his company at Smock Alley performed it in 1762 or 1763; and Robert Owenson's company at Fishamble Street performed it in 1785. Macklin prosecuted or threatened each of these managers, emphasizing the "Great Labour Assiduity Care and Study" that had made the work his own and arguing that the property violation was doubly damaging because he had gained "very considerable reputation Profit and Benefit [from *Love à la Mode*] both as an author as well as an actor."[96] Macklin's complaints emphasized the multiple ways that unauthorized use hurt the actor-playwright. His bill against Owenson charged the manager with profiting not only from use of a play text without paying the author, but also profiting as a performer: "Owenson acted or attempted to perform one of the Principal Characters in the said Farce [which he] could not have done if he had not obtained unjustly the said copy so surreptitiously."

Although performances were not technically a violation of Macklin's property, he compensated for his lack of legal recourse by making a show of his ownership. He embraced his threatening and litigious public character to scare managers away from using his work. When Macklin discovered that Whitley's strolling company intended to perform his farce, he suggested to his lawyer that they should file a bill without warning Whitley, as that "would be more alarming to him, and to others of the same character in life, who have taken the same liberty."[97] On another occasion, Macklin assured Tate Wilkinson that the only reason provincial companies had recently gotten away with performing the farce was that he was in Ireland: "But now I am returned, and shall settle here, depend upon it I shall put the law against every offender of it, respecting my property, in full force."[98] Macklin probably benefited from popular equation of the actor with Shylock, his most famous character. The public saw Macklin as a vengeful figure. In fact, in a rare case when Macklin forgave Wilkinson for performing the farce, Wilkinson commented, "Mr. Shylock to me proved himself no Jew."[99] In 1800, Charles Dibdin recalled that Macklin did not write many plays and instead tried to make a single play support him financially. As a result, Macklin became "a torment to himself and to every body else."[100] Admittedly, Macklin's celebrity persona was often cartoonish in its focus on litigiousness and vengeance. He was certainly more complex than many contemporary descriptions made him out to be. Yet it was this very persona that aided his success, and he seems to have cultivated it when it was convenient to do so. Macklin was famous for vigilantly protecting his plays, and his public character and almost theatrical level of litigiousness made his crusade to limit performances of *Love à la Mode* surprisingly successful.

Macklin wanted his claims made public in order to effect more widespread change. As much as he invoked the law, his strategy was more effectively one of changing the professional norms surrounding use within the theater community.[101] He appealed to the law, but also to "liberality," "morality," and community, calling fellow members of the theater community who infringed on one another's property rights "unsocial." When he wrote to James Whitley, he did not want the manager alone apprised of the contents of his letter, but wanted him to "communicate this letter" to the entire company. He asked for "proper acknowledgement" of their transgressions and "publick assurance that they will never again invade my Property."[102] Later, when Wilkinson asked Macklin's permission to perform the farce for one night only, he actually printed a statement about literary property on his playbills, which I discuss at greater length in chapter 4. This was unprecedented and was an acknowledgment of the playbill's power to communicate norms with theatrical publics.[103] Through retaining his property in *Love à la Mode*, protecting the manuscript, and threatening managers who performed the play without his consent, Macklin managed to control the production of his work in the absence of performance copyright. Doing so benefited him hugely not only as an author but also as an actor looking to ensure his employability. His strategies were unorthodox but effective.

Appleton claims that Macklin "championed the property rights of authors."[104] This is true in the sense that he put the question of performance copyright at the forefront of theater professionals' minds. His ability to sustain a dramatic career largely through the use of one farce illustrated the value of performance. As a result, fellow actors and playwrights began to think about the value of their work differently. Yet Macklin's legacy in terms of authorial empowerment was not immediately straightforward. This is because few playwrights could reasonably replicate his strategies. Macklin was able to make nonpublication a successful strategy not because he had the law backing him. Instead, it was his vigilance in shutting down unauthorized performances that supported this strategy. For, as the many examples of unauthorized performances show, theaters found creative ways to recreate unprinted works. Although the law was clear that an unprinted play remained the author's property to print (as *Macklin v. Richardson* ruled), the law remained murky on whether an unprinted work could be reproduced in performance. It was Macklin's constant attention to provincial performances and his angry letters to managers that supported his case. Not all playwrights had the time or personality to do this. Macklin's eccentric approach to keeping *Love à la Mode* out of the public domain drew attention to the limits of copyright and set in motion a gradual movement by theater professionals to attain clearer, more empowering laws on dramatic literary property. The following chapters trace how Macklin's performance of ownership and his strategy of nonpublication were appropriated and altered by subsequent playwrights, actors, and theater managers.

Chapter 2

Samuel Foote's Strategic Ephemerality

On April 24, 1747, Samuel Foote placed an advertisement in the newspapers, inviting the public to drink chocolate with him:

> On Saturday Noon, exactly at Twelve o'Clock, at the New Theatre in the Haymarket, Mr. Foote begs the Favour of his Friends to come and drink a Dish of Chocolate with him, and 'tis hoped there will be a great deal of good Company, and some Joyous Spirits; he will endeavor to make the *Morning* as *Diverting* as possible.—Tickets for this Entertainment to be had at George's Coffee-house, Temple-bar, without which no Person will be admitted.[1]

Under the guise of drinking chocolate together, Foote was offering his audiences some sort of dramatic entertainment. But what exactly would they be seeing? The advertisement generates interest through its mystery. It also hints at what might be included. The italicized "morning" and "diverting" informed potential audiences that this would be a continuation of the entertainment he had offered two days earlier, *Diversions of the Morning*, which was quickly shut down by the justice of the peace. Both performances were offered in subterfuge, for the 1737 Stage Licensing Act, now a decade old, dictated that no spoken, legitimate drama could be performed outside of the patent theaters. So Foote first advertised a "concert of Musick" accompanied by a free "New Entertainment." When that did not work, he disguised his entertainment as something that sounded even less like drama: drinking chocolate. Continuing to develop the metaphor in his subsequent advertisements, Foote notified the public on May 2 that "the Waiter is well, so that Chocolate may be had as usual."[2] On May 15, the eighteenth day of its performance, the papers teased, "there will be a New Desert. There will be a New Character there."[3] On June 1, he once again changed the title of this continually evolving entertainment, announcing that "at the Request of several Persons, who are desirous of spending an Hour with Mr. Foote, but find the Time inconvenient, instead of Chocolate in the Morning, Mr. Foote's Friends are desired to Drink a Dish of Tea with him, at Half an Hour after Six in the Evening this Day."[4]

Foote's advertisements were effective in attracting audiences, and some version of this entertainment—whether performed under the title *Diversions*, *A Dish of Chocolate*, or *Tea*—ran for thirty-six nights that first summer at the Haymarket and continued to be revived for years to come.[5] These performances marked the start of a successful dramatic career. But while London publics could quench the mystery of what the advertisement was offering by going to see Foote perform live, modern theater historians have no such luck. Neither *Diversions*, *Chocolate*, nor *Tea* was printed. These were sketchy, plotless works, in which the humor lay primarily in Foote's mimicry and performance. Moreover, Foote regularly updated the humor and content, making a stable, reliable text impossible to identify. What remains archivally is not an original performance text, but the advertisements, playbills, and versions of the second act printed decades later, in Tate Wilkinson's *The Wandering Patentee* (1795) and William Cooke's *Memoirs of Samuel Foote, Esq.* (1805). What we know about the original performances is limited. The very nature of the work—particularly its reliance on Foote's performing body and its continually changing content—meant that remediation into print was nearly impossible: too much would be lost.

This chapter reconsiders Foote's career and oeuvre as one of what I call "strategic ephemerality." That is, he embraced performance's existence in a particular moment in time, its changeability from one iteration to the next, and its unfixity. Doing so had multiple benefits. Early in his career, it allowed him to perform outside of the patent theaters, creating works that evaded the oversight of the dramatic censor. Indeed, his career has most frequently been studied in relation to the 1737 Stage Licensing Act.[6] But his authorial strategies, I argue, had as much to do with ownership and control of his works, particularly later in his career. Creating intentionally ephemeral works allowed Foote to assert some control over their circulation. Like Macklin with *Love à la Mode*, he kept many of his dramatic works out of print, including *Diversions*. But he did not rely on nonpublication alone. After all, as the case of *Love à la Mode* shows, rival theaters regularly found ways to recreate unprinted work. So Foote went beyond this by making his physical presence as an actor integral to the production of his works. By composing elements of his works onstage, in performance, through improvisation, mimicry, and bodily humor, he tied his body and celebrity to the production of his plays, making his own presence a selling point. In doing so, he compensated for the lack of a dramatic literary property law, using his body to assert control over his texts. He performed ownership.

By approaching Foote's career through this lens, as one of strategic ephemerality, this chapter not only enriches our understanding of Foote's works. It also highlights the increasingly print-centric nature of legal systems—especially systems for regulating and rewarding the production of literature—arguing that their focus on print altered the relationship between print and performance. Foote's authorship proved a challenge to regulatory systems and notions of property. The 1737 Stage Licensing Act was based on preperformance review of dramatic manuscripts. Yet, as Jane Moody asks in regard to works like Foote's, "How could a system of censorship be imposed on performances for which no texts existed?"[7] Just as performance was difficult to regulate, so too was it difficult to protect as a form of literary property. This had to do in large part with its unfixity. In the famous copyright case, *Donaldson v. Becket* (1774), Sir John Dalrymple argued that literary works needed to be published in a tangible form to confer property rights. He recognized that there are modes of publishing that are not print-based, "such as by gesture, action, and manner." As an example of such a nontextual publication, Dalrymple pointed to a work that was not part of the case at all: Foote's *Primitive Puppet Show*, which had recently been performed at the Haymarket. Yet he firmly asserted "the absurdity of claiming a property in such modes of publication," because performance as a mode of publication is not fixed and tangible.[8]

If performance's ephemerality was worrying to some theater professionals, it was empowering to others. This chapter contributes to work on performance's ephemerality, as I shift the discussion away from one of loss. Ephemerality is a controversial topic among scholars. Some, like Peggy Phelan, define the medium by its ephemerality: it disappears at the very moment it is enacted.[9] Many eighteenth-century actors, including Colley Cibber and David Garrick, expressed frustration that their art did not have the staying power of print or the visual arts. On the other hand, for scholars including Diana Taylor and Rebecca Schneider, defining performance by its ephemerality, or as that which is always disappearing, privileges a print-centric worldview and ignores the medium's ability to preserve itself through reperformance. As Taylor writes, "Embodied memory, because it is live, exceeds the archive's ability to capture it. But that does not mean that performance—as ritualized, formalized, or reiterated behavior—disappears. Performances also replicate themselves through their own structures and codes."[10] Taylor's insistence that performance "persists" through the repertoire has roots in the eighteenth century: as I will show in chapter 4, eighteenth-century actors were particularly conscious of preserving works in this way. Yet I argue that the term "ephemeral" is useful, for it captures what Foote was celebrating about performance: that each night his original embodiment of his own plays existed within a particular moment and could not be identically replicated—especially not without his own participation as an actor. While this quality of his work prompted criticism from contemporaries who suspected that the works would not outlast their author, it also enabled him to control their circulation in the absence of a literary property law protecting performance. His works' ephemerality was in one sense associated with loss. In another sense, it was the very quality that protected their value for the performer.

This chapter begins with Foote's earliest works, considering their ephemeral nature and attempts to remediate them into print. I then examine how his authorial strategies developed in relation to legal systems that were structured around print. Moving from his relationship with the Stage Licensing Act to his relationship with literary property law, I argue that Foote's authorial strategies grew out of and also disrupted print-based legal systems. His turn away from print went further than Macklin's, for not only did Foote often reject print publication, but he created works whose very nature evaded that possibility. Foote's authorial strategies—particularly making his celebrity presence integral to the performance of his work—enabled him to control the circulation of his work to a large extent. Yet he could not control it fully. In the final section of this chapter, I suggest that Foote's strategic ephemerality was undermined by the very art he practiced: mimicry. Through his performances of Foote's works in imitation of Foote's performance style, the actor and mimic Tate Wilkinson challenged Foote's exclusive control over both his literary works and his celebrity persona. Mimicry became a mode of piracy.

FOOTE'S EARLY CAREER: LICENSING, LEGITIMACY, AND THE PERFORMING BODY

Samuel Foote's first appearance on the London stage as an actor, as well as the premieres of his earliest works, blatantly violated the 1737 Stage Licensing Act. In 1744, Foote made his acting debut at the Little Theatre at the Haymarket, where Macklin, who was then running a school for acting, gave a series of performances under the guise of concerts.[11] Three years later, spurred by the need to create roles more suitable to his talents, Foote wrote *Diversions of the Morning* (1747), which he advertised as "a New Entertainment" to be given for free at the Haymarket alongside a "concert of Musick." Thus, his authorial career began in subterfuge. This illicit performance marked a decade from the passage of the Licensing Act, a law that strictly limited the performances of "any interlude, tragedy, comedy, opera, play, farce, or other entertainment of the Stage" to the two royally sanctioned patent theaters at Drury Lane and Covent Garden.[12] The act's strict limitations gave rise to actors performing illegally and authors—sometimes from among the actors—providing dramatic material for them. These prohibited activities, which began as early as James Lacy's 1737 "orations" in the York Buildings in Villiers Street, formed a theatrical culture in opposition to the "legitimate" theater of Drury Lane and Covent Garden.[13]

Foote operated between legitimate and illegitimate realms of theater, crafting an authorial persona that highlighted the audaciousness of his performances but also allowed him to socialize in respected literary circles. While his acting debut was at Macklin's illegal operation, he subsequently performed at Drury Lane, Covent Garden, and Smock Alley in Dublin. He premiered the majority of his plays at the Haymarket, a space Jane Moody calls "the playhouse on the institutional border between the monopolists (Drury Lane and Covent Garden) and the minor establishments," but wrote a few specifically for the patent houses.[14] Moreover, his illicit performances were so popular that managers of the patent theaters—the very theaters whose monopoly he was invading—sought out Foote to perform his works in their state-sanctioned venues. Foote commodified the illegality of his performances. Upon performing *Diversions of the Morning* at Drury Lane in 1758, Foote made a show of outsmarting the law and the monopolists by beginning the second act with a conversation between Puzzle (played by Foote) and the Prompter:

PUZZLE. A Truce to your impertinence! I tell you, I'm above law!
PROMPT. Why, Sir, 'twas but last night I heard a goodish-looking well-dressed man, that sat in the next box at the porter-house, affirm, that to his knowledge, if you proceeded to exhibit, you and your pupils would all be sent to Bridewell.
PUZ. So much the better—the ministry will then interpose.[15]

This opening exchange paints Puzzle, or Foote, as a brazen, fearless personality. The act ends with Puzzle being called to Westminster Hall to account for his illegal performances. As a Drury Lane afterpiece, *Diversions* capitalizes on Foote's notoriety to attract audiences into the patent house. Kinservik argues that Foote's performances of himself represent not who he really was as a satirist, but the version of himself he wished to project: a modern Aristophanes.[16] Foote was the most successful playwright to make a place for himself in legitimate theatrical culture and also to operate on his own terms on the outskirts of legitimacy, altering generic conventions, making strong use of his body through mimicry, and evading government regulations.

The emerging opposition between legitimate and illegitimate theater influenced the way the public understood dramatic authorship. Moody argues that the difference between legitimate and illegitimate theater was increasingly understood as the difference between text and body. The "legitimate" was spoken, text-based drama, ideally in pure generic form: comedy or tragedy. The playwright Douglas Jerrold argued that in legitimate drama, "the interest of the piece is mental; where the situation of the piece is rather mental than physical."[17] The illegitimate was the theater of the London fairs, pantomime, and "entertainments" like rope dancing and juggling.[18] As Moody puts it, the gulf between the legitimate and illegitimate "soon beg[an] to be imagined as a nightmarish confrontation between quasi-ethereal textuality and grotesque corporeality."[19]

In creating a form of authorship on the border of legitimacy, Foote combined creative invention through the text and body. He crafted incomplete texts, meant to be completed in performance. His earliest plays, in particular, were plotless and sketchy, relying on the actor to develop characters and improvise scenes, ensuring that the humor and satire would be topical. The textual incompleteness allowed Foote to adjust his performances to venues and audiences as necessary. When the justice of the peace stopped his performance of *Diversions* on April 23, 1747, he was able to start it back up just two days later by advertising an invitation "to come and drink a Dish of Chocolate with him."[20] His early biographer William Cooke writes that having discovered public demand for his mimicry, "he had nothing to do but evade the act," and his evasion was highly successful: "The joke succeeded to a tittle; and he not only proceeded without further molestation that morning, but through a course of *forty* others that season, in thus *giving tea* to crowded and splendid audiences."[21] When audiences grew eager for novelty, Foote advertised a new character. And when John Rich contracted with Foote to perform *Tea* as an afterpiece at Covent Garden in the winter of 1747, Foote could alter the content to make it less offensive to his fellow actors at the patent house, many of whom he had mimicked in earlier versions.[22]

We can see in his first play just how malleable and performance-based his early work was. Indeed, it is inappropriate to refer to it as a single play at all, as the work transformed from *Diversions* to *Tea* to *Chocolate*. No full edition was printed, and the segments that did eventually appear in print are better considered as textual remediations than representations of the work. Wilkinson, in particular, was aware of the impossibility of capturing the work in print, and thus his version, included at the end of his *Wandering Patentee* (1795), deliberately presents the text as the record of a single performance in the play's long and evolving stage life.

Wilkinson's printing of "The Second Act of Diversions of the Morning, as Acted at the Theatre-Royal, Drury Lane, 1758–9," conveys his struggle to commit the work to print. The dramatis personae represents his May 14 benefit night, which was advertised with Wilkinson playing Puzzle. This was a part that Foote usually performed. The advertisement for his benefit performance notes that Puzzle is performed "with additions by Mr. Wilkinson, (in the manner of the Original)."[23] The text that Wilkinson prints, then, may not be entirely of Foote's composition, but adapted by Wilkinson. Moreover, the work had already been altered that season in response to audience demand: after the 1758 premiere at Drury Lane, there had been "Great Calling for ye Imitations & they were done" in subsequent performances.[24] Foote undoubtedly altered the objects of mimicry many times over between the 1747 premier and the 1758–59 season.

With so much of the humor of Foote's plays laying in imitation and performance, remediation into print was challenging. As the Multigraph Collective notes, printing a play means that "the transitory nature of performance comes into dialogue, if not conflict, with the more permanent nature of print."[25] The two media forms function differently, each limited by its distinct affordances. Heather Davis-Fisch asks, "How can one locate and recuperate the repertoire—the embodied performances of the past—in and from the archive?"[26] Performance cannot be fully conveyed or preserved through print. This is true regardless of the play. But the performance-dependent nature of Foote's works made the rift between media especially visible. Wilkinson's edition answers Davis-Fisch's question precisely by acknowledging print's limits. The text that Wilkinson prints is not the play itself, but a historical document attempting to reconstruct a moment in the play's ever-changing stage history.

Wilkinson used footnotes to indicate mimicry and explain what were, by 1795, historical references. After a line in which Puzzle states that he intends to write a treatise on elocution, Wilkinson adds the note that "Mr. Sheridan was then giving lectures."[27] A note on the very next page informs readers that "the scene between Puzzle and Bounce was meant as mimicry of Macklin's teaching Barry Othello." The notes function as stage and historical referents, indicating how something was performed or explaining context for 1795 readers. The single footnote that best captures the limits of remediating the play to print, while also suggesting the layers of humor that performance would convey, comes after Puzzle calls Wilkinson onstage to give his imitations. When Wilkinson fails to appear, Puzzle—who is being played by Wilkinson—says that he will give those imitations himself. The footnote summarizes: "Here Mr. Wilkinson in the character of Mr. Foote, as Puzzle, gave an imitation of Mr. Foote and Mrs. Clive, in Mr. and Mrs. Cadwallader, and other characters, which filled up more than a quarter of an hour."[28] This confusing note tells readers that Wilkinson as Puzzle imitates Foote's and Clive's imitations of two real people by the name of Mr. and Mrs. Apreece whom Foote had "taken off"—or satirically mimicked—in the characters of the Cadwalladers in *The Author*. Fifteen minutes gets condensed to a footnote, and layers of humor have to be imagined—likely to little effect for the reader who had not also seen the play in performance.

Wilkinson's textual reconstruction of his 1759 benefit night raises broader questions about what Foote's printed texts were and how they were meant to be read. Foote did not print a version of a work called *Diversions* or *Tea* or *Chocolate*, likely because he understood that these medleys would be incomprehensible in print. Yet he did print many of his other works. His works that more closely resembled traditional comedy or farce—including *The Englishman in Paris* (1753), *The Mayor of Garret* (1763), and *The Commissary* (1765)—would have been comprehensible independent of performance. Aside from the typical, formulaic "as it is acted at" clause on his title pages, Foote's printed texts rarely invoke previous performances the way that Wilkinson's reprinting does. He does not indicate performance elements, such as mimicry, ad-libbing, or costume. It appears that his printed texts are not explicitly intended to summon a memory of the performance. In practice, the texts did summon memory, as we find instances of readers annotating their own texts with reference to Foote's performances. Horace Walpole, for instance, added footnotes to his own copies to indicate whom Foote was mimicking.[29] It would be nearly impossible for Foote's performances and his printed texts to operate independently of each other, yet he seems not to have intended the printed texts as representations of the performance. Such a reading is supported by Kinservik's argument that Foote's characters as acted are "distinct" from his characters as written; while public figures were "taken off" in performance, they were not always satirized in the text.[30] The printed text and the performance operate as separate artistic objects whose modes of publication enable different forms of humor and create different experiences for the consumer.

But while many of Foote's plays are readable as printed texts, critical reception suggested that the works would only survive while Foote's body survived to sustain them. That is, audiences saw Foote's works fundamentally as performances, not as literary texts. Foote's acting was an integral part of the work itself. Benjamin Victor notes the dependence of Foote's plays on his acting, observing that "Mr. Foote has produced some Characters, which, perhaps, would fail of the Effect from any Performer but himself."[31] George Carey, in *Momus* (1767), speculated that Foote's plays would not outlive their author, because the actor-playwright's body was an integral component of their performance: "Grief! that his name must with his body die, / And all his bantlings with their father lie, / When, lacking his distortion and grimace, / Their sole protection and their only grace, / Spurn'd and detested in some wiser age, / Will never more get footing on the stage."[32] Such language sounds familiar, as actors often lamented that their performances, and thus their art, would die along with them. Garrick, for instance, famously declared, in the preface to *The Clandestine Marriage* (1766), "But he, who struts his Hour upon the Stage, / Can scarce extend his Fame for Half an Age; / Nor Pen nor Pencil can the Actor save, / The Art, and Artist, share one common Grave." But while Garrick was lamenting that the actor's art would die with the actor, Carey takes the idea a step further, observing that in the case of Foote, the actor-playwright's plays themselves would die alongside the actor.

LEGAL FORMULATIONS OF AUTHORSHIP

The degree to which writing and acting were inseparable in Foote's works becomes clear when looking at the trouble his mode of authorship caused systems of theatrical regulation. Foote's authorship disrupted increasingly print-based modes of regulation and authorial liability. The regulation of drama is always complex. Performance—because of its intangibility and its inherently dispersed authorship—causes problems both for preperformance regulation and postperformance punishment. Who is liable for words spoken onstage? The Licensing Act relied on certain assumptions about the relationship between the author's text and the actor's performance, in particular that the words spoken onstage would align with the manuscript submitted for review, and that the text itself was enough to gauge a performance's meaning. Foote's mode of composing works through improvisation and bodily humor upset this system, which, for the most part, functioned effi-ciently. Foote's works illustrated the challenges in holding him accountable as an author, when there were not clear distinctions between his multiple capacities as actor, author, and publisher.

The 1737 Stage Licensing Act—the law that motivated many of Foote's early-career choices and shaped the form of his early works—had a fun-damental flaw: it did not account for onstage invention. The law required managers to submit manuscript copies of the plays they intended to pro-duce to the Examiner of Plays. He might strike out words and mandate changes before granting the theater permission to perform the work. But in sanctioning performances based on written texts, the law assumed a basic conformity between text and performance. In essence, the approved manu-scripts were contracts for performance, stipulating that only the words on the page would be spoken on the stage. The system was created as such, at least in part, for its efficiency. Reading a text is quicker than sending some-one to watch rehearsals or sit in on performances. It also leaves a record. Yet a text-based regulatory system can only manage one dimension of perfor-mance: the words themselves. In any performance, actors and managers add layers of meaning through nontextual forms of expression.

In spite of its failure to address nontextual invention, the Licensing Act was largely effective. As Kinservik observes, rarely did the government have to suppress a play outright or after its initial performances. This absence of suppression, he argues, is evidence of an effective regulatory system: "The most effective censorship law is one that disciplines writers and readers so that they create and consume 'appropriate' material."[33] The law also taught managers, who were the ones submitting plays to the Lord Chamberlain, to be self-policing, submitting plays that they suspected would be accepted. With authors and managers policing their own actions, trouble rarely arose. But in 1758, Foote proved that a licensed text might not be so innocuous in performance, when it was his body rather than his words that provoked outrage. On January 27, 1757, Garrick and James Lacy applied for a license to produce Foote's new play, The Author, at Drury Lane. Unlike many of his previous plays, which he had premiered at the Haymarket, The Author was opening at one of the patent houses and thus went through the appropriate legal channels of the Lord Chamberlain's office.[34] The manuscript submitted to the Examiner of Plays (the Larpent Manuscript) shows few corrections or emendations, so we know that the Lord Chamberlain's office did not find the text offensive. After the piece was performed, however, it met with a signifi-cant complaint. Foote had mimicked a man named Mr. Apreece in the char-acter of Cadwallader. According to contemporary reports, Apreece initially laughed at the piece—some anecdotes even suggest that he had asked Foote to bring him onstage to heighten his public visibility.[35] But after the play took off and Apreece and his wife could not walk through London without being identified as the Cadwalladers, he asked Garrick to stop producing the piece. Garrick suggested to Apreece that he should apply to the Lord Chamberlain to stop the performances, saying that the Lord Chamberlain had "too much humanity to suffer any gentleman to be hurt by personal representation."[36] And so Apreece did. On December 18, 1758, as Foote was preparing to perform *The Author* for his benefit night, the Lord Chamberlain revoked Drury Lane's license for the play.[37]

This revocation shows us that when dealing with an actor-playwright, whose invention was largely enacted through his body, the Licensing Act could fail to detect a play's offensive elements. Kinservik notes that "if the Lord Chamberlain had known that Foote intended to mimic Apreece in the play, he might have refused his license or demanded alterations."[38] But the Lord Chamberlain could not have known of the mimicry, because the text itself makes no mention of it, and the character of Cadwallader, as written, does not resemble Apreece. Kinservik argues that this incident illustrates that the text and the mimicry have distinct satiric ends. This is undoubtedly true. But the incident tells us more than that. The actor-playwright's invention extended beyond the text, and a text-based regulatory system was not equipped to discipline performance.

If the system of preperformance review could not account for his mimicry and his mode of composing works through his body, there was always the possibility that Foote might be punished for his work after a performance. Given how many people he took off, it is surprising that this did not happen more often. The story of his punishment for mimicking George Faulkner in *The Orators* (1762), however, deserves greater attention, for it reveals the difficulty in limiting liability for the performance of a dramatic work to the original writer. The scope of "authorship" here expands to accommodate actors, as it had prior to the Licensing Act.

The Orators, a play lacking a single unifying plot, strings together a series of scenes that provided Foote and his company with opportunities for mimicry and individual satire. The play satirizes different forms of oratory. In the opening scene, Foote performs an oratory instructor, teaching his pupils the principles of the art, which in England, he tells them, is practiced in "the pulpit, the senate, the bar, and the stage."[39] As he delivered long speeches on the topic, Foote mimicked Thomas Sheridan, who was delivering lectures on elocution at the time.[40] The second scene narrows the focus to legal oratory, and Foote teaches his pupils the art by having them enact the imaginary trial of Fanny Phantom, the ghost of Cock Lane.[41] The text itself proves readable, both because the scene presents a brief, ridiculous plot, and because the text's replication of legal language conveys humor on the page as well as on the stage. For instance, the indictment against the ghost, which one of Foote's pupils recites as he is performing the role of clerk, adopts the long string of adverbs and verbs typically found in treason trials: "You, the said Fanny . . . maliciously, treacherously, wickedly, and willfully, by certain thumpings, knockings, scratchings, and flutterings against doors, walls, wainscots, bedsteds, and bedposts, disturb, annoy, assault, and terrify divers innocent, inoffensive, harmless, quiet, simple people."[42] The choice of words to describe the offense, including "flutterings," shows how legal oratory can transform something as ridiculous as the indictment of a ghost into a "serious" matter. After some debate, the Justice concludes that because Fanny is a ghost, she is "entitled to a jury of ghosts."[43] Any reader familiar with legal language and procedures would undoubtedly find this scene funny.

In this scene, Foote introduces readers to Peter Paragraph, whom the text describes as "an eminent printer" with "the misfortune to have but one leg."[44] Paragraph's inclusion is by no means integral to the plot, the satire of legal oratory, or the satire of the Cock Lane ghost debacle. Foote writes him in as a witness to the case, called to testify because he has "collected for the public information, every particular relative to this remarkable story."[45] The character was based on George Faulkner, a Dublin printer who published the *Dublin Journal*, was close to Jonathan Swift, and regularly came to London to hobnob with some of London's most prominent citizens. Foote satirizes Faulkner's pretensions to celebrity. Throughout the brief scene, Peter Paragraph unnecessarily name-drops important Londoners and assures the court, "I know *peers*, and *peers* know me."[46] When asked why he came to London during the time of the Cock Lane ghost incident, he responds with a story about "a little love affair."[47] Moreover, he boasts that although his wife was prone to jealousy as a result of his affairs, he was generous enough to write about her glowingly in his *Dublin Journal*. He flatters himself in thinking that giving his wife a "prodigious good character" in his journal appeases her jealousy. Although the depiction of Paragraph does not directly satirize oratory, the character does satirize a particular way of speaking and presenting oneself.

These textual elements of satire did not cast Faulkner in a good light, but neither were they biting. It was Foote's mimicry of Faulkner, hobbling about the stage and replicating his mannerisms, that added force and color to the caricature. Foote described his own method in taking off Faulkner: he "cull'd, with curious care, / his voice, his looks, his gesture, gait, and air,

/ His affectation, consequence, and mien, / And boldly launch'd him on the comic scene."[48] Foote boasts of his success, writing that "all felt the satire, for all knew the man."[49] William Cooke, who is critical of the piece, summarizes the source of the humor in writing, "Crowded audiences were found repeatedly roaring at a few common-place stories, told in a ridiculous manner by a man hopping upon one leg."[50]

Without the verve that Foote brought to the performances through his mimicry and ad-libbing, the play would have been unlikely to sustain interest and popularity for as long as it did. During its first summer at the Haymarket, *The Orators* ran for thirty-nine nights. While a review of the play's premiere only briefly mentions Foote's "infinite humour and accuracy" in "taking off" Faulkner, later reviews focus almost exclusively on that impersonation.[51] Cooke reasoned that "such is the propensity of human nature for personal scandal, that the comedy was principally supported by this character."[52] Foote's mimicry accrued even more interest after Faulkner threatened to sue him for libel. Foote had traveled to Dublin with the intent to stage the show in Faulkner's home city. Faulkner declared that if Foote brought him onstage, he would prosecute—so naturally Foote did just that, integrating this very threat into the updated performance. A "Letter from Dublin" reprinted in the *London Magazine* reports that when Foote's Peter Paragraph was called to testify in the Fanny Phantom trial, he did not immediately appear. Audiences at first supposed that Faulkner had successfully scared Foote. But just as audiences grew restless, Paragraph appeared onstage with "so laughable an extravagance of the manners of Falkner [*sic*]," declaring that he had been held up because he was with his lawyer, deciding how to prosecute Foote.[53] Foote's ability to adapt his plays to evolving situations proved a great strength, as it increased his own celebrity and reinforced the satire on Faulkner.

Faulkner followed through on his threat, first by getting an injunction suppressing the performance (which Foote ignored), and then by suing Foote for libel. Foote was released on bail for £400 and owed Faulkner a settlement of £300.[54] In examining what Foote was punished for, it is interesting to consider the advice that the Earl of Chesterfield gave Faulkner. Because the brunt of Foote's satire on Faulkner occurred during performance, when the Earl of Chesterfield wrote to Faulkner recommending that he bring Foote to court, he added, "I do not mean for writing the said Farce, but for acting it."[55] Faulkner's correspondence with Chesterfield illustrates the complicated nature of Foote's punishment. On July 1, 1762, Chesterfield wrote to Faulkner to inform him that "Mr. Foote ... takes you off, as it is vulgarly called, that is, acts you in his new Farce, called *the Orators*."[56] Chesterfield writes that "the government here [in London] cannot properly take notice of it" and suggestively asks Faulkner, "Would it be amiss that you should shew some spirit upon this occasion, either by way of stricture, contempt, or by bringing an action against him[?]" Chesterfield's suggestion that Faulkner pursue Foote for *acting* the farce invokes a fascinating history of actor-punishment—a history that Chesterfield had taken a clear stance on twenty-five years earlier in his speech against the Stage Licensing Act. Kinservik writes that Chesterfield had urged Faulkner to sue Foote "despite his memorable speech against the Licensing Act."[57] A close look at the speech, however, reveals that the suggestion is consistent with his stance on licensing. Chesterfield had not objected to punishing authors or actors for stage performances. Indeed, he believed that actors and authors should be held liable for onstage publications. What Chesterfield had objected to was preperformance censorship, which he saw as an infringement on English liberty and a precursor to press censorship.[58] He believed that actors and managers should have the right to perform any plays that they wanted, with the understanding that should the plays be found offensive, they were liable to punishment.

Chesterfield's speech focuses, interestingly, not on authorial liability, but on actor liability. He argues,

> If the stage becomes at any time licentious, if a play appears to be a libel upon the government, or upon any particular man, the king's courts are open, the law is sufficient for punishing the offender; and in this case the person injured has a singular advantage, he can be under no difficulty to prove who is the publisher; the players themselves are the publishers, and there can be no want of evidence to convict them.[59]

Chesterfield does not mention punishing the author, but instead jumps right to the publishers, who in the case of performance are actors. There are two possible ways to read his focus on publishers. He may have assumed that the prosecutor would naturally first pursue the author, but in the case of an anonymous text, would next turn to the publisher. Authors, particularly before the passage of the 1710 Statute of Anne, were more difficult to identify than publishers, and as a result, the government had historically held publishers liable for authorial sentiments. As Jody Greene and Joseph Loewenstein both argue, prior to the 1710 act, liability for a work was "distributed over the widest possible field"—from publishers, printers, booksellers, and even proofreaders—to ensure that someone would be held responsible for a treasonous, blasphemous, or libelous work.[60]

The widely dispersed nature of authorship and authorial liability in the seventeenth century was a way to use a publisher as a substitute for an unidentifiable author. Moreover, it recognized the many figures necessary for the creation and dissemination of a text. Publishers were authors because they were creators, and this was arguably truer in the theaters. Actors published and republished texts from one night to the next. Eighteenth-century acting manuals stressed that actors (unlike print publishers) had to understand the author's meaning in order to succeed in their art. Actors' degree of understanding, and their additions to the text through their body, expression, and sometimes ad-libbing, made them authorial figures. Thus, it is possible that Chesterfield was not suggesting that actors could be punished when the authors were not identifiable or alive, but that actors should always be held responsible for their performances, as they understood their parts and chose to publish them. Chesterfield promotes a system of self-policing, arguing that the threat of punishment will prevent actors from bringing "any seditious libel upon the stage": actors have an obligation to censor the texts that they perform.[61] Chesterfield adopts the older notion of the publisher as a type of author, or a figure who, by the act of publishing sentiments that he understands, shares in authorial liability.

Chesterfield's logic was not of his own time, but of an earlier era. He argues that there is precedent for actor-punishments, but most of these precedents are to be found in the seventeenth or very early eighteenth centuries. John Lacy, for instance, had been imprisoned in 1667 for adding "gags" that were offensive to Charles II in Edward Howard's *The Change of Crowns*.[62] Katherine Corey was punished for impersonating Lady Harvey in *Catiline* in 1669.[63] In 1682, the epilogue to Aphra Behn's *Romulus and Hersilia* was found to contain "abusive reflections on several persons of quality"—specifically the Duke of Monmouth. Both Behn, as the author, and Lady Slingsby, the actress delivering the epilogue, were taken into custody.[64] Some instances of actor-punishment show us that during the Restoration and early eighteenth century, actors assumed an authorial role simply by performing plays, regardless of whether they improvised or impersonated anyone. George Bright was arrested in 1700 for performing the part of Bellair in George Etherege's *The Man of Mode* for speaking words (specifically the name of God) that were written in the text.[65] Each of these instances suggests that the government in the late seventeenth and early eighteenth centuries viewed performance as a collaborative endeavor with multiple participants subject to authorial liability. Yet after the early eighteenth century, there is a decrease in actors being punished for the content of a play. This coincides with the narrowing of "authorship" to signify only the creative originator, or writer, of a work. Jody Greene argues that copyright, by incentivizing authors to "own up" to their works, narrowed and solidified the concept of the "author" as the imaginative source of a work and the person responsible for its content. Chesterfield's insistence on actor liability in 1737, and again in 1762, is savvy, for it recognizes a form of authorship and invention that the text-based Licensing Act failed to. When Chesterfield urged Faulkner to sue Foote for acting rather than writing, he understood that the performance rather than the written text was the libelous mode of composition.

That Foote was punished not for writing, but for performing, is evident not only from Chesterfield's advice to Faulkner, but also from Faulkner's subsequent publication of the play in print. The same year that he sued Foote, Faulkner published a Dublin edition of the play, without removing the character of Peter Paragraph. Unsurprisingly, Foote mocked this publication. When he revived *The Orators* the next year in London, he added a brief, farcical reinterpretation of his own libel trial to the performance, "Trial of Samuel Foote, Esq. for a Libel on Peter Paragraph." He ends this farce by turning the table on Faulkner: his lawyer sues Peter Paragraph, arguing, "If my client is a libeller for writing the Orators, Peter Paragraph, for printing and publishing it is as guilty as he every whit."[66] Yet, as I have argued, without Foote's performance, the satire on Peter Paragraph lacked teeth. Faulkner's publication in print was not, as Foote would have his audiences believe, a libel on himself.

Foote's prosecution for libel was based on a broad formulation of "authorship." Foote wrote the play, and he published it through his acting, adding new words and mimicry during the performance. He was thus author, actor, and publisher, and each of these roles overlapped with one another. It was not a print-based definition of "authorship" that Foote was being punished for. His mode of authorship blurred the lines between actor, author, and publisher, complicating the relationship between authorship and liability. Foote's run-ins with systems of censorship and punishment point to the problems in thinking about authorship purely in textual terms. This way of defining authorship did not work in the theaters. Authorial regulation was not the only legal arena in which this was true: systems for protecting literary property were similarly flawed in their print-centric nature. Thus, just as Foote had embraced the ephemerality of performance to evade regulatory systems, so too did he turn away from print and embrace performance's ephemerality in order to control the circulation of his work.

FOOTE'S FACE:
CONTROLLING PRODUCTION THROUGH SINGULARITY

Foote's distinctive mode of composing his works through a combination of writing and acting not only made it more difficult to regulate his authorship, but also made it impossible for the legal system to reward him with property in his works. Like any author, he could copyright his works by printing them. But, as the previous chapter has shown, he could not copyright the most valuable mode of publication: performance. The nature of his performance, moreover, would frustrate even today's copyright system, because his works were neither stable nor fixed. In this regard, they resemble today's stand-up comedy, which also runs into problems effectively using the copyright system. As Dotan Oliar and Christopher Sprigman write, "To enjoy copyright protection, a joke must be fixed in a tangible medium of expression. While writing the joke on a piece of paper would suffice, the nature of the art sometimes makes this requirement difficult to meet. First, many stand-up acts are not fully scripted, and depend, to a non-trivial degree, on ad-libbing and audience interaction."[67] For this and other reasons, stand-up comedians rarely turn to the law for protection, but instead rely on professional norms established within and enforced by their own community, not unlike Macklin's method of creating new norms. Like today's comedians, Foote worked in a medium impossible to capture in fixed form, and he therefore could not turn to the laws themselves.

Although the unfixity of Foote's performances made it impossible for him to copyright and protect his creations, this very quality also made it more difficult for theaters to replicate the works. In the case of Foote's plays, audiences were not going to the theater only to see a particular set of words performed. They were going to see the physical mimicry that the plays enabled. Eighteenth-century audiences were fascinated by Foote's performing body. Commentary on his face, and its comedic power, permeated popular discourse surrounding his career. In a letter to Garrick following Foote's riding accident and leg amputation, the actor William O'Brien commented that

> as to Foote, tho his [accident] was a shocking thing, yet one expects him to turn ev'ry disaster into Joke, & draw subsistence from calamity: nothing can ever effectually hurt him but meeting with the misfortune of some beggars I have seen in the streets, of having his tongue cut out by the Turks, but even then he could get money by making faces.[68]

O'Brien's confidence that even a mute Foote could attract an audience attests to his ability to express ideas and create laughter through his body and face. O'Brien was not the only person to refer to Foote's face as an independent creator of meaning. Henry Fielding satirized the extent to which Foote expressed meaning (or, to Fielding's mind, a lack of meaning) through physical gesture rather than through text. In a mock trial "at the Court of

Criticism" in Fielding's *Jacobite's Journal*, Foote is charged with "mauling" and "hacking" people with his "hatchet-face" at his "Scandal-Shop" in the Haymarket. When asked to defend himself, Foote "remain[s] silent," but "perform[s] many ridiculous gestures," and is subsequently found guilty.[69] Fielding's satire suggests that Foote's reliance on gestures rather than words makes him unintelligible in any mode of performance other than mimicry. He concludes that Foote is neither a skilled actor nor author, but makes his living entirely by the labor of his face. Yet Fielding's criticism misses an important fact: it was this labor of his face that allowed Foote to develop his celebrity as an actor-playwright and assume creative authority over his works.

During a period when dramatists struggled not only to get their plays staged, but to have some degree of control over their performance, Foote's bodily satire afforded him greater control over his texts and their stage productions than most playwrights could hope for. It is a truism of theater scholarship to acknowledge the collaborative nature of performance and the ways in which actors and managers challenge the sole authority of the playwright. Nora Johnson, for instance, argues that "on the early modern stage, where the economics, the collaboration, the physicality of theatrical production speak more forcefully than they do in the printed book—where an audience applauds or hisses—authorship takes its proper place: as a relational form, a contest, a negotiation."[70] Johnson's contrasting of performance with print is indicative of another widely held belief: dramatists were more able to assert singular authorship on the printed page than in the theater. Early modern scholars often turn to Ben Jonson to illustrate this argument. Douglas Brooks, for instance, discusses Jonson's "authorial singularity" and argues that this singularity "could only be achieved and maintained in the printed text."[71] It is logical that playwrights could most fully control their texts in print, where they did not have to negotiate the terms of production and interpretation with actors and managers.

Although modern notions of proprietary authorship were firming up over the course of the century, the author's ability to control his works in the theater remained weak. In fact, Tiffany Stern argues that during the Garrick era, the playwright and his intentions "were not of great importance."[72] Managers altered texts before and after the first performance, and actors revised their own parts. Paulina Kewes argues that by the middle of the century, playwrights were making fewer proprietary and artistic claims.[73] A playwright might still use print to assert creative control over his work, particularly when censors or managers altered a play heavily. But within the theaters themselves, most playwrights could not hope to assert authorial singularity. Foote proves an exception. It was in the theaters rather than in print that Foote was able to assert his authorial singularity fully.[74] He did so by creating "unfinished" texts that only he could complete in performance. Foote wrote, acted in, and managed his own works. His body, gestures, and expression became integral parts of his authorship. He further ensured that his presence was necessary for the production of a work by developing a distinct celebrity persona and creating demand for not only his plays, but for himself.

Foote celebrated his own status as a dramatic author to an extent that Kewes would call uncharacteristic of eighteenth-century dramatists. His newspaper advertisements consistently featured his name, even when his performances were illegal. Indeed, because it was initially unclear to many people what his early performances were actually offering—as in the case of *A Dish of Chocolate*—Foote relied on a combination of mystery and his name to attract audiences. What he was offering was not a play that any theater could reproduce, but an experience in which he himself was the main feature. Moreover, Foote put his name on the title pages of all of his printed plays. In fact, Foote explicitly stated his belief that playwrights ought to acknowledge their works before they could be sure of their stage success, because doing so incentivizes the author to write work he is proud of. In his first piece of dramatic criticism, *A Treatise on the Passions* (1747), Foote humorously chides Garrick for not owning up to *Miss in her Teens* (1747). By expressing mock disbelief that an actor as successful as Garrick could have written such a "paltry farce," he asserts the importance of associating an author with his works. Indeed, Kewes's claims about playwrights' diminished sense of their artistic abilities do not stand up when looking at Foote's career.[75] Foote tied his name to his works, empowering himself as both an actor and a playwright. Over his roughly thirty-year career in the theater, Foote asserted his authorial singularity by creating works that required both his own writing and his own acting and by using his celebrity to control the production and publication of his works.

That Foote developed his celebrity largely through his mimicry, however, invoked a set of questions about originality, imitation, theft, and property. Moody has argued that "Foote used the celebrity of other people as the artistic raw material for the creation of his own fame."[76] As recent work in celebrity studies has demonstrated, celebrity relies on such repetition: Leo Braudy points out that those striving for fame often model their images on those of the earlier greats, while Joseph Roach defines celebrity as a state in which individuals' "images circulate widely in the absence of their persons." The "tension between their widespread visibility and their actual remoteness,"

Roach argues, creates public desire for seeing the celebrity in person.[77] As a phenomenon that emerged "at the moment private life became a tradeable public commodity," celebrity relies on an extensive media apparatus.[78] Reproduction of the celebrity's image often occurs in material form, from theater reviews and prints to figurines.[79] But mimicry, too, functioned as a form of this repetition, going beyond static, print-based reproductions of celebrity to pass on a sort of cultural memory that could only be transmitted through the body.[80] As Leslie Ritchie convincingly argues about the eighteenth-century theaters, nonparodic mimicry increased the celebrity of both the imitator and the imitated.[81]

Yet in spite of mimicry's clear potential for increasing celebrity, it also poses a threat to the imitated, not just, as Roach argues, because it offers a candidate for substitution, but also because it takes control over self-representation out of the hands of the original "author" of a celebrity persona.[82] Like the work of a novelist or painter, the celebrity's public image is an artistic creation, often carefully crafted to reveal elements of her private life in order to create an illusion of public intimacy.[83] Braudy writes that "eighteenth-century culture introduced the individual to an awareness that his life could be contemplated, shaped, and sold."[84] Celebrity was increasingly being conceived of as both an artistic expression and a product, and as a result, eighteenth-century celebrities came to think of this abstract concept as a form of property—something they should have control over and rights to. As an artistic expression written in part on and through the body, and intimately bound up with a sense of personal identity, celebrity seemed to some to be singular and controllable by its "author." Mimicry undermined such presumptions. Writing about Foote specifically, Moody argues that his mimicry was sometimes seen as "a kind of identity theft."[85]

Mimicry's dual potential to increase celebrity and remove the agency of the imitated makes it a particularly vexed art form and one that Foote consciously dwelled on in his performances. On the one hand, he drew attention to his mimicry, cultivating "the impression of his own criminality" and developing an Aristophanic persona that further contributed to his celebrity.[86] But Foote did not draw attention to his mimicry simply as a form of self-aggrandizement; by repeatedly tapping into the language of ownership, he engaged with anxieties about the singularity and reproduction of identity. Foote's self-reflexive engagement with his own practice highlighted celebrity's increasing value as a form of intellectual property.

Foote directly addresses the relationship between mimicry and theft in *The Trial of Samuel Foote, Esq.*, his brief addendum to *The Orators*, in which he staged a parodic version of Faulkner's libel suit against him. Performing not only himself, but the counselor against him, Foote begins the piece by asking, as Counsellor Demur, "what kind of right now this Fot has to be any body at all but himself."[87] The trial begins, then, not directly with the question of libel, but with what it means to perform another's body. Is this a form of theft? Demur's ensuing logic mocks the premise of Faulkner's suit and creates laughter. But it also raises provocative questions about mimicry as a form of plagiarism. Demur reasons that "every body knows it is forgery to take off a man's hand; and why not as bad to take off a man's leg." If someone aims to replicate another's signature, he is considered to be stealing that person's identity. Thus, if one aims to reproduce another person's body onstage—in this case Faulkner's missing leg—is this not also identity theft or forgery?

Although always couched in humor, Foote's work is surprisingly concerned with ownership. Possessive pronouns abound in the opening speech of *The Trial of Samuel Foote*. Prosecutor Demur, performed by Foote, starts off the piece with a long speech to the judge and jury, not only asking what right Foote has to be anybody but himself, but warning of the likelihood that Foote will next impersonate them: "Gentlemen of the Jury, if you have a mind to keep yourselves to yourselves, and not to suffer any body else to be you but yourselves, . . . you will find the prisoner *Fot* guilty."[88] Demur's speech also plays on fear that one's identity might multiply beyond one's control through mimicry: he tells the judge that if he "does not choose to be in London whilst you are living in Dublin"—or in other words, if he does not wish representations of himself to circulate beyond his control or even knowledge—he will find Foote guilty.[89] Through this satire, Foote was responding to objections mounted by his contemporaries. On April 21, 1747, the day before Foote premiered *Diversions* at the Haymarket, Orator Henley placed a notice in the *General Advertiser* insisting that Foote's intended mimicry was not only defamation, but also a property violation:

> Whoever attacks my reputation, or livelihood . . . ought to be knock'd down, prosecuted, &c. &c. &c. I live by my oratory, he that attacks me there, by stage-exposing, is a robber. I hear that I am to be hung up on Wednesday, at the Haymarket, by one Foote, a Fool: but it is hoped all Gentlemen, or Lovers of Gentility, will treat him as an Invader of Property, a Scandalizer, or Robber.[90]

By hurting his livelihood, Henley reasoned, Foote was invading his property. In his response the next day, Foote did not entirely claim he was innocent of the offense, but instead described his play as a trial and asked the audience to judge his cause.[91] This move was savvy, as it increased interest for his upcoming performance and allowed him to straddle the line between a criminal and a respectable reputation.

While Henley called Foote a robber for damaging his reputation, Foote responded to accusations of property theft by focusing not on the abstract concept of reputation, but instead on the physical body. Doing so framed the discussion in terms of something "ownable." Property was generally understood in material terms. But at the same time that Foote's focus on the body allowed audiences to imagine acting as being related to property, it undermined the idea that mimicry was a real threat to self-possession. The debacle following Foote's performance of *The Orators* illustrates his rhetorical use of the body. Because Faulkner, whom Foote had mimicked as Peter Paragraph, only had one leg, Foote's mimicry depended heavily on hopping around the stage. In *The Trial*, Foote puns on legs and other body parts, satirizing Faulkner's disability and highlighting his own performative appropriation of Faulkner's body. The judge claims that Foote needs to be "taught how dangerous a thing it is for him to tread upon other people's toes; and so . . . to prevent his being so free with other people's legs, we will lay him by the heels."[92] Quirk, Foote's defense lawyer, quickly mangles and twists this bodily logic, arguing that "it is there said that Fote [sic] did, by force of *arms*, imitate the *lameness*, &c. of said Paragraph. Now as we conceive this imitation could not be executed by the *arms* but the *legs* only, we apprehend the laving out *legs* and putting in *arms* corrupts and nullifies said indictment."[93] In these lines, Foote asserts his right to mimic Faulkner through the repeated and punned-upon image of his lost limb. Through his physical and linguistic embodiment of Faulkner's disability, Foote asserts the normalcy of "gestural thefts" in acting and the integral role of such theft in stage satire.[94] *The Trial* parodies the accusations of libel leveled against him by Faulkner and ultimately undermines the notion that mimicry is a real threat to the body when, in a later line, the judge calls libel a more "heinous" crime than "common cases" like rape and murder—crimes that very literally violate the body. Through Foote's satire, mimicry is presented as an art that enables the reproduction of identity and the body, violates one's ownership of oneself, yet causes no real physical harm.

Foote justified the practice of mimicry by drawing a parallel between writing and acting. His comic comparison of mimicry and forgery in *The Trial* is one such instance. Foote was satirically parroting back criticism that mimicry, like imitation in writing, lacked invention and did not signify artistic genius. Theater critics drew parallels between imitation and plagiarism on the one hand and mimicry on the other. A Frenchman visiting London in 1767, for instance, wrote that "as their present writers are either plagiaries or translators, the present comedians are either imitators or mimics."[95] A 1751 essay in *The Inspector*, meanwhile, insisted that an actor who lacked invention was "a copyist, a plagiary, or a mimic."[96] Whether Foote's mimicry deserved artistic acclaim was a particularly contentious issue when Foote was imitating his fellow actors. In such cases, not only was Foote damaging actors' livelihoods, but he was also undermining the creative labor they put into their character development. In *Momus*, Carey asks, "Why should one actor villainously try / To damn another in the public eye? / Either by malice or by envy led, / To hurt his brother in his fame or bread?"[97] Moody argues that the danger of Foote's imitations of actors lay in the way they "challenged the presumption of originality by demonstrating just how easily that originality could be reproduced."[98] Foote's mimicry threatened to diminish the commercial value of actors' creative labor.

If Foote's mimicry of actors was sometimes seen as a form of appropriation akin to plagiarism, it could also be defended on the grounds that the imitation served his parodic aims. A writer calling himself "Philo-Mimicus" defended the practice of mimicking actors by extending the parallels between writing and acting: "I cannot see why there should not be a sort of Parody upon Acting, as well as Writing, which, sooner than Volumes, will serve to open Men's Eyes in both Arts, will detest a false Sublime in either."[99] Foote was not attempting to recreate previous actors' styles in order to develop his own acting ability; on the contrary, he was parodying actors' performance styles to draw attention to their ridiculous elements. Parody, under modern fair-use standards, is an acceptable reason to use elements of a work, because the object needs to be recognizable for the parody to be effective. Foote recognized that it was an imitation's relationship to the original that made it effective, and in describing his imitations of Faulkner, he wrote that "all felt the satire, for all knew the man."[100]

Foote further justified his mimicry and dramatic method through a nationalistic appeal to British individualism. In his critical essay *The Roman and English Comedy Consider'd and Compar'd* (1747), which he published just weeks before he premiered *Diversions*, Foote prepared audiences for his forthcoming satiric reviews. Pointing to William Shakespeare, he argues that English dramatists are peculiarly talented in character writing.[101] Building on what he identifies as a national literary strength, he preemptively justifies his satire of individuals against those, like George Carey, who insisted that "the stage was ne'er design'd / To point at this, or that, but all mankind."[102] Foote argues that individual satire is necessary in English plays, because the English people themselves are so diverse: "In *France*, one Coxcomb is the Representation of the whole Kingdom. In *England* scarce any two are alike."[103] English subjects create individual personae by "affecting" "particular singularities." As a result, mimicry becomes necessary to satirize the myriad affectations of England's many citizens.

Foote defended the practice of mimicry seriously in his critical writings and more humorously in his performances, rebuffing critics who saw mimicry as an impolite, unoriginal practice or a form of property violation. In *The Trial*, in particular, he played on the language of ownership and joked about the replication of bodies to establish his artistic right to mimic anyone who fell within his own definition of fair objects of satire. Yet while Foote built his own fame on the celebrity of others, he did not take well to being mimicked himself. This was not, as fellow mimic Tate Wilkinson suggested, because Foote had thin skin.[104] Rather, it was because mimicry enabled fellow actors to reproduce not only Foote's celebrity, but also his dramatic works. In order to maintain control over his plays, Foote relied on his celebrity and demand for his presence. Mimicry became a threat not just to individual identity, but also to his sense of property in his literary works.

MIMICRY AS A MODE OF PIRACY

Foote could only maintain creative authority over the performances of his works if he was involved in their production. And as Charles Macklin had discovered, one of the most effective ways to control and limit the production of a work was by maintaining the copyright and keeping it out of print. Foote's publishing choices show a few clear trends. Foote did not print his first few plays—*Diversions of the Morning, Tea, A Dish of Chocolate*, and *An Auction of Pictures*—each of which shared elements and scenes with the others and constantly evolved. However, in 1752, with the premier of *Taste* at Drury Lane, Foote began printing his plays. From 1752 through 1767 he printed the majority of his plays, increasing his visibility as a playwright. In the preface to *The Englishman in Paris* (1753), Foote draws attention to his entrance into the print world by feigning ignorance of its conventions. He writes that his bookseller, Paul Vaillant, "informs" him that readers will expect a brief preface. But as he has no obligations to any patron, he declares that he will dedicate the work to Vaillant himself, to whom he is obliged for "the Correctness of the Press, the Beauty of the Type, and the Goodness of the Paper, with which you have decorated this Work."[105] Foote had by this time printed two pieces of theater criticism, a criminal biography, and one play; he was no novice to the print world. But with this declaration, Foote reintroduced himself to the public, who knew him primarily as an actor and mimic, as a professional playwright. With *Taste* and *The Englishman in Paris*, he deliberately and pointedly entered the print world as a dramatist.

During these fifteen years—1752 to 1767—Foote generally waited until after a work had been performed at one of the winter theaters before printing it. *Taste* and *The Englishman* both premiered at the patent theaters, and he printed those works the same years they were performed. This was the case as well for *The Englishman Returned from Paris* (1756) and *The Author* (1757). In the case of *The Knights*, alternately, he waited for five years after its premier at the Haymarket in 1749, until he had also performed it at Drury Lane in 1754.[106] Similarly, he waited to publish *The Mayor of Garret*, which he had premiered at the Haymarket in the summer of 1763, until after he had also performed the piece at Drury Lane and received an author's benefit night there.[107] This strategy meant that he could profit not only from his Haymarket performances, but also from the first run at one of the patent houses.

Beginning in 1768, with *The Devil upon Two Sticks*, Foote stopped printing his plays. Aside from two exceptions—*The Lame Lover* (1770) and *Bankrupt* (1773)—none of his post-1768 plays were printed in legal editions until after Foote's death in 1777. Why, at this point, did Foote decide to stop printing his works? The change in publication choices coincided with the conferral of a royal patent for Foote to operate the Little Theatre in the Haymarket during the summer months. Upon receiving this patent, Foote no longer had to worry about whether he could find venues for his new works. His concern was now whether his works would draw audiences and support his theater. By keeping his plays out of print, he aimed to ensure the profitability of his summer patent by limiting Drury Lane's and Covent Garden's ability to perform his plays. The anonymous author of *Memoirs of the Life and Writings of Samuel Foote, Esq.; the English Aristophanes* (1777) notes Foote's publication choices multiple times, suggesting that publication and literary property were at the forefront of Foote's mind. The author observes that beginning with *The Devil*, Foote kept almost all of his plays out of print to maintain "the avidity of the public to see the representation."[108] He surmises that Foote only printed *The Lame Lover* (1770) and *The Bankrupt* (1773) because they did not make much money onstage, remarking that as *The Lame Lover* "did not *draw*, he resolved to make the most of it by selling the copy, and suffering it to be published." Foote published *The Bankrupt* in 1776, three years after its premier, and the author comments, "This piece he has given to the public, having published it last year; according to the stage phrase it did not draw so much as his other plays, and perhaps on that account he thought it best to sell the copy."[109] Keeping his popular plays out of print allowed

Foote to limit their performances to the Haymarket.[110] But in order to sustain interest in the Haymarket, he needed not only to maintain the novelty of his plays. He needed to maintain the novelty of himself.[111] Foote's celebrity drew audiences, and with the receipt of his patent, he had to ensure that he could control the circulation of his own celebrity body.

Controlling the circulation of one's own body might sound like a straightforward task. And in a literal sense, it was. For the final decade of his career, Foote stopped performing at the winter theaters and thus, in order to see Foote in the flesh, audiences had to visit the Haymarket. Even after Colman bought Foote's patent in 1776, the articles stipulated that Foote was "to perform on no other stage in London, but that of the Hay-market Theatre."[112] But Foote's face circulated in other forms that diminished the novelty of seeing him in person: mimics who had acted with Foote earlier in his career began to take off Foote, using his plays and performing his parts "in the manner" of Foote. The actor-playwright had so successfully developed his celebrity that audiences outside of London were eager to see Foote and were willing to see imitations of the famous mimic. In an age before video, audiences across England and Ireland accessed this celebrity through his imitators, most notably Tate Wilkinson.

Wilkinson, famous as a strolling player, mimic, and manager of the Yorkshire circuit, established his early career in the mold of Foote. In *The Rosciad* (1761), Charles Churchill describes Wilkinson as a "shadow" of Foote, a "mere mere mimic's mimic," or the simulacrum of someone who was already an imitation.[113] Wilkinson insists in his *Memoirs of his Own Life* (1790) that, contrary to Churchill's criticism and popular belief, Foote did not teach him how to act.[114] Yet Foote's influence on the younger mimic is undeniable. The first two plays that Wilkinson saw performed in London were Susanna Centlivre's *The Busie Body* with Foote's *Tea* at Covent Garden. From that night on, he was captivated by the stage. He made his own entrance into the London theater scene by impressing Garrick with an imitation of Foote.[115] Garrick asked Wilkinson to show Foote his imitations, after which Foote invited Wilkinson to travel to Ireland with him.[116] Early in his career, Wilkinson worked closely with Foote and observed his acting style and imitations. As early as their time acting together at Crow Street in Dublin, Wilkinson began mimicking Foote onstage.

As Wilkinson constructed his reputation and career, he did so largely by using Foote's works. From his first season at Drury Lane (1758–59), Wilkinson began performing Foote's plays and parts without his consent. For his benefit night that season, he chose *Othello* along with Foote's *Diversions of the Morning*. He had been expecting Foote, who had just returned from Edinburgh, to perform alongside him. Foote not only refused, but complained that "the publishing his farce was an unwarrantable freedom" and refused to give Wilkinson a copy of the play.[117] When Wilkinson told Foote that he would perform the play without him, Foote "sternly replied . . . he had a reputation to lose, and would not hazard the representation of any piece of his not printed, to be mutilated, spoiled, and condemned by [Wilkinson's] ignorant bungling."[118] Foote's response, as Wilkinson relays it, focuses not on anger at being mimicked, but on his sense of property in the piece. He explicitly calls Wilkinson's performance a "publication" of his work and emphasizes that because it was not yet printed, no one else had a right to publish it in print or performance. The roughly three-decade gap between the incident and Wilkinson's account of it in his *Memoirs* saw multiple legal cases involving performance rights. In each of these, the question as to whether performance was a mode of publication was crucial to the outcome, as I will discuss in the next chapter. By conceiving of both print and performance as modes of publication, Foote was reifying the performance's status as a product—something that ought to secure profit for its author. But he also maintains an important distinction between the two modes in order to ensure that only print made the work a "gift to the public": it was not until a work was printed that others had a right to use it. In spite of Foote's response, Wilkinson went forward with the performance, having surreptitiously obtained a copy from the underprompter. When Garrick asked him what he could possibly do with the script "for want of Foote's characters being supplied" by Foote's acting, Wilkinson replied that he would act Foote's characters himself. Thus began a career of defiantly appropriating Foote's plays and parts.

The playbills for Wilkinson's subsequent benefit nights reveal the extent to which he relied on Foote's creations. Wilkinson performed complete versions of Foote's plays, segments, and isolated imitations of Foote in particular roles. In many of these instances, Wilkinson included Foote's name in the advertisement, using his popularity to attract audiences. For instance, on a benefit night in Portsmouth on July 24, 1758, Wilkinson staged Foote's *The Author*, performing Foote's character of Cadwallader "After the Manner of the Original." A performance at Bath on November 28, 1764, meanwhile, advertised Wilkinson performing Foote's part of Major Sturgeon from *The Mayor of Garret* "in Mr. Foote's Dress." For his 1763 benefit night in Shrewsbury he combined "the principal scene from the New FARCE, call'd The MAYOR of GARRATT. (Written by Mr. *Foote*)" with "The Favourite Scene from THE ORATORS. PETER PARAGRAPH, (Writer of the Dublin Journal) by Mr. Wilkinson."[119] In 1764 at Chester, Wilkinson gave a comic lecture that included "Mr. Foote's PROLOGUE to the AUTHOR, and Comic Introduction and Imitations. Major STURGEON from the *Mayor of Garret*. Lady PENTWEA-ZLE from *Blowbladder-street*. Also a NEW PIECE, written by Mr. *Foote*, call'd, TRAGEDY A-LA-MODE."[120] Each of these nights combined segments of Foote's plays and imitations of Foote. Wilkinson did not hesitate to cut up plays and rework them, using the most popular scenes and parts. In his *Memoirs*, he recognized the extent to which he depended on Foote's work and popularity, describing a performance of *Diversions* by saying, "Mr. Foote was my chief food."[121] This self-description easily extends beyond that single performance; Wilkinson's early career can be characterized by his "feeding" on Foote.

Wilkinson's mimicry offered provincial audiences secondhand access to London's theatrical fare. His variations on *Tea*, or as he would sometimes call it, *A Dish of all Sorts*—riffing on Foote's *A Dish of Chocolate*–circulated London's plays and celebrities throughout the country. But if Wilkinson's live reproductions of Foote's body enhanced both of their reputations, they also diminished Foote's exclusive control over his works and undermined the singularity of his presence. Wilkinson's imitations inflected Foote's celebrity, destabilizing Foote's control over his own image and the dramatic works that his celebrity image supported. They also undermined the notion that celebrity might be "ownable" as property.

Foote responded to Wilkinson's persistent mimicry by writing him into one of his plays: the character of Samuel Shift in *The Minor* (1760) is a sendup of Wilkinson. Cooke attributes the character to Foote's growing resentment at being taken off by the younger mimic.[122] There may be some truth in this. Yet the satire is less vindictive than playful, albeit with a bite. And Wilkinson, always good natured, does not seem to have been bothered by the portrait. In fact, he writes in his *Memoirs* that "Shift, Mr. Foote did me the honour to write as a satire on me."[123] Regardless of whether Wilkinson was offended, the play as written and its performance history reveal a great deal about Foote's response to his works being appropriated through mimicry.

Through the character of Shift, Foote takes control of the public narrative about the relationship between the two mimics. As Shift describes how he gained footing in the theaters, he attributes his success to his "master," a "whimsical man" who is "remarkably happy" in the art of mimicry.[124] Shift declares that he studied under this master "for two whole years" before setting out on his own and thus is in his debt.[125] By writing Wilkinson as a character into his play, and mimicking him in performance, Foote takes credit for Wilkinson's theatrical success. But he also sets himself apart from Wilkinson by characterizing Shift as a talented mimic, but essentially the theatrical equivalent of a hack writer. As Shift describes his day-to-day activities, it becomes clear that he does not hold a prized position within a theatrical company, but instead hires out his mimic services to individuals and groups wishing to attack one another.[126]

Shift is much more than a sendup of a rival mimic. His background and actions comment on the practice of mimicry and its relationship to identity and self-possession. Shift tells Sir William, who is hiring him to impersonate an auctioneer, that he learned the ways of the world by growing up around the theaters: "My first knowledge of the world I owe to a school, which has produced many a great man, the avenues of the playhouse. There, sir, . . . I learnt dexterity from pick-pockets, connivance from constables, politics and fashions from footmen."[127] Shift, in other words, learned to interact with the real world by imitating the theater—itself a realm of imitation—and the streets around it. To learn the "real" by imitating the feigned, and to do so successfully, reinforces the Shakespearean trope that all of reality is performance. That Shift's entire reality, moreover, is based in performance seems to anticipate the comment that Foote would later satirically make about himself: "He is so used to put[ting] on other people's faces, that I question very much if he has got ever a one of his own."[128]

Perhaps it was this element of Wilkinson's identity—that it was always something other than itself—that enabled Foote to justify mimicking the mimic after he had explicitly condemned mimicking actors in the dramatic introduction to *The Minor*. In this introduction, a character named "Foote" explains his satiric practice to two eager audience members, Smart and Canker. While Smart and Canker are expecting a dangerous satirist, who will mimic whomever he pleases, the "Foote" character presents himself as satirist whose mimicry is guided by a strict set of principles. Foote tells his two companions that he will not mimic actors (a practice he regularly engaged in in the past), "because, by rendering them ridiculous in their profession, you, at the same time, injure their pockets."[129] Yet Foote's renunciation of mimicking actors was likely less about their pockets and more about his own. Foote was discovering that by mimicking his potential colleagues, he was making himself less employable, as particular actors would refuse to work with him after being the target of his mimicry. Mimicking a mimic, alternately, appeared more justified, both because there was a one-for-one element about it and because, as Foote's characterization of Shift suggested, if the mimic's entire identity was already an appropriation of something else, then the mimicry could not really be a form of identity theft—the performer did not have ownership to begin with. This sort of layered mimicry became important to Foote in *The Minor*, as it distanced him from fault. For instance, in performing Squintum, Foote's sendup of the Methodist preacher George Whitefield, in the play's epilogue, Foote was not directly mimicking the Methodist. The character of Shift was mimicking Whitefield as Squintum; Foote was simply performing Shift.

The takeaway from a close analysis of mimicry in *The Minor* might be that Foote's stance on the practice was not nearly as uniform or principled as he might like his audiences to believe. The story becomes even more complex when one begins to look at the performance history. Foote was perfectly happy to mimic the mimic Wilkinson, and perhaps was willing to deal with being mimicked by Wilkinson in turn, occasionally even in his own works. Yet one thing is clear: he would not stand for Wilkinson's mimicry when it challenged rather than aided his profit. It was on such occasions that Foote introduced property into the conversation.

When Wilkinson contracted with John Rich at Covent Garden in November 1760 to perform Foote's parts in *The Minor* in direct competition with Foote's Drury Lane performances, trouble arose. Wilkinson was well prepared to imitate Foote in Foote's parts. He was so dedicated to the goal of authentically reproducing Foote that when *The Minor* took the town with its first Haymarket season, Wilkinson, who was then performing at Winchester, obtained a furlough to "see Mr. Foote perform his characters in the meridian of its glory."[130] As Wilkinson records, he had already seen the play in Dublin, but "it had received much retouching and many alterations by the ingenious hand of Mr. Foote," and he intended to perform the most up-to-date version.

The media hyped the competing Drury Lane and Covent Garden performances. One newspaper puff hoped that "the public will benefit by the spirit of opposition" with which "Mr. Foote's pupil in mimickry, is to oppose his master, in the characters of Shift, Mrs. Cole, and Smirk."[131] Foote, however, was not as open to competition. When he heard about Wilkinson's plan, he complained to Covent Garden manager John Rich, insisting that Rich call off the performance in order to protect both Foote's reputation and his stage characters. In a "violent, blustering, and boisterous" manner, Foote declared to Rich, "if you dare let Wilkinson, that pug nosed son of a b———h, take any liberty with me as to mimicry" or "appear in my characters, in the Minor," "I will bring you, yourself, Rich, on the stage!"[132] If we are to believe newspaper reviews, Wilkinson's performances truly were a threat to Foote's singularity. A review in the *Whitehall Evening Post* focuses almost exclusively on Wilkinson as a simulacrum of Foote. The review does not compare the two actors in their parts. Instead, it evaluates how effectively Wilkinson mimicked Foote in the introduction, declaring that Wilkinson's "Representation or Mimickry of the Author's Person and Voice, in the Introduction, was so extremely striking, that the nicest Judge could scarce discover whether or no it was the Original himself."[133] Wilkinson reports that his performances of *The Minor* consistently drew full houses at Covent Garden, and he made a good deal of money from performing Foote in Foote's works. As the imitation threatened to replace the original, Foote began to learn that imitation—which had established his career—could also weaken it.

Always adaptive, though, Foote once again teamed up with Wilkinson, inviting him to perform together in *The Minor* at the Haymarket in the summer of 1763. Rather than continue to be angry, Foote turned the strange relationship between the two mimics to profit, splitting Foote's parts between them. That summer, the playbills announced *The Minor* with "The Parts of Mrs. Cole and Smirk, by Mr. Foote, Shift and Squintum, with Imitations, by Mr. Wilkinson."[134] The division is strange, because "Smirk" does not exist in the play as an independent character, but only as a false identity performed by Shift. Thus, Wilkinson performs himself as the mimic Shift, but when his character slips into an imitation of Smirk, Foote takes over. Foote's casting choices were likely made to stir up renewed interest in the piece. Audiences by this point would have known well that Shift was a sendup of Wilkinson, so for the satirist to cast his satiric target to perform himself might seem a bold move. By casting Wilkinson to perform the mimic, meanwhile, Foote could take advantage of the popularity of Wilkinson's mimicry without participating in the mimicry of actors himself. The fact that Foote so vehemently objected to Wilkinson's performance of his characters in 1760 but invited him to perform them in 1763 suggests that what he was opposed to was not so much being imitated, but having his plays used without his consent or involvement. The 1760 conflict had the potential to eat into Foote's profit at Drury Lane; the 1763 collaboration increased his profit and reasserted his artistic control. Wilkinson's mimicry might threaten Foote's singularity . . . until Foote reappropriated it into his works.

Without legal protection for performance, Foote developed a new sort of authorship that took advantage of rather than lamented the ephemerality of the medium. He was wildly successful. By linking his celebrity persona to his dramatic compositions, Foote created demand for his works and for himself in those works. So successful were Foote's creations and his new mode of authorship that they spawned, in turn, a new mode of piracy. Wilkinson used the very skill that distinguished Foote, mimicry, to recreate Foote's works, performing them in the manner of the actor-playwright. But as Foote repeatedly demonstrated throughout his career, he was adaptable. This was true in Foote's response to theatrical regulation, the suppression of his works, and the limitations of property law. Without legal protection, Foote constantly had to alter his composition and publication strategies to maintain control. So when Wilkinson proved a threat, Foote responded by incorporating the theatrical pirate into his work, not only as an object of satire, but as a subject, whose invention and mimicry contributed to the development of the work. Foote's works never lost their appeal during his lifetime, and he never lost control over them. Yet in spite of his successful manipulation of his property, one serious problem remained: the ephemerality that ensured Foote's control also threatened the longevity of the works. Three years after Foote's death, Thomas Davies, calling Foote's works incomplete "sketches," proclaimed that "the death of the author put the finishing stroke to them."[135] How would Foote's and other such works circulate after the death of the author? What would the turn away from print mean for theater managers building their repertoires? And what would become of a rich eighteenth-century theatrical tradition after the eighteenth century? The following chapters take up these questions.

Chapter 3

Managerial Interventions
George Colman, Thomas Harris, R. B. Sheridan,
and the Practice of Buying Copyrights

In his 1790 *Memoirs*, Tate Wilkinson complained of the trend among playwrights and managers of keeping plays out of print: "The fashion of not publishing is quite modern, and the favourite pieces not being printed, but kept
under lock and key, is of infinite prejudice to us poor devils in the country
theatres, as we really cannot afford to pay for the purchase of MSS."[1] Wilkinson was troubled that he could not simply buy a printed play and perform
it free of charge because many popular plays were being jealously held by
their owners. By the final quarter of the eighteenth century, the lack of performance copyright had caught up with theaters. Playwrights were upset
that they had no control over the production of their plays after the first run,
and managers who had paid for the initial right to perform the play were
upset when rival theaters could easily buy a printed script and perform the
same play, undermining the initial theater's profit potential. These managers
adopted Macklin's method of keeping plays out of print. They began buying
the right to print directly from playwrights and prosecuting theaters that
pirated and performed plays to which they held the printing rights.

The trend of keeping plays out of print was widespread by the end of the
century, affecting the performance of plays in and out of London and the
relationships among playwrights and managers. Its pervasiveness resulted
not primarily from authorial choices, but from managerial appropriations
of Macklin's strategy. The theater manager was a more powerful and well-
resourced figured than the playwright. It is through the manager rather than
the author that this became a significant trend. Managers, moreover, were
the ones who took cases of unauthorized performance to court. This brief
chapter examines the shift from an authorial strategy to a managerial one,

showing the effects of property issues on play publication in the final quarter of the eighteenth century. I discuss the new practice of "buying copyrights" and its legal reverberations. "Buying copyrights," I argue, became a power struggle between managers and playwrights, for it was eroding a foundational right that playwrights had acquired during the Restoration period: the right to print their works. This right had allowed playwrights to make names for themselves as literary authors and to enter not just a market for entertainment, but a literary sphere. In this chapter, I examine how the shift from an authorial strategy to a managerial one came about and how it affected the publication of plays and the circulation of drama. Actor-playwrights had developed a way to protect the performance of their works; managers captured that strategy and reasserted it for themselves, ushering in a new era in the economic relationship between playwrights and managers, and the availability of works to theatrical publics.

Among the earliest figures to adopt Macklin's strategy of keeping his plays out of print were playwrights seeking to protect their own work.[2] Macklin's ability to make a single farce secure him multiple performance contracts and actor benefits must have been tempting to contemporary and subsequent playwrights. As Milhous and Hume note, through unprecedented contract arrangements, he earned "the largest recorded authorial profit made on any afterpiece in the century."[3] But with these rewards came constant vigilance and policing: Macklin paid great attention to London and provincial theaters, ensuring that his works were not performed without his consent. In using the popular farce to secure acting contracts, he often found himself in drawn-out negotiations with managers. When he was negotiating a contract with Colman to act at Covent Garden for the 1773–74 season, for instance, he sent a set of proposals, received a set of counterproposals from Colman, and responded with a thirteen-page letter, picking apart each element of Colman's points.[4] All of this would have been a much less tempting proposition for fellow playwrights.

Playwrights who were also managers, however, could employ Macklin's strategy of nonpublication with ease, withholding their own works from print in order to perform them solely at their own theaters. Doing so benefited both them and their theaters for multiple runs. As a result, Macklin's strategy was most readily taken up by playwrights who were also managers, including Foote, George Colman the Elder and Younger, and R. B. Sheridan. As chapter 2 demonstrates, Foote sought to be the exclusive performer of his plays throughout his career, but it was not until he received a patent to operate a summer theater at the Haymarket that he consistently adopted the strategy of nonpublication. When he had to support not just himself, but also his theater, and when he knew that he would have a consistent venue in which to perform his works, he kept them from print and stopped performing on any boards but his own.

Playwright-managers like Foote were among the earliest figures consistently to adopt Macklin's strategy. When George Colman the Elder took over management of the Haymarket in 1776, he considered the repertory of Foote's unpublished plays to be part of what made the property so valuable. Thus, along with buying the right to operate the theater, he also bought the rights to Foote's unpublished works, negotiating that Foote would continue to perform only at the Haymarket. The *Morning Chronicle* reports that Colman paid £500 for all of Foote's unpublished works.[5] Keeping these works out of print was essential, Colman believed, for if he printed them, the "winter houses would hack [them] out, and take from his *nut-shell* (as he termed the Haymarket Theatre) that novelty which was necessary to attract an audience in the hot summers."[6] The Haymarket's success depended on its ability to attract an audience, and novelty was one of the most effective ways to do so. Thus, when the printer John Wheble published two of Foote's unpublished works and advertised a third in 1778, the year after Foote's death, Colman sought an injunction.[7] Wheble's lawyer argued that anyone had the right to print "what he might take down by way of note, or carry away by memory."[8] Yet this argument proved unsuccessful, for just as the court had ruled in *Macklin v. Richardson*, an unprinted manuscript remained the author's common-law property until printed.[9]

At the same moment that Colman took over the Haymarket and sued to protect his property in Foote's unpublished plays, he also stopped printing his own plays. This is a marked shift, for Colman had previously printed all his original works shortly after their premieres at Drury Lane and Covent Garden. The first three plays he wrote after taking over the Haymarket, *The Spanish Barber* (1777), *The Suicide* (1778), and *The Separate Maintenance* (1779), were never printed during the eighteenth century, remaining primarily on the boards of the Haymarket.[10] Although not as consistent as his father in his publication choices, George Colman the Younger also kept many of the works he premiered at the Haymarket out of print. Likewise, as manager of Drury Lane Theatre, Richard Brinsley Sheridan kept many of his works out of print, increasing public desire to see them at his theater.[11] As managers, these dramatists valued their own productions for their theatrical potential.

In addition to increasing economic value for the theaters, nonpublication allowed playwright-managers to exercise greater creative control over the production of their works. It is a truism that playwrights have more control in print than onstage. It should come as no surprise, though, that playwrights, as artists who wrote specifically for the stage and often with particular actors in mind, would want to have some control over theatrical representation. Yet without legal protections for performance, dramatists were unable to restrict the staging of their works or demand to be involved in production decisions. Sheridan was particularly wary of what theaters might do to his works without his supervision. Thus, when he became manager of Drury Lane in 1776, he began staging his plays there and keeping them out of print. The most famous and well-documented instance of this is his hugely popular *The School for Scandal* (1777). The play had premiered late in the 1776–77 season, and it makes sense that Sheridan would have wanted to prevent its performance at other theaters over the summer. The *Morning Chronicle* commented on May 17, 1777, "We hear it is Mr. Sheridan's intention not to publish the *School for Scandal*; in which case, as there will be but a small part of the town, comparatively, who will have an opportunity of seeing it this season, there is no doubt but its attraction, next winter, will operate as forcibly as it appears to do at present."[12] But Sheridan's continued nonpublication was not just about Drury Lane's profits. The actor John Bernard speculated that Sheridan protected his manuscript "in order to preserve his language from mutilation, and prevent the play being produced at any theater where the proper attention could not be paid to its 'getting up.'"[13] Sheridan occasionally loaned the manuscript to country managers, but he was wary of how they might use it. In fact, when he allowed the Theatre Royal at Bath to produce his play, he traveled to Bath to oversee the production.[14] Moreover, he demanded that these theaters not allow the manuscript to be copied. Bernard writes that "the [country] managers, who had copies of it, had obtained them on condition that they did not permit the same to become the parents of others."[15] The play—which is one of the most popular and enduring works from the period—was not legally printed during Sheridan's lifetime.

The limited number of performances of *The School for Scandal* increased demand, which worked in Sheridan's favor. But its popularity led to piracies, both in print and onstage. Bernard himself, who knew how protective Sheridan was of his text, was one of Sheridan's many pirates: he attempted to recreate the text for the theater in Exeter in 1779 in a manner similar to Wilkinson's reconstruction of *Love à la Mode*.[16] By his own account, he made the Exeter manager "give me his word that the manuscript should be destroyed at the end of the season."[17]

If playwright-managers' own works could prove enduringly lucrative for their theaters, so too could the works of others. As a result, all three theaters began buying the copyrights for many of the works they staged. It is worth pausing here to examine the phrase "buying copyrights." Eighteenth-century writers used the phrase to describe the practice by which theater managers bought the right to print plays alongside the right to perform them, thereby preventing the author from printing his work. These managers sometimes subsequently sold the right to print to a bookseller; but often they held onto it, keeping the play out of print for years. Scholars have similarly adopted the phrase. For concision, I have adopted this terminology as well. However, literary works were not technically copyrighted until they were printed. Thus, what the managers were actually buying was not a copyright, but the right to print and copyright the works. They did this in order to prevent authors from selling the copyright to a bookseller.[18] Harris was likely the first manager to begin buying copyrights. In 1774, he bought the copyright to Sheridan's *The Duenna* to prevent other theaters from performing it. Theatrical publics appear to have been well aware of what was at stake in such choices: an article in the *General Evening Post* complained that "the comic opera of the Duenna is not to be published; the managers of Covent-garden house having bought the literary property of it, to prevent its exhibition at any other theatre."[19] Harris withheld the extremely popular play from publication for two decades. He continued to buy copyrights during his tenure as Covent Garden manager, including the rights for works by Charles Dibdin, John O'Keeffe, Elizabeth Inchbald, Thomas Morton, and Frederick Reynolds. Colman the Elder followed suit, buying the copyright to a number of John O'Keeffe's plays for the Haymarket, including *The Son-in-Law* and *The Agreeable Surprise*, for a mere £40 each.[20] In his *Recollections*, O'Keeffe explained that Colman had asked him to sell him the copyright "instead of disposing of it to a bookseller."[21] In calling the act of selling a copyright to a bookseller "disposing," O'Keeffe (or Colman, whom he is ventriloquizing) locates the value of a copyright in the leverage it provides to control and profit from performance. As I will discuss in the final chapter, O'Keeffe went along with the arrangement both because he was grateful to Colman for producing his first play and because he feared that if he refused, Colman would not stage his future plays. Colman kept O'Keeffe's plays out of print for years, and as late as 1798, when O'Keeffe wanted to publish his complete works, Colman's son refused to allow him to print the five plays to which he held the publication rights. By the 1780s, Drury Lane Theatre began buying copyrights, paying James Cobb, Prince Hoare, Joseph Richardson, and Benjamin Thompson for the right to print some of their plays. Managers also occasionally paid playwrights to delay publication. In 1780, for example,

Harris paid Hannah Cowley £100 to hold off publishing *The Belle's Stratagem* and paid Charles Dibdin £120 to delay publishing *The Islanders*.[22]

The managerial appropriation of Macklin's strategy had a substantial impact on printing trends in the last quarter of the eighteenth century, resulting in a measurable decline in the publication of drama. Milhous and Hume calculate that while 89 percent of new plays staged between 1660 and 1700 were published, the percentage drops to 68.5 percent between 1701 and 1750 and 51.5 percent between 1751 and 1800.[23] As scholars including Paulina Kewes have shown, it was an innovation and a major development for Restoration dramatists to have the rights to publish their own plays, and many took advantage of this by publishing their plays soon after their premiers. These printed editions often featured their names on the title pages and elaborate dedications or prefaces.[24] Printing their plays allowed Restoration dramatists to develop authorial reputations, which in turn further benefited them in theatrical and print marketplaces. Why would authors abandon such a beneficial practice? One answer, put forth by Kewes, is that there was a devaluation of playwriting in the eighteenth century.[25] Evidence from surviving letters between playwrights and managers, however, suggests that rather than a devaluation, there was a changing valuation: by the final quarter of the century, playwrights and managers saw their work as highly profitable commodities whose primary value and profit potential lay in performance. Rather than making works widely available in print, managers sought exclusivity of performance rights, ensuring that the play's profit supported their theaters only.

Managers who bought copyrights were operating under the belief that keeping plays out of print allowed them to claim not only the right to first print publication, but also the right to exclusive performance of the work. There was no legal backing for this belief. Instead, it developed through theatrical practice that created new norms. The belief that performance rights for an unprinted work remained with the author (or the manager who had bought the author's right to print) was grounded in the idea that an author retained common-law property rights in an unprinted work. This common-law right extended, some believed, to performance. As I have shown in chapter 1, Macklin took the *Millar v. Taylor* ruling to mean that he had the right to control any use of his unprinted work, including performance. He reached this conclusion even before the ruling in *Macklin v. Richardson* (1770), as his letters to Tate Wilkinson illustrate. Macklin's public insistence that he had performance rights shaped practice, influencing some managers—notably Wilkinson—to request his permission before performing his and others' unprinted works, which I will discuss at greater length in the next chapter. The managers who followed Macklin's nonpublication example did so believing that that secured them exclusive performance rights. When rival theaters performed the works that they were deliberately keeping out of print, then, managers reacted by turning to the courts. Harris and Colman took managers to court for performing deliberately unprinted works. Their lawsuits were the first legal cases involving unauthorized performance.

The first documented case challenging a theater's right to perform an unprinted work was the *Proprietors of Covent Garden Theatre v. Vandermere* (1777). Harris and the other Covent Garden proprietors had bought the copyright to *The Duenna* from Sheridan in 1774, before Sheridan became a manager of Drury Lane. Sheridan's comic opera turned out to be one of the most popular plays of the period. It was acted 164 times in London in the eighteenth century.[26] When Irish managers staged illegitimate versions of the unprinted play, Harris prosecuted. In April 1777, Harris's case against John Byron Vandermere, manager of Fishamble Street Theatre, was tried in the Irish Court of Chancery. Harris asked that Vandermere and his company "be restrained and injoined from printing, publishing, or acting said piece."[27] An article in *The Gazetteer* on May 3 reported that "yesterday se'nnight the great question concerning literary property, received a final decision."[28] This "great question" was how literary property law applied to performance. After hearing both sides, the Lord Chancellor declared that he would not grant an injunction against the performance of the work, ruling, according to the *Hibernian Journal*, that "anyone could repeat what was already made public."[29] Because the play had not been legally printed, "making public" referred to earlier performances: theaters could freely produce *The Duenna* or any other play, printed or unprinted. The ruling reaffirmed the limits of literary property law, leaving playwrights and managers unable to turn to the law to protect their most valuable medium.

George Colman the Younger brought a similar complaint to the Court of King's Bench in 1793. Colman the Elder had bought the copyright to John O'Keeffe's *The Agreeable Surprise* in 1781. Over a decade later, he had still not printed the play. So when George Wathen, manager of the summer theater at Richmond, staged *The Agreeable Surprise*, Colman brought him to court under the Statute of Anne, claiming, according to one newspaper report, £4,000 in damages.[30] Colman's lawyer, Thomas Erskine, argued that the performance was evidence "that the work had been pirated" in print, for, he argued, "it could not be supposed that the performers could by any other means have exhibited so perfect a representation of the work."[31] This argument suggested that there had been a violation of the Statute of Anne, though no evidence of a print publication was presented. Justice Buller responded by suggesting that the play may have been reproduced entirely through memory, and "reporting any thing from memory can never be a publication within the statute."[32] Erskine's second argument, however, moved beyond application of the law to a call for legal change. Because he understood that performance did not count as publication under the Statute of Anne, Erskine did not try to argue that Wathen's performance was a violation of the act. Instead, he argued that because performance was so profitable, it *should* be considered a form of publication. His arguments constituted one of the first major attempts to amend the laws of literary property to include performance. He argued that "if this [performance] were not held to be a publication within the statute, all dramatic works might be pirated with impunity; as this was the most valuable mode of profiting by them."[33] Oliver Gerland argues that Colman and Erskine's decision to take this case to King's Bench rather than Chancery is significant, for while Chancery was a "court of equity overseen by the Lord Chancellor who issued orders in accordance with his sense of justice as informed by the law," King's Bench was "a court of law whose job it was to interpret statutory language."[34] Erskine was trying to reshape copyright law to include performance.

Chief Justice Kenyon ultimately dismissed the case, ruling that "the great copy-right case by the House of Lords," *Donaldson v. Becket*, had determined that "the statute for the protection of copy-right only extends to prohibit the publication of the book itself. . . . But here was no publication."[35] Erskine's mistake may have been in invoking the ruling in *Millar v. Taylor* that authors held literary property rights independent of the Statute of Anne. By 1793, the *Millar* ruling had been overturned by *Donaldson v. Becket*, which reinforced a limited copyright term under statute law.

While Durnford and East's *Reports of Cases Argued and Determined in the Court of King's Bench* record that Kenyon made his ruling without hearing from the defense, articles in *Lloyd's Evening Post* and the *Morning Chronicle* reported that both sides were heard and that the jury ruled in favor of Colman before the judges found for Wathen on a legal technicality.[36] If we take the newspaper reports to be accurate, two important details emerge. First, we see that the jury—and perhaps the public more broadly—was beginning to view performance as an essential part of literary property. Second, the focus of newspaper reports on memorization and oral repetition suggests that the public was increasingly interested in the relationship of orality to literary property. *Lloyd's Evening Post* reports that Kenyon ruled that "the defendant had not multiplied the copies of this entertainment, but had only, by the mouths of the actors, repeated the words of it."[37] This idea firmly distinguishes oral repetition from print reproduction. When Justice Buller argued that repetition by memory could never be a "publication within the statute," he was trying to show that the strength of people's memories meant that performance did not prove that anyone had pirated the work by taking it down in writing. But his ruling had broader implications. It meant that theaters could profit by the oral repetition of words that had never been published in print. Although *Coleman v. Wathen* did not immediately change the law, it prompted important conversations about the relationship between intangible performance and property.

Harris and Colman had taken managers to court because they believed that by buying copyrights at the same time or shortly after they contracted with authors to perform their works, they not only held the right to print the work, but also held exclusive performance rights. Gerland argues that through the practice of buying copyrights and taking theater managers who performed unprinted works to court, the Colmans and later David Edward Morris at the Haymarket took what was operating as a custom and established it as a legal right. Gerland writes, "Following the example of actor/author Charles Macklin, Colman maintained that, so long as these works remained unpublished, he had both a legal right to exclude others from publishing them and a legal right to exclude others from performing them," helping "to construct a common law public performance right."[38] In other words, Macklin's strategy was not simply a workaround, but a precursor to real legal change. The immense power of eighteenth-century theatrical practice in creating norms and setting the groundwork for legal change is precisely what most scholarship on dramatic literary property law misses. Jessica Litman, for instance, argues that "in the 18th century, not even the most ardent defender of common law copyright suggested it extended to control over public performances of works."[39] Yet Macklin repeatedly suggested that very thing. He not only developed the strategy of withholding works from print to control their performance, but also articulated the legal underpinnings that would become the basis for Colman's lawsuits and injunctions. Colman's substantial contribution, as Gerland argues, was to take cases to court, testing the legal standing of what was previously just an accepted practice, and not always that.

Coleman v. Wathen established that performance was not a mode of publication, and that an unprinted play therefore remained "unpublished." This had two important implications. The first was that once a play was printed, anyone could perform the work, since performance was not legally a mode of publication. Gerland argues that this fact further encouraged managers to keep plays out of print. The second implication was that if the play remained unprinted, the author (or the manager who had bought the print rights) held the right to print the work in perpetuity. The case did not establish a common-law performance copyright. Colman, after all, lost the case. But it did clarify certain legal questions about the nature of performance, and it laid the groundwork for later cases. Gerland's argument recognizes what little scholarship to this point has: that there were customary precedents for a common-law performance right decades before the passage of the 1833 Dramatic Literary Property Act and that these precedents were occasionally tested in the courts. But what Gerland does not examine is who this benefited.

Without an accompanying statute law that allowed copyright holders to benefit from repeat performances even when a work was printed, a common-law performance right could be more detrimental to authors than one might imagine. The legal rulings, like *Coleman* v. *Wathen*, that laid the groundwork for common-law performance rights benefited managers rather than authors, just as common-law copyright often benefited publishers more than authors.[40] The next two chapters investigate the effects that the new practice of "buying copyrights" had on theatrical culture, playwrights, and managers in the final quarter of the century.

Chapter 4

Tate Wilkinson's Reperformances
Performance as Piracy and Preservation

In 1776, Tate Wilkinson wrote *The Duenna*. He records in his *Memoirs*, "I locked myself up in my room, sat down first the jokes I remembered, then I laid a book of the songs before me, and with magazines kept the regulation of the scenes, and by the help of a numerous collection of obsolete Spanish plays I produced an excellent opera."[1] And an excellent opera it was. *The Duenna* ran for seventy-five nights at Covent Garden during its London premier and remained popular for the rest of the century.[2] Yet anyone familiar with eighteenth-century drama knows that Richard Brinsley Sheridan wrote the popular comic opera *The Duenna* in 1775. So what, exactly, did Wilkinson write? The play, which came to be known as "Wilkinson's Duenna," was a derivative of Sheridan's original text. Driven by "necessity," he tells his readers, Wilkinson rewrote the play from a combination of memory and fragmentary sources. Why did Wilkinson "need" to rewrite this play? Why did he need to perform it at all? And what did his text look like?

In 1775, Covent Garden manager Thomas Harris bought not only the right to perform the work, but also the right to print it. Keeping the hugely popular opera out of print, Harris put fellow managers in a bind, leaving them unable to give their audiences what they most wanted to see. After asking Harris for a manuscript copy and finding himself unable "to move Mr. Harris's tenderness," Wilkinson set about creating his own version of the opera to perform on his Yorkshire circuit.[3] We do not know how close this version was to the original or what changes Wilkinson may have made. But its influence is undeniable: when, subsequently, managers across England and Ireland applied to Harris for a copy of the original opera, he told them to perform Wilkinson's version instead.[4]

As Yorkshire theater manager from 1765 to 1803, Wilkinson sought to bring the London repertory to the provincial theaters. In *The Wandering Patentee* (1795), he discusses the difficulties for a country manager of constructing a repertory. Audience taste in the country, he writes, differs from that in London, and, as a result, he was often damned for his choices. Yet he insists that regardless of whether or not a London play succeeds with his Yorkshire audiences, it is his "indispensable duty to produce whatever has a run" in London.[5] He did so with impressive speed, often performing new works just a few months after their London premiers. Annibel Jenkins writes that "the variety of spectacle, including music and dance, the combination of drama and pantomime, the play by a famous playwright . . . all contributed to the success of [Wilkinson's] company."[6] Wilkinson was exceptional among country managers for his determination and ability to give Yorkshire audiences something akin to London offerings. His attempts to nationalize London theatrical culture, however, reveal just how troubling issues of dramatic literary property were for both London and provincial managers. By the last quarter of the eighteenth century, many playwrights and London managers were compensating for the lack of performance copyright—or the right to control and profit from the repeat performance of one's works—by keeping their plays out of print. As access to printed plays was limited, country managers like Wilkinson found themselves at the mercy of copyright holders. The lack of dramatic literary property law, counterintuitively, became a barrier for provincial managers wishing to stage London favorites.

This chapter takes up the effects of dramatic literary property on the creation of a national theatrical culture. Responding to Jane Moody's call to "write the history of British theatre—as opposed to the metropolitan narratives which have too long stood as surrogates," I aim to decenter our understanding of eighteenth-century drama by recovering the role of regional adaptation and appropriation in the formation of a British theater tradition.[7] Audiences outside of London often experienced drama in altered and abridged forms, for, I argue, the circulation of drama was heavily shaped by issues of dramatic literary property. I take Wilkinson as my subject for a number of reasons, the most practical being the vast archive he left behind through his eight volumes of theatrical memoir, his near-complete collection of playbills spanning 1766 to 1803, and his correspondence with managers, actors, and playwrights. Wilkinson carefully constructed his own archive, collecting his playbills and referring to them as he wrote his memoirs: taken together, these documents offer an amazingly full picture of a provincial manager and his theater circuit. Thanks to the richness of his theatrical memoirs, Wilkinson has been memorialized in modern scholarship, but almost always as a source rather than a subject in his own right. His crucial importance in nationalizing London theatrical culture has not yet been recognized.

More than offering an extraordinary archive, Wilkinson makes a strong subject for the study of an English theatrical tradition because of his experience and investment in both the London and the provincial theaters.[8] Wilkinson's career trajectory instilled in him a love of London theater that he was determined to share with Yorkshire audiences, overcoming property-related barriers to deliver "correct" or authentic productions to the country theaters. His theatrical career began in London, where he acted under David Garrick and alongside Samuel Foote. From 1757 until 1765, he traveled around England and Ireland, performing on metropolitan and provincial stages, before finally settling into a nearly forty-year managership of the Yorkshire circuit. As manager of the Yorkshire company, Wilkinson acted on a circuit of six theaters—York, Leeds, Wakefield, Pontefract, Doncaster, and Hull—occasionally also traveling to Edinburgh and London to perform with other companies.[9] During this time, he put all his efforts into circulating and preserving the eighteenth-century repertory, whether by pirating texts, altering texts to extend their popularity, or using mimicry to reconstruct performances.

While the theater has been theorized as a "microcosm of the nation," it has rarely been thought of as contributing to the construction of an imagined national community, precisely because, by taking place "in a particular place, at a particular moment," it speaks to a real and localized community of audience members.[10] The intentionality with which Wilkinson sought to reperform significant works from the London repertory, however, challenges the image of theater as wholly local. Building on Diana Taylor's work on the archive and repertoire, I argue that Wilkinson's performances were at once local and nationalizing. Through mimicry and reperformance, he drew the theater into a project of "conserving memory and consolidating identities."[11] As a manager, Wilkinson did much more than provide an evening's entertainment; he was also a teacher, using his playbills, and later his memoirs, to teach provincial audiences what to value in drama and how to recognize cultural references. Wilkinson's managerial skill, combined with his mimicry, circulated the London repertory—a good deal of which was being kept out of print—beyond the metropole, allowing audiences in the provinces to participate in a national theatrical culture.

ANTHOLOGIES OF PERFORMANCE, 1759–1765

Long before he wrote his *Memoirs* (1790) or *The Wandering Patentee* (1795), Tate Wilkinson was a theater historian. It may be more fitting to adopt his own term and call him a "stage chronologer," for he worked to preserve recent and ongoing history rather than the distant past.[12] Yet few studying Wilkinson would characterize his early career that way. The limited scholarship on him has, instead, dwelled primarily on his incredibly popular, but polarizing, mimicry. Mimicry was, on the one hand, the basis for his early success: Highfill, Burnim, and Langhans write that "his extraordinary native ability as a mimic enabled young Tate to put his foot in the theatre door and remained for years his dependable calling card in the provinces."[13] On the other hand, his mimicry sometimes left potential colleagues—managers and actors—unwilling to work with him. Garrick vacillated between encouraging Wilkinson's mimicry (which audiences loved and demanded) and forbidding it (because it created uproar among the rest of Garrick's actors).[14] In spite of its liabilities, Wilkinson relied heavily on his mimic skill for the first eight years of his acting career. These early years of mimicry, though, need to be studied as something more than the basis for both his individual success and his dubious reputation. His mimicry was part of what would become a larger project for Wilkinson: it was precisely through this mimicry that Wilkinson's earliest theater historical impulses found expression.

It is not new to suggest that mimicry is a form of history telling. In an analysis of nineteenth-century mimic Charles Mathews's one-man shows, Jacky Bratton has argued that "it seems to have been a genuine conviction not only of Mathews but of other actors at the time that the essence of performance could be passed on, in a kind of living history, by serious mimicry, that preserved the art of theatre."[15] Mathews, who was a protégé of Wilkinson, explicitly discussed the ephemerality of performance in his *Home Circuit* shows, quoting both Cibber and Garrick on the subject before arguing that "imitation, which has grown into disrepute of late days from having been made the instrument of personality, can perpetuate both the art and the artist."[16] Mathews was working to legitimize mimicry, defending it from the charges of illegitimacy and libel that it often incurred. His argument was not exclusively defensive, though. Mathews was searching for a way to preserve performance and with it, an English theatrical tradition tracing back, as he pronounced, to Shakespeare: "I knew Tate Wilkinson, who knew Garrick; Garrick knew Betterton; Betterton knew Booth; Booth knew Davenant, who was Shakspeare's godson."[17] At the same time Mathews proposed using imitation to preserve performance, he also provided audiences with a set of imitations of actors performing their popular characters. In a scene called *Mathews' Dream*, he stood in front of five full-length portraits of actors and proceeded to bring the static portraits to life through his performance. These included portraits of George Frederick Cooke performing Sir Pertinax MacSycophant and Thomas King performing Sir Peter Teazle.

Mathews distinguishes mimicry from parody by associating it, instead, with the continuity of performance, or the passing down of an interpretation from one actor to the next. This echoes John Downes's declaration in *Roscius Anglicanus* (1708) that "Sir William [Davenant] (having seen Mr. Taylor of the Black-Fryars Company Act [Hamlet], who being instructed by the Author Mr. Shakespear) taught Mr. Betterton in every Particle of it."[18] As the author of what some have argued was England's first printed theater history, Downes was aware of an older tradition of historical preservation that had little to do with a printed text.[19] Downes, Wilkinson, and Mathews all realized that continuity of performance and serious mimicry were forms of preservation that, in Taylor's words, "transmit information, cultural memory, and collective identity from one generation or group to another."[20] Wilkinson and Mathews actively participated in the preservation of English performance and the construction of a theatrical history by reperforming works of art that could "be passed on only through bodies."[21]

In spite of their crucial role in preserving an intangible art form, performative theater histories, like Wilkinson's and Mathews's, have been seriously understudied both because they are difficult to reconstruct and because, as Bratton argues, twentieth-century theater historians have tended to privilege works that deliver definite facts about the theater and its employees.[22] Yet, through studying these performance-based forms of preservation and theater history, we can better understand how figures within the theaters worked to build a community and to convey their art to the nation. Wilkinson's mimicry, in particular, demands further investigation because, in working to establish his place in a theatrical community that was dominated by actor-playwrights, he not only circulated performance but developed a way to give provincial theaters access to plays, like Foote's, that depended on performance for their full expression. As he traveled around England and Ireland performing in a range of metropolitan and provincial theaters from 1757 (when he first performed in London for Ned Shuter's benefit night) to 1765 (when he bought into the proprietorship of the York Theatre), Wilkinson relied on his mimicry and his association with London actors to secure employment. Often staying in each location for only a brief period of time, he packed each night with more than the traditional mainpiece and afterpiece. In a single evening, Wilkinson presented his audiences with highlights from the London and Dublin theaters, performing "the principal scene" from Macklin's *Love à la Mode*, for instance, alongside his own version of Foote's *Tea*, an imitation of Foote in the character of Lady Pentweazle, the epilogue to Foote's *The Minor*, and Ned Shuter's *London Raree Show*. By excerpting the most popular scenes from a series of plays, compiling them into a single evening, and performing in the style of the original actors, Wilkinson created what I am calling "anthologies of performance." This new form could succinctly convey to far-reaching and diverse audiences all that (Wilkinson thought) Britons needed to understand about their theatrical culture.

Wilkinson marketed his performances as reenactments, recreations that are "simultaneously *representational* and *live*."[23] By advertising his performances of others' bodies, he not only built his celebrity on the fame of others (as Foote did), but very consciously highlighted the representational nature of his art. Wilkinson's mimicry could do what print-based recreations could not do: allow audiences to experience the live presence of an artist, if not the original one. Charles Churchill criticized the mediated nature of Wilkinson's performances, writing in *The Rosciad* that Foote served tea "Which W—k—s—n at second hand receives, / And at the New pours water on the leaves."[24] Yet while Wilkinson recognized that the celebrity of London actors was crucial to the success of his imitations, he nevertheless made the works his own. Describing a season in which he acted at Portsmouth, he writes, "I lived almost on my Tea."[25] As his possessive pronoun signals, he claimed ownership over his performances, constructing his own array of imitations on the model of Foote's satiric reviews. The playbill for a 1762 performance at Bath, for instance, gives us a clear sense of how Wilkinson combined scenes from some of the decade's most popular plays, imitating Foote, Macklin, and Ned Shuter, in order to create his show. Wilkinson adopts Foote's licensing-evasion device of serving tea rather than performing a play, but extends the idea by turning the playbill into a detailed menu. The space that would normally be taken up by actors' names and parts is now filled with a description of the dramatic fair, making Wilkinson and his imitations the focus.

Wilkinson's anthologies of performance were incredibly important, for in many instances they were the only means through which audiences outside of London could experience contemporary drama. As actor-playwrights increasingly composed their works in ways that limited reperformance, yoking the works to their own physical presence, drama had the potential to become more localized, more centered in London than it already was. Wilkinson used his mimicry to recreate these performances. Variations on the phrase "in the manner of the original" regularly appeared on his playbills. He assured audiences that the pieces had been performed *"with universal Applause, at the* Theatres *in* London *and* Dublin."[26] He even touted the authenticity of his costumes: a performance at Bath on November 28, 1764, for instance, featured Wilkinson performing Major Sturgeon from *The Mayor of Garratt* "in Mr. Foote's Dress." Wilkinson played on the titles of Foote's plays, changing *Tea* into "a new Dish of Tea," and *A Dish of Choco-*

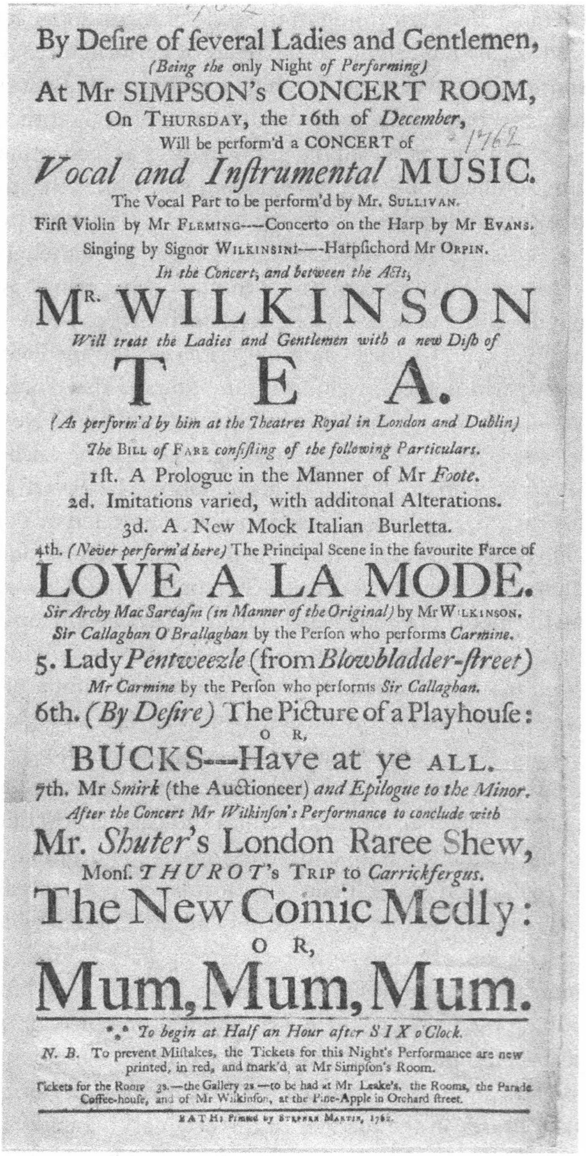

By Desire of several Ladies and Gentlemen,
(Being the only Night *of Performing)*
At Mr SIMPSON's CONCERT ROOM,
On THURSDAY, the 16th of *December*,
Will be perform'd a CONCERT of
Vocal and Instrumental MUSIC.
The Vocal Part to be perform'd by Mr. SULLIVAN.
First Violin by Mr FLEMING---Concerto on the Harp by Mr EVANS.
Singing by Signor WILKINSINI---Harpsichord Mr ORPIN.
In the Concert, and between the Acts,
MR. WILKINSON
Will treat the Ladies and Gentlemen with a new Dish of
T E A.
(As perform'd by him at the Theatres Royal in London and Dublin)
The BILL *of* FARE *consisting of the following Particulars.*
1st. A Prologue in the Manner of Mr *Foote*.
2d. Imitations varied, with additonal Alterations.
3d. A New Mock Italian Burletta.
4th. *(Never perform'd here)* The Principal Scene in the favourite Farce of
LOVE A LA MODE.
Sir Archy Mac Sarcasm (in Manner of the Original) by Mr WILKINSON.
Sir Callaghan O'Brallaghan by the Person who performs *Carmine*.
5. Lady *Pentweezle* (from *Blowbladder-street)*
Mr Carmine by the Person who performs *Sir Callaghan*.
6th. *(By Desire)* The Picture of a Playhouse:
O R,
BUCKS---Have at ye ALL.
7th. Mr *Smirk* (the Auctioneer) *and Epilogue to the Minor*.
After the Concert Mr Wilkinson's Performance to conclude with
Mr. *Shuter*'s London Raree Shew,
Monf. *THUROT*'s TRIP to *Carrickfergus*.
The New Comic Medly:
O R,
Mum, Mum, Mum.

*** *To begin at Half an Hour after SIX o'Clock.*
N. B. To prevent Mistakes, the Tickets for this Night's Performance are new printed, in red, and mark'd, at Mr Simpson's Room.
Tickets for the Room 3s.—the Gallery 2s.—to be had at Mr Leake's, the Rooms, the Parade Coffee-house, and of Mr Wilkinson, at the Pine-Apple in Orchard street.

BATH: Printed by STEPHEN MARTIN, 1762.

Fig. 2. Playbill for a 1762 performance by Tate Wilkinson in Bath. Playbills: Drury Lane, Covent Garden, Dublin, Edinburgh, Glasgow, and Others, 1748–1778, Folio 767 P69B W65. Courtesy of the Lewis Walpole Library, Yale University.

late into "A Dish of All Sorts." The playbills for Wilkinson's "anthologies of performance" were dense, giving a literal form to William West's claim that "early audiences seem to have understood what they saw [at the theater] as a reverberant constellation of speeches, gestures, and interactions rather than as neatly circumscribed plays."[27] They very intentionally advertised the intertheatricality of his performances, or their dependence, for meaning, on knowledge of a network of plays and entertainments within the current theatrical culture.[28]

Wilkinson's anthologies present a paradox, though, for while he used the authenticity of his performances to attract audiences, he could not assume that his provincial audiences would have seen the original London performers. He boasted that when performing in London "my imitations were never told either in bill or newspaper who they were designed for."[29] He took it as a sign of his success if audiences would shout out who he was imitating without knowing in advance. While performing in Bath or York, by contrast, he could not depend on audience recognition of the objects of his mimicry.[30] Nor could he expect his audiences to recognize a repeated gesture or a reused costume. Instead, he used his playbills to teach these audiences what to recognize. When he was performing outside of London, Wilkinson's anthologies took on an intentionally pedagogical function. Wilkinson guided playbill readers through the document with explanatory and puffing parenthetical notes, telling them whom he was imitating, where the plays had been performed, and how original audiences reacted. Reading through his dense and complex playbills, one cannot help but wonder whether Wilkinson might characterize these performances in the same way he described his *Memoirs*, as a "confused, motley, incoherent medley—this something, or this nothing of a work."[31] Yet if the performance itself was motley, Wilkinson's playbills certainly worked to make the show coherent and legible. Through his playbills, Wilkinson provided audiences with information in advance that glossed the performances. As they watched his multifaceted and quickly shifting anthologies, then, provincial audiences knew what to look for and understood how to "read" Wilkinson's body. When watching Wilkinson perform in the manner of Foote, provincial audiences would not, in Marvin Carlson's terms, have been haunted by the memory of Foote's performances.[32] Rather, they would have learned for the first time, through Wilkinson, what Foote's performances were like.

Both onstage and off, Wilkinson was widely recognized as a storehouse of celebrity imitations; his body preserved and circulated the art of his most celebrated contemporaries. John Bernard, in his *Retrospections of the Stage*, expressed a desire to see Wilkinson for this very reason:

> Tate was the accredited magazine for all the jokes, whims, and peculiarities which distinguished his great master, Foote,—and was considered as a sort of short-cut to the acquaintance of Garrick, Barry, and Macklin, and a dozen more, of whom he gave imitations, both in and out of character; so that you had the originals before you in the full strength of their visible distinctions.[33]

Wilkinson collected gestures, mannerisms, and stories, making himself the surrogate for celebrities one might not have direct access to. Bernard's description of him as "accredited" speaks to both his skill in mimicry and his talent for self-promotion. His performances acted as embodied theater histories and embodied anthologies of contemporary performance. While these acts of preservation are lost to us today, they have left behind traces, like Wilkinson's eccentric playbills, and have influenced more permanent forms of theater history. As modern scholars mine Wilkinson's *Memoirs* for anecdotes and information about Garrick, Foote, and other heavyweights of British theater (often without much attention to Wilkinson himself), few realize the extent to which this printed history is indebted to Wilkinson's mimicry. Wilkinson writes in his preface to the *Wandering Patentee* that his much-praised textual "portraits" in his *Memoirs* of "the great luminaries Garrick, Foote, and their opponents, Whitfield and Wesley . . . are a species and specimen of my former mimicry."[34] In other words, his ability write with depth and humor about individuals grew out of having embodied and mimicked those figures onstage.

Wilkinson continued performing his anthologies until roughly 1765, when he bought into the proprietorship of the York Theatre. Hogan writes that after this point, Wilkinson "abandoned all efforts as a mimic," except in private.[35] Hogan argues that he made this shift as a result of his permanent position on the Yorkshire circuit, where his imitations "were not sufficiently well known to Yorkshire audiences." I doubt that this is true to the extent that Hogan states it, particularly since Wilkinson continued to perform many of the same parts. It seems unlikely that he would have altered his performance to remove the imitation. He continued, moreover, to perform works, like *Tea*, that depended on imitation.[36] But his playbills, at least, bear out the fact that around this time he stopped advertising his mimicry. As a joint and later full manager of the York Theatre from 1765 onward, Wilkinson veered away from mimicry, which was regarded by many as "impolite, unoriginal, and incapable of representing or eliciting sentiment."[37] It would certainly have been bad managership to mimic his own actors. Wilkinson's priorities shifted at this point, as he focused more on improving and dignifying the

Yorkshire theater than furthering his own acting career.[38] As part of this process, he returned to the traditional, legitimate mainpiece and afterpiece model of theater. During this time, though, he was still dedicated to creating a national theatrical tradition and delivering authentic productions of London drama. To do so, he carefully acquired and staged unprinted dramatic works in the face of property restrictions. Given his propensity early in his career to pillage the stock of contemporary English drama with little regard for authorial property, his later-career choices, and especially his increasing respect for dramatic literary property, is surprising. Yet, as the next section will demonstrate, his shifting strategies were in line with his career-long aim of circulating and preserving British drama and performance.

PROPERTY VERSUS AUTHENTICITY: CIRCULATING UNPRINTED DRAMA

When Wilkinson bought into the proprietorship of the York Theatre in 1765, he imagined the moment as a crucial shift in the nature of the York stage. If previously they had been a backwater, disorganized group of strollers, they would now be an organized, professional troupe under the management of a theatrical monarch. Wilkinson records the moment thus: "I suddenly became monarch over a set of people that had never been accustomed to restraint. . . . They approved not of being under monarchial sway, but were of levelling principles."[39] The changes Wilkinson began to institute in order to bring the theater in line with "London, Dublin, Edinburgh, Liverpool, Bath, and every other theatre under regular and gentleman-like establishment" were extensive.[40] He enacted "laws" with the aim of dignifying the acting profession, like forbidding his actors from peddling benefit tickets door-to-door.[41] In 1769, he spent £500 to buy royal patents for his theaters at York and Hull, resulting, as he put it, in his "troop being relieved from the subterfuge of acting under a concert of music, and presenting a play *gratis.*"[42] Moreover, he made alterations to the theater building and began investing in scenery and costume. Costume, in particular, seems to have been a preoccupation for the manager: his bills often boast about clothing, and the 1788 *Theatrical Register* for York comments over and over on costume, as, for instance, when the author describes Wilkinson's benefit performance of *Henry VIII*:

> The banquet scene was so much superior to any thing of the kind known here, that our description would fall short of its magnificence. . . . The intention of the Manager, in dressing this play, was no doubt to shew the very great expence he has been at, for some years past, in procuring the

most superb dresses, and he may with very great truth aver that no play can be more brilliant, even in the metropolis.[43]

Under Wilkinson's managership, performances in Yorkshire became more spectacular and elaborate, mimicking the costume and spectacle of London theater.

Alongside dignifying his actors and beautifying his space, sets, and costumes, Wilkinson aimed to improve the Yorkshire theaters by performing the most popular plays from the London repertory soon after their London premiers. Describing Wilkinson's improvements to the theater, Sybil Rosenfeld writes, "Wilkinson's energy did not stop at securing the patent and having the Theatre repainted. On January 4 [1770], he set out for London to see the new productions. He wanted to present these at York at the height of the season and not wait until the spring."[44] As manager, he wanted to stage these new plays in complete, correct form. But with playwrights and managers keeping plays out of print and (at the extreme) chasing down managers who performed their works without permission, this was no easy task. When unprinted plays were advertised outside of London, what was actually being performed?

The answer to this question depends on quite a few factors, the most significant of which grew out of property claims. The version of a contemporary play that theaters outside of London performed depended first and foremost on whether the play was in print, and, if it was, whether the edition was legitimate or spurious. If the play was unprinted, the copyright holder's attitude toward use stood in where the law was unclear. Some copyright holders allowed other theaters to perform their plays on a limited basis, sometimes even sending them authentic copies; copyright holders were much more likely to be generous toward country theaters than toward other theaters in London, which were their direct competition. Policies and attitudes toward use were further influenced by whether the copyright holder was a theater manager, the playwright, or both. Unsurprisingly, authors often wanted their names associated with their authentic texts rather than what Wilkinson called "jumbles," or recreations of the texts. Managers, alternately, demonstrated that they could be more interested in protecting their exclusivity of performance than the authenticity of a text. Thus, we sometimes see instances of managers sanctioning the use of "jumbles," while happily maintaining a monopoly over the performance of the original text, as in the case of Wilkinson's *Duenna*. One of the central conflicts that emerged from a lack of performance copyright was between property and authenticity. Wilkinson aimed for authenticity and correctness, going to great lengths not only to acquire original playscripts, but to reproduce the way they were performed in London. In order to perform unprinted texts without incurring charges of piracy during this period, though, Wilkinson needed to develop a new strategy to assert his legitimacy. To do this, he once again turned to his playbills.

In looking at Wilkinson's playbills from 1766 onward, one notices an unusual trend: he began to put notes on the bills about literary property and the authenticity of his productions, often linking the two ideas.[45] Performing Sheridan's *The School for Scandal* for the first time in York on his April 21, 1778, benefit night, for instance, Wilkinson tells his audiences that the play can "positively" be performed for only one night before assuring them that this production will do justice to the hugely popular London production:

> It is almost needless to inform the Public of the unprecedented Success of the above COMEDY, not only in *London*, but at the Theatres-Royal in *Dublin* and *Bath*. It cannot, however, on any Consideration, be acted after this Night. The Public may depend upon Mr. WILKINSON's strict Attention in Regard to the Representation; and that not any Expence or Care will be wanting to render it worthy the Approbation of the Audience, and no Way injurious to the Credit of the ingenious Author.

As I previously discussed, Sheridan had chosen not to print the play, instead limiting its use to Drury Lane Theatre, where he was manager. He did occasionally lend out a manuscript for single use at a provincial theater, lending a manuscript to the Bath theater, for instance. This may be the case for Wilkinson's York performance, which would explain why Wilkinson focuses on the production's effect on Sheridan's authorial reputation.[46]

Some of Wilkinson's playbills are more explicit about how he obtained a copy of an unprinted play. On an April 6, 1779, bill, he describes how he obtained a copy of the afterpiece, *The Touchstone of Truth*. A note at the bottom of the bill explains that "Mr. Wilkinson on Application to Mr. Harris Patentee of the Theatre-Royal, Covent-Garden, was immediately Favour'd with the Manuscript of the Touchstone," noting also that the production required "much Attendance in every Department of Stage Business" to do it justice. On July 29, 1782, Wilkinson adds a note under the evening's play, Frederick Pilon's *The Fair American*, explaining that it was "Obtain'd of Mr. Sheridan at the particular Request of Miss Farren, of Drury Lane Theatre, for her Sister's Benefit at Leeds, with a strong Injunction that it be acted for her Benefit Only, as the Piece is not in Print, but the private Property of the Author."[47] A note at the bottom of a May 12, 1782, bill, puffing an upcoming

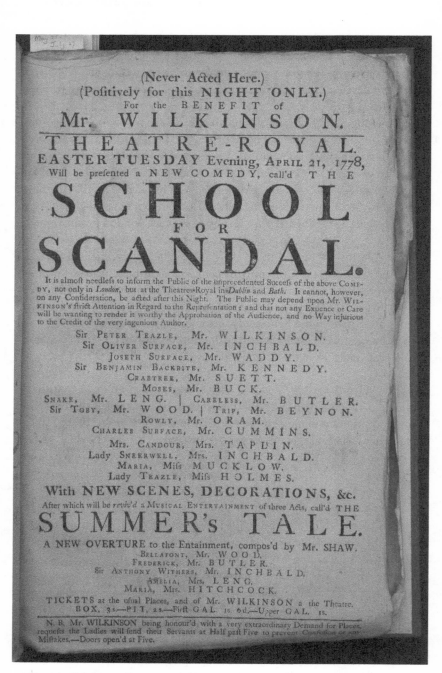

Fig. 3. Playbill for April 21, 1778, performance of *The School for Scandal* in York. "A Collection of Playbills for Theatres Mainly in Yorkshire, 1777–79." York Minster Library, York. Reproduced by permission of the Chapter of York.

performance O'Keeffe's *The Agreeable Surprise*, takes up almost a third of the playbill. Following an explanation of where else the piece has been performed, Wilkinson highlights the difficulty he had in obtaining the work: "He can only say, (it being unpublished) that he has not been able to obtain a Copy and Music without great Application, Expence, and Trouble." Wilkinson's playbill for an April 10, 1787, performance of Elizabeth Inchbald's *Such Things Are*, meanwhile, reads, "*This Comedy is to be acted for Mr.* Wilkinson, *not only by permission, but by the express desire of Mr.* Harris *and Mrs.* Inchbald; *as the author's own letter to Mr. W. can testify*"—a seemingly straightforward statement that trails a complex and heated story, which I recount in the next chapter. Such explicit notices about theatrical property directly on the playbills are extraordinary and rare. Wilkinson was going out of his way, altering the conventions of the playbill form, in order to assert the legitimacy of his productions.

The appearance of these notes on Wilkinson's playbills signals a few things. The public was becoming increasingly aware of who owned the rights to plays and how that affected their performance. Wilkinson may have felt the need to legitimize his use, heading off charges of piracy. A good portion of Wilkinson's audience, though, may not have known which plays were unprinted and protected; Wilkinson's notes educate that portion of his audience, teaching them to appreciate the cost of obtaining manuscripts and the labor of producing them accurately. Such notes have the additional function of puffing the performance, creating demand by highlighting the novelty and exclusivity of the work. Particularly for plays that could be performed only once, the notes work to fill the house. Wilkinson's playbills differentiate his Yorkshire circuit from other provincial theaters, elevating Yorkshire through its connection to the metropole. By explaining the provenance of his play texts, Wilkinson asserts not only the legitimacy of his operation, but the authenticity of his productions.

Wilkinson's earliest playbill note about the provenance or use of a play text was the direct result of a confrontation with the man who had made it his mission to protect his literary property: Charles Macklin. On September 30, 1772, for Wilkinson's benefit night at Leeds, a note appeared below the farce *Love à la Mode*: "This Entertainment being the private Property of Mr. MACKLIN, he has, at the Request of Mr. Wilkinson, given Permission for it to be performed at Leeds Theatre one Night." The language is strong and precise. This was the first time that Wilkinson, or any manager as far as I can tell, advertised a play as "private property" directly on a playbill. He conveys a clear directive from Macklin himself about when and where he can perform the work. Why, at this moment, does Wilkinson, who had performed

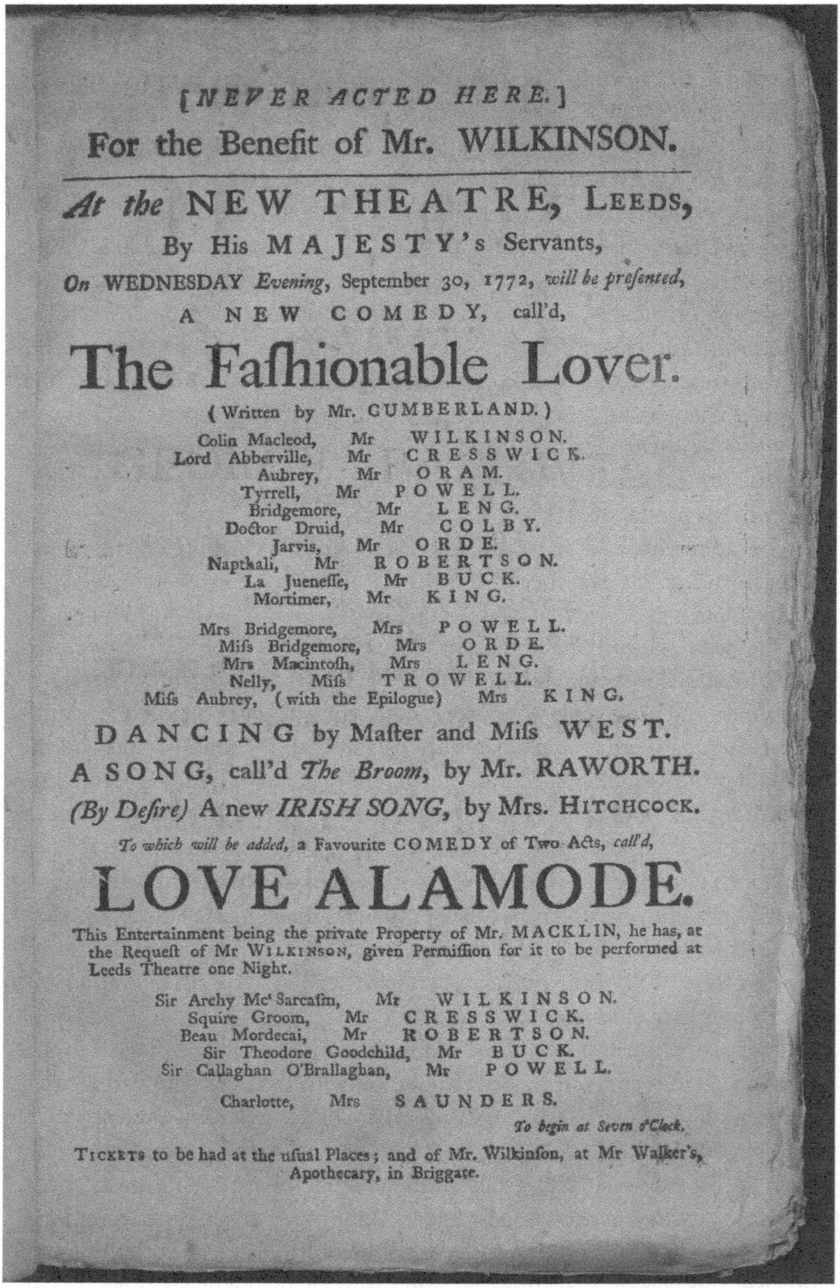

[*NEVER ACTED HERE.*]

For the Benefit of Mr. WILKINSON.

At the NEW THEATRE, LEEDS,

By His MAJESTY's Servants,

On WEDNESDAY *Evening*, September 30, 1772, *will be presented,*

A NEW COMEDY, call'd,

The Fashionable Lover.

(Written by Mr. CUMBERLAND.)

Colin Macleod,	Mr	WILKINSON.
Lord Abberville,	Mr	CRESSWICK.
Aubrey,	Mr	ORAM.
Tyrrell,	Mr	POWELL.
Bridgemore,	Mr	LENG.
Doctor Druid,	Mr	COLBY.
Jarvis,	Mr	ORDE.
Naptkali,	Mr	ROBERTSON.
La Juenesse,	Mr	BUCK.
Mortimer,	Mr	KING.

Mrs Bridgemore,	Mrs	POWELL.
Miss Bridgemore,	Mrs	ORDE.
Mrs Macintosh,	Mrs	LENG.
Nelly,	Miss	TROWELL.
Miss Aubrey, (with the Epilogue)	Mrs	KING.

DANCING by Master and Miss WEST.

A SONG, call'd *The Broom*, by Mr. RAWORTH.

(By Desire) A new *IRISH SONG*, by Mrs. HITCHCOCK.

To which will be added, a Favourite COMEDY of Two Acts, *call'd,*

LOVE ALAMODE.

This Entertainment being the private Property of Mr. MACKLIN, he has, at the Request of Mr WILKINSON, given Permission for it to be performed at Leeds Theatre one Night.

Sir Archy Mc Sarcasm,	Mr	WILKINSON.
Squire Groom,	Mr	CRESSWICK.
Beau Mordecai,	Mr	ROBERTSON.
Sir Theodore Goodchild,	Mr	BUCK.
Sir Callaghan O'Brallaghan,	Mr	POWELL.

Charlotte, Mrs SAUNDERS.

To begin at Seven o'Clock.

TICKETS to be had at the usual Places; and of Mr. Wilkinson, at Mr Walker's, Apothecary, in Briggate.

Fig. 4. Playbill for September 30, 1772, performance of *The Fashionable Lover* and *Love à la Mode* in Leeds. "A Collection of Playbills for Theatres Mainly in Yorkshire, 1772–75." York Minster Library, York. Reproduced by permission of the Chapter of York.

the farce often in the past, adopt a new stance? The answer lies in correspondence between the two men, preserved in the National Art Library at the Victoria & Albert Museum and the Lewis Walpole Library.

Three years earlier, on April 22, 1769, Macklin had sent Wilkinson one of his typical cease-and-desist letters, telling him that he had "evidence" that Wilkinson had "frequently taken the Liberty of acting my Farce of Love a la Mode at York, Newcastle &c" without permission.[48] But this letter varies from the many similar letters Macklin wrote in one fascinating way: two days earlier the *Millar v. Taylor* ruling in favor of perpetual common-law copyright had been delivered, and Macklin, who was following the case, interpreted this ruling to protect *any* use of a text, including performance.[49] As I discuss in chapter 1, he wrote to Wilkinson that performing the farce was an "illegal act" and "a more offensive Invasion of Property than you perhaps may imagine, as the pirating Booksellers of Edinburgh proved two days ago in Westminster Hall, when the Court of King's Bench finally determined the writings of an Author to be his inherent and perpetual Right." This letter is remarkable, for not only does it show how closely Macklin had been following the print copyright debates, but it illustrates the depth of his legal understanding and his ability to extend the ruling logically to his own situation. The Statute of Anne did not protect performance because it applied only to the printed book. But the *Millar* ruling established that authors had a perpetual right to their work independent of the statute and thus without the statute's limitations. Macklin took this to mean that his right applied to any use of his text, although the case did not explicitly state as much. Within just two days of the ruling, Macklin was sending off letters to at least one country manager, and probably more, using the case as new force behind his cause.

Macklin's interpretation of *Millar* effectively put a stop to Wilkinson's performances of *Love à la Mode* for the next three years. When he did begin to perform the farce again, it was with Macklin's explicit and limited permission. In 1772, Wilkinson wrote to Macklin, requesting permission to act the farce for one night only, which Macklin granted in a letter dated July 27, 1772, insisting that "you do not play or permit it to be played more than once on any Account. For as I have observed above I am determined not only to put the Law in force against any one that pirates it, but I will put the Statute of Vagrancy against them likewise wherever they perform out of licensed Theatres."[50] With this explicit permission, Wilkinson ended his three-year hiatus from performing the work, telling audiences, for the first time on one of his playbills, that he has secured permission for the use of "private Property." The note was likely not meant only for the audience, but also for Macklin himself; it was often through playbills that Macklin learned about provincial performances of his farce. Should Macklin have gotten hold of this bill, he would have been reminded of his consent and flattered by Wilkinson's respect for his property.

Wilkinson kept to his word, performing the farce only once until granted explicit permission to perform it again. He requested that permission the very same day that he performed *Love à la Mode* at Leeds, writing to Macklin on September 30, 1772, to thank him for "your Permission relative to Love A la Mode" and asking for "the same Permission for One Night in the same Manner at Hull & York." He assured Macklin that should he be allowed those two additional nights, "then it shall Sleep till you Please to Amuse yourself by Playing it in this Noble County, or till you Please to Publish it."[51] Macklin appears to have granted this permission, and Wilkinson performed the farce two more nights, each time with a playbill note indicating his permission, after which he let the farce "sleep" until 1775.

Wilkinson seems to have accepted Macklin's argument that unpublished plays were the common-law property of authors, making even performance a legal violation of their rights. Thus for the next few years, he sought permission to perform unprinted works and noted that permission on playbills. Notes similar to those found on the *Love à la Mode* playbills show up particularly often for unprinted plays by Foote, whose works he had previously pillaged. As I discuss in chapter 2, Foote began keeping most of his plays out of print after 1768, beginning with *The Devil upon Two Sticks*. I have suggested that this had to do with the new stake he had in his work as patentee of the Haymarket. It is not unlikely, though, that he had also been following *Millar* or at least talking to Macklin; his abrupt shift in publishing choices certainly aligns with the ruling. While I have not discovered correspondence between Wilkinson and Foote, Wilkinson's notes on post-1772 performances of Foote's unprinted plays (specifically, *The Nabob*, *The Devil upon Two Sticks*, and *The Maid of Bath*) suggest that he had the same sorts of arrangements with Foote as he had with Macklin. On a December 8, 1772, playbill for *The Nabob*, he includes this note: "The Nabob being private Property, and not intended for Publication, Mr. Wilkinson has with much Difficulty obtain'd Permission to have it Acted his Benefit Night only." A December 21, 1773, performance of *The Maid of Bath* similarly focuses on the unprinted state of the work: "This Piece is perform'd under particular Restrictions, as it never has been Printed, and the property of Mr. FOOTE, who has granted Permission to Mr. WILKINSON, to have it acted for his Benefit ONLY." The contrast between Wilkinson's early-career attitude toward Foote's property and his managerial attitude is striking. He would continue to perform Foote's works but would do so in a way that brought acclaim rather than derision to the Yorkshire theaters.

From 1772 onward, Wilkinson aligned his mission to make the Yorkshire theaters the purveyors of contemporary British drama with his aim of making these theaters polite and legitimate in large part through these sorts of playbill notes. By requesting permission to perform unprinted plays, and prominently advertising that permission on playbills, Wilkinson dissociated himself from the dramatic piracy so often associated with country managers. Macklin seems to have understood Wilkinson's concerns about legitimacy and theatrical community, and in granting Wilkinson permission for his 1772 Leeds benefit performance of *Love à la Mode*, Macklin appealed directly to Wilkinson's desire to transform York from a theatrical backwater to a legitimate, royally sanctioned institution:

> I have experienced such a Lack of honour in the Community of Actors out of London, from their Invasion of my Property in Love a la Mode, as has made me almost an Infidel respecting their morals in that Point. However to convince you, Sir, that I am fond of encouraging even a Profession of honour or morality in our Brethren of the Buskin & Sock, and to Shew you that I am not quite an unbeliever in the Reform that you have prescribed to yourself concerning Love a la Mode, I do hereby permit you to play Love a la Mode at Leeds once.[52]

Macklin's letter repeatedly uses the words "community" and "brethren," offering Wilkinson the possibility of participating in and contributing to that community by respecting playwrights' and managers' control over the works they had written or purchased. Macklin's rhetoric of theatrical community may have played as large a part in persuading Wilkinson of the necessity of obtaining authorial permission as the threat of legal action did. Respecting property became part of Wilkinson's mission to draw the Yorkshire theaters into a national theatrical culture.

If Wilkinson wished to project a certain image of the York stage to the rest of the country, he needed to avoid property disputes with playwrights and managers. By and large Wilkinson worked to respect authorial property during his managerial career, in spite of the expense he incurred. Yet when he could not "borrow, beg, or buy" an authentic copy of an unprinted play, he occasionally created his own version.[53] Here we return to the opening anecdote.

When Wilkinson wrote his own version of *The Duenna*, he did not try to pass it off as an authentic version, but instead advertised it as play "on the plan of the Duenna." Acknowledging the work's derivative nature would have been important to Wilkinson, who prided himself on the authenticity of most of his performances. More surprisingly, it may have played a hand in saving him from a lawsuit. As I discussed in chapter 3, Covent Garden manager Thomas Harris had bought the printing rights to *The Duenna* and kept it out of print to ensure exclusive performance at his own theater. In 1777, he would bring a lawsuit against John Byron Vandermere, proprietor of the theater in Fishamble Street, Dublin, for performing the unpublished work. However, the year before Harris sued Vandermere, Wilkinson performed his own pirated version. Harris undoubtedly knew about Wilkinson's performance. On April 10, 1776, the *Morning Post* reported that Wilkinson was foiling Covent Garden's attempt to be the sole purveyor of *The Duenna*:

> It is hoped the Covent Garden managers have been sufficiently repaid their purchase money for the Duenna, for though they have not chose to publish it, they have not been able to prevent others getting a copy and reaping profit from what they thought they had secured a monopoly of. This Opera is acted this evening at the Theatre Royal at York. Wilkinson (the proprietor and manager) came up to town purposely, and did take down this favourite Opera in short hand, and that he might have an accurate copy, was for eight nights successively at the play-house to compare and correct it.[54]

This report does not align with Wilkinson's own account that he reconstructed the play from memory, magazines, and the Spanish source plays. He probably did not take down the entire play in shorthand. Given Wilkinson's tendency to see popular plays multiple times, though, it is not unlikely that he was at the theater "for eight nights successively," paying attention to the stagecraft, costumes, and performances. Returning to York, he performed the play that eventually came to be known as *Wilkinson's Duenna* for his benefit night on April 9, 1776. What differentiated Wilkinson's piracy from Vandermere's? The difference seems to be in their advertising strategies. While Wilkinson was clearly performing a derivative of Sheridan's play, on his playbills and advertisements, he did not claim to be performing a play called *The Duenna* at all.

Wilkinson's advertising strategies made it clear that the opera was not Sheridan's, but his own. In his 1776 performances of this *Duenna*, Wilkinson changed the title to *The Mistake, or, the Double Discovery*. The playbill ensured that audiences knew they were getting a version of Sheridan's hit by following his new title with the note: "In which will be introduc'd all the

Songs, Trio's, and *Chorusses*, (as published) in the celebrated *Opera*, call'd The DUENNA." The word "Duenna" is as large as the word "Mistake," allowing Wilkinson to profit from the popularity of the original opera. But his wording is careful. Instead of highlighting what is unprinted (as he so often did), Wilkinson points out that the music he incorporates in his piece is already published and thus free for use. By March 1, 1777, for his benefit night in Edinburgh (and again for his April 1 benefit in York), Wilkinson had dropped the title *The Mistake*. Yet even at this point, he does not actually claim to perform *The Duenna*, instead calling the work "A *Selected Piece* of Three Acts, on the Plan of the Duenna." These two playbills take advantage of the opera's name and popularity, but distance themselves from the original opera, emphasizing their own derivative nature.[55]

Wilkinson's choice to emphasize the inauthenticity of his performances may have saved him a lawsuit, for the year that he first performed his "Selected Piece . . . on the plan of *The Duenna*" was the same year that Harris and the managers of Covent Garden Theatre brought their suit against Vandermere for performing *The Duenna* at Fishamble Street in Dublin. Indeed, it was on the very same day that Wilkinson used this piece for his Edinburgh benefit, March 1, 1777, that a notice in the *Morning Chronicle and London Advertiser* announced Harris's intention to sue Vandermere. Whether Harris's choice to direct his suit toward Vandermere rather than Wilkinson was indeed a result of Wilkinson's advertising is not wholly clear. Other factors, like the comparative audience sizes, for instance, could have influenced Harris's choice. Yet the *Morning Chronicle* suggests that the mode of advertising played a significant role in directing Harris's response:

> The Managers of the New Theatre in Fishamble-street, Dublin, are now performing *the Duenna* under its proper title, and without any attempt to provide a loop-hole against the effect of a legal prosecution for their having invaded private property. We hear the Managers of Covent Garden theatre, who paid a valuable consideration for the copy-right of the Duenna, have directed their Solicitor immediately to proceed against these Irish pirates. The Managers of the Theatre Royal in Edinburgh, have also advertised their intention of exhibiting some scenes *selected* from the *Duenna*, for the benefit of Mr. Wilkinson, now playing there under an engagement to perform for a few nights, on condition of receiving a handsome sum of money, and having a clear benefit.[56]

In contrasting Vandermere's and Wilkinson's performances, the article emphasizes the title of the play, implicitly suggesting that by advertising "their intention of exhibiting some scenes," the Edinburgh managers created a legal "loop-hole." Wilkinson and the Edinburgh theater advertised their performance as fragmentary, as an alteration of the original. Vandermere, by contrast, had the audacity to perform a version of the work under "its proper title." As the *Morning Chronicle* points out, the difference between Wilkinson's and Vandermere's performances was purely a difference of advertising and self-presentation, since neither theater was performing the authentic text.

Wilkinson was an incredibly shrewd manager, particularly when it came to property issues. He understood the ways that playwrights and managers were operating in lieu of dramatic literary property law. And he performed authentic editions of unprinted texts in generally sanctioned ways to an impressive degree during a period when managers and playwrights were clamping down on this sort of circulation. By respecting the unofficial conditions under which copyright holders allowed their plays to circulate, Wilkinson managed to evade Harris's anger as he performed a self-pronouncedly derivative version of *The Duenna* at the same time Harris was suing Vandermere for piracy through performance. Cecil Price derides Wilkinson's version of Sheridan's text, calling it "feeble."[57] But Wilkinson's *Duenna* had real value: it allowed provincial audiences to participate in contemporary theatrical culture. He rarely resorted to reconstructing texts, opting instead to "borrow, beg, or buy" the authentic manuscripts of popular unprinted plays. But when that was impossible, staging an altered version was a worthwhile trade-off, ensuring that his Yorkshire audiences had access to Sheridan, Macklin, Inchbald, and the period's other major playwrights.

"PIECE-MEAL" PLAYS: THE CANON AND THE REPERTOIRE IN THE 1780S AND 1790S

In the 1780s, Wilkinson began to experiment with form once again, compiling excerpts from various plays into a single production. The format was similar to his earlier anthologies of performance in that in both endeavors Wilkinson abandoned a whole work in favor of a set of fragments. Yet these "fêtes," as he would often call them, differed from his earlier anthologies in one crucial way: while his earlier anthologies centered on mimicry and the reproduction of celebrity, his fêtes of the 1780s and 1790s were about drama, the repertoire, and the canon. In his final decades, Wilkinson became increasingly interested in reviving old plays, digging through the English literary canon to produce works that rarely found their way onstage. He experimented with the relationship between the repertoire and the canon, between theatrical and literary traditions, adapting dramatic form to allow the two realms to better support each other. His fêtes, moreover, built on the school of thought that Garrick was Shakespeare's best commentator, or, more generally, that performance is the best mode of interpretation and critique. Through his fêtes, and similar modes of excerpting, Wilkinson asserted the necessity of performance in the preservation and formation of not only British theater, but also a literary tradition and dramatic canon.

On May 1, 1781, Wilkinson performed the first of his fêtes, explaining, in a long note to the public at the top of the playbill, what this new form was:

> A Gentleman of Taste and Experience in the Theatrical World, having mentioned to Mr. WILKINSON that he intended giving an Evening's Entertainment at a London Theatre, under the Title of "HUMOURS and PASSIONS; or, THE SCHOOL of SHAKESPEARE."—Mr. W. thought such a plan might be agreeable to the York Audience.

The "gentleman" was West Digges, who would perform his "entertainment" on August 7, 1781, at the Haymarket. Wilkinson beat Digges to the punch, staging his version three months before Digges had the opportunity to create his entertainment. Yet he seems to have had a clear sense of Digges's plan. And although the two men's creations differed in some important ways, they both actively drew the theater and performance into emerging fields of literary criticism and scholarly editing that were centered on Shakespeare. If the English literary tradition was forming around a single dramatist, then the theater might well take its place as a central cultural institution. To establish the continuing cultural importance of the stage, actors and playwrights alike worked to define the theater as not solely an object of literary criticism, but as a subject contributing to that criticism. The stage itself, as Digges's title announced, was the true "school of Shakespeare."

The title "School of Shakespeare" did not originate with Digges, but with William Kenrick, whose popular 1774 "School of Shakespeare" lectures were founded on the idea that "a proper, tho' simple, recital of the text is . . . often a better comment than whole pages of written annotations."[58] From January through March 1774, Kenrick delivered a series of weekly lectures on Shakespeare's plays at the Devil Tavern in Temple Bar. In these lectures, Kenrick recited portions of the play he was discussing, commenting on how different inflections change the meaning. He discussed what earlier critics, from Pope to Johnson, had said about the works and talked about different performances. Although his original plan had been to edit a ten-volume edition of Shakespeare's plays (his contract was canceled when George Steevens volunteered to do the same work for free), his turn away from print to lecturing widened the scope of what he was able to do.[59] In the introduction to his lectures, which he printed the same year, he expatiated on the value of performance as a mode of dramatic criticism. The lecture format allowed Kenrick to incorporate performance into literary criticism, creating a solution to his argument that "there are a number of passages in dramatic writers, particularly in Shakespeare, which cannot be successfully elucidated without the aid of declamation."[60]

The incorporation of performance into literary criticism was all the more important, Kenrick argued, because of criticism's crucial part in nation formation: echoing Pope, Kenrick reasoned that helping readers and audiences understand Shakespeare through literary criticism "would be the best method to form the judgment and taste of our nation."[61] More than just forming taste, Shakespeare improves English morality, for, as Kenrick argues, Shakespeare was a "*moral philosopher*; his works containing a practical system of ethics, the more instructive and useful as the precept is almost every where joined to example."[62] The effectiveness of Shakespeare's works in shaping national taste and character, however, depended on comprehension. Performers, by acting as interpreters of the texts, make them accessible to audiences and convey Shakespeare's lessons more forcefully on the imagination than they would be conveyed through a printed text.[63]

When Digges picked up Kenrick's title seven years later, he structured his "new Plan of Entertainment" to illustrate the various "humours and passions" that Shakespeare's works best exemplified. His first act, entitled "vanity," was drawn from *Henry IV, Part 1*. Each subsequent act came from a different Shakespeare play to illustrate parental tenderness, cruelty, filial piety, and ambition. The selections, which Digges advertised as "his most FAVOURITE and CAPITAL SCENES," were likely chosen in large part to display Digges's acting. But in structuring and advertising them using the qualities they exemplified, Digges's new form performed the sort of work Kenrick's lectures had called for, explicitly using performance to comment on Shakespeare and help shape English character. When John Bannister reused Digges's new entertainment for his own benefit night ten days later, he kept the format, changing a few of the selected scenes and qualities (introducing "madness" through *King Lear* and "love" in *Romeo and Juliet*, for instance). Each of these performances advanced the idea that actors could and should act as commentators, not only through their interpretation of a character, but by actively drawing audiences' attention to particular scenes for particular purposes.

Wilkinson's versions of *Humours & Passions* (he dropped the title *School of Shakespeare* and used Digges's subtitle instead) went further than any of his contemporaries' versions not only to draw performance into the realm of literary criticism, but to assert the interdependence of the canon and the repertoire. His structure and aims differed significantly from Digges's. He did not limit his selections to Shakespeare, instead envisioning the English literary tradition much more broadly. His fêtes included early English dramatists, like Shakespeare, Philip Massinger, and Thomas Randolph, alongside eighteenth-century dramatists, including Samuel Foote, Joseph Mitchell, Susannah Cibber, and Thomas Arne. The works he chose were much less well known, and less often performed, than Digges's choices. And instead of organizing the evening around humors and passions, as the title suggested, Wilkinson was guided in his selections by a combination of literary criticism and performance potential. He searched for potential in rarely performed but anthologized works, using printed literary criticism to help guide and justify his choices. These works provided new material for his actors, and his performances of these selections, in turn, would give life and exposure to works that were rarely staged.

In his note to the public on his May 1, 1781, playbill, when he premiered *Humours & Passions, or, A Theatrical Fête*, Wilkinson touted the instructive value of this entertainment and justified the practice of excerpting works. He narrativizes the process by which he created the entertainment, likely in part to assert its difference from his earlier anthologies of performance. Those who remembered Wilkinson's early-career benefit nights would associate a medley performance like this with his mimicry—a period when he showed no qualms about pulling apart and appropriating bits of plays as it suited him. After working for fifteen years to stage full productions of legitimate drama, Wilkinson now felt the need to explain and legitimize a "compilement" like *Humours & Passions*.[64] In describing the work's creation, Wilkinson explains how and why his work differs from Digges's:

> He [Wilkinson] has judged it an Injury to the Stage to take Piece-Meal, established Stock Plays, for the Purpose, such as The Merchant of Venice, Hamlet, Henry VIII, Othello, &c. &c. but is of Opinion, and humbly submits to the Public, if he could bring forward detached Acts from SHAKESPEARE, MASSINGER, and others, where the greatest Beauties may be found, and from such Plays as are entirely, or in a great Measure, lost to the Stage, it would be affording a *nouvelle* and instructive Amusement for one Night's Performance.

Pillaging popular plays for their best bits had served Wilkinson as an actor early in his career and was now doing the same for Digges. But Wilkinson argues that this sort of excerpting does not serve the work itself, but only the actor. On the playbill for a later fête, Wilkinson gives the example of performing the "closet scene" in *Hamlet* in isolation: "Were it read or played *separately* from the preceding Part of the Tragedy we should not only be deprived of some of the finest Thoughts in the English language, but we should likewise be at a Loss to account for his Behaviour to his Mother. . . . In short, the Mode here censured tends to the Annihilation, rather than to the Recovery, of Dramatic Beauties."[65] Wilkinson's increasing respect for authorial property from the 1770s onward seems to have been accompanied by increasing respect for the author. The man who had once used authors' works however he wished without apology now felt the need to include substantial paragraphs on his playbills explaining why he would perform plays "piece-meal."

Excerpting and staging rarely performed works might serve both the drama and the public. Restoring these works to the stage by performing excerpts allowed the public to benefit from their beauty and instructive value. Wishing to be sure that his audiences absorbed the lessons appropriately and understood why they were watching particular scenes, he once again used his playbills pedagogically. In his note to the public, Wilkinson declares that particular works, by Shakespeare and by other English authors, could not succeed onstage in their entirety. Yet particular scenes within these plays possess "the Fire and masterly Strokes of [Shakespeare's] wonderful Pen, equal to the best of his Works." As an example, Wilkinson takes *Julius Caesar*, which he included in the first of his fêtes: "The Third Act of Julius Caesar, by Shakespeare, may be averred equal to any Play he ever wrote; but the Last Act, performed even by the best Actors, cannot claim Attention, and requires great Care to prevent Laughter."[66] In order to preserve the "masterly Strokes" of such plays, which "are so little calculated for Stage Effect at present, that most of those mentioned may be pronounced as entirely confined to the Closet," and in order to restore them to the English stage, Wilkinson "collected" valuable scenes and experimented with dramatic form to preserve and restore those bits of English dramatic tradition.

The format of Wilkinson's fêtes, and their focus on underperformed rather than popular plays, forwarded the idea that the literary canon and the theater ought to be mutually supporting realms. He acknowledges on his playbills that the dramatic canon held a "Fund of Entertainment in Store." But he also calls the works he is choosing from "obsolete" and describes their existence in the closet as "confinement." They cannot escape obsolescence until they regain footing on the stage. The structure of Wilkinson's bills reinforces the interdependence of canon and repertoire. On these unusually wordy bills, he excerpts criticism from David Erskine Baker's *Biographia Dramatica*, using printed criticism to support his selections and interpretations of the scenes. Describing his *Julius Caesar* selection, for instance, Wilkinson quotes Baker's assessment that "the Speeches of *Brutus* and *Antony* over *Cesar's* Body are perhaps the finest Pieces of Oratory in the English Language."

Wilkinson performed these fêtes, which were long and difficult to assemble, a few times in 1781 and 1782 and then again in 1795.[67] They did not become a regular feature of his repertoire, likely because of the logistical difficulties. But his stance on the importance of the work he was performing did not change. He reiterated his language about restoring "dramatic beauties" on his 1782 bills, this time adding even greater emphasis to the theater's support of literature: "He hopes he is . . . serving the Cause of Literature, by preserving Sterling Ore, which might otherwise have been lost. In each of his *Fetes* he has endeavoured to give as much Variety as possible, and *that* which he now offers he trusts will display Beautiful Oratory in Point of Language— Morality—Boldness—Whimsicality—and Pathos." As he thought about the way English literature would be preserved, Wilkinson did not trust print alone; for the sentiments and force of dramatic works to be truly preserved, they would need to be performed.

In addition to excerpting works in his fêtes, Wilkinson also excerpted rarely performed works to use as interludes. Throughout the 1770s and 1780s, alongside the new full-length pieces that Wilkinson went to great trouble to acquire and stage "correctly," he often performed brief interludes based on the "favourite scenes" from English farces. These interludes were drawn from the works of playwrights who were popular in the 1750s through 1770s, especially Macklin, Foote, and Arthur Murphy, and they were largely character-driven. He turned Murphy's *The Upholsterer* into an interlude called *The Political Barber*, highlighting the character of Razor. Foote's *The Devil upon Two Sticks* became *Dr. Last's Examination*. He chopped Foote's *The Orators* down to the popular *Trial of Fanny Phantom*. He also performed pieces of Macklin's *Love à la Mode* and Foote's *The Minor, Diversions, Tea*, and *Taste* as interludes.[68] The language he includes on his playbills indicates that he was choosing to perform popular parts of works that were falling out of favor. Many of Foote's works, in particular, were so dependent on reference and mimicry that even Wilkinson, great admirer of Foote that he was, had to admit that they were not likely to endure:

> That Mr. Foote's pieces were neat traits, and of a peculiar excellence in the years 1740, 1750, to 1780, cannot be denied, and will, I dare say, be readily admitted by every lover of wit and whim: But I mean that the dramatic works of those two luminaries [Foote and Garrick] of the English stage will be barely recollected, when Cibber's "Provok'd Husband," and Mr. Sheridan's "School for Scandal," will be alive to the end of the world.[69]

Many of these works were popular not because of plot (indeed some lacked a plot), but because of well-written and well-performed characters. By excerpting and performing only the popular scenes, Wilkinson was able to repurpose the works that he had grown up on, prolonging their life spans and ensuring the survival of the characters, like Razor and Dr. Last, that had become central to English theatrical culture.

In 1771, the actor Henry Woodward wrote a letter to Wilkinson, working out the terms for an upcoming visit to Wilkinson's Yorkshire theaters. Woodward left it entirely in Wilkinson's hands to determine what characters he should perform. He had faith in the Yorkshire manager because he knew Wilkinson to be a good judge of talent and audience taste: "You know my *forcible* characters as well as I do;—you know the taste of the public where you preside, and therefore make choice of plays and characters that seem most advantageous in your own judgment." Woodward's next sentence attests to the York Theatre's national reputation: "I am told your catalogue of plays far exceeds any of our theatres royal, and if that be true, when we meet we shall not be at a loss to choose."[70] By "catalogue" Woodward was referring not only to the plays Wilkinson had access to, but to the range of plays he was equipped (in terms of actors, sets, and costumes) to perform in any given season.[71] While there is undoubtedly a degree of flattery in his letter, Woodward ranked Wilkinson's repertoire as not only the best among country theaters, but as better than the theaters royal in London. He did not view Wilkinson's stage as a provincial backwater, but as a competitive venue. Wilkinson's catalog of plays was a significant part of this transformation. Wilkinson worked hard to increase the range of British drama that his theaters performed by restoring excerpts from out-of-favor plays, repurposing popular characters from ephemeral and occasional works, and acquiring popular full-length pieces that were being kept out of print.

Property was crucially intertwined with the creation of a national theatrical culture because it had a significant effect on the circulation of plays and because it affected how the metropolis viewed and interacted with provincial theaters. When Macklin generalized about the "Lack of honour in the Community of Actors out of London from their Invasion of my Property" and when Garrick stereotyped an entire city by its theater managers' propensity to perform unprinted work, referring to "those theatrical pirates in Dublin,"[72] we can see how London playwrights' and managers' sense of property in the performance of their work led them position those outside of London as "others," characterizing them as "brethren," but brethren who did not play by the rules and customs of the metropolis. To disrupt this perception and to establish York as a legitimate part of British theatrical culture, Wilkinson made a point to ensure that his audiences and London managers knew he was respecting unofficial property restrictions. He staged an impressive proportion of new, unprinted drama with permission, not only acquiring authentic texts, but often traveling to London to see how they were staged in their original forms. His version of *The Duenna* is certainly a striking example of a play text morphing as a result of property restrictions. But this was a unique instance.[73] In nearly all cases, Wilkinson aimed to perform accurate versions of popular plays, only altering or excepting plays when doing so would restore them to the stage or preserve them for a while longer. By doing so he earned the respect of the theater community and at the same time, in his own words, served "the cause of literature."

Chapter 5

Printing and Performing Drama in the Final Quarter of the Century
Elizabeth Inchbald and John O'Keeffe

Preserved in the Victoria and Albert Museum's National Art Library lies an unusual copy of *The Dramatic Works of John O'Keeffe* (1798), owned and annotated by his daughter Adelaide. It is a copy that very literally materializes the problems arising from the lack of a law protecting the repeat performance of plays and the concerns and anxieties of eighteenth-century dramatists. In the "Address Prefatory" to his *Dramatic Works*, O'Keeffe addresses an issue that seems to have vexed him until his death: his inability to print five of his own plays.

> The Author regrets that an inconsiderate disposal of the Copy Right of his Pieces, called The SON IN LAW, The AGREEABLE SURPRISE, The YOUNG QUAKER, The DEAD ALIVE, and PEEPING TOM; to the late Manager of the Hay-Market Theatre, prevents their appearance in this Collection*. However, should those of his compositions, which he is here enabled to give to the Public, afford any gratification in the reading, it is derived from the kindness of Mr. HARRIS, (Proprietor of the Theatre-Royal, Covent-Garden) in permitting the AUTHOR to Print them; the Copy Right of most of them, he also having purchased.

> * Had they been sold to a Bookseller, and consequently then Published, the Author would, by the laws respecting literary property, have had a right to print them at the expiration of fourteen years, a term now long elapsed.[1]

O'Keeffe's aggravation with George Colman the Younger for continuing to hold onto the printing rights to these five works lessened with time, but his frustration at having been unable to print a complete edition of his plays continued for decades. Twenty-eight years later, in his *Recollections*, O'Keeffe dwelled on the insulting nature of this predicament for an author, bringing up his "five Haymarket pieces locked up in MS" multiple times.[2]

The same year that O'Keeffe published his *Recollections* (1826), his daughter and amanuensis Adelaide marked up a copy of her father's *Dramatic Works*. In handwritten additions, Adelaide inserted each of the five missing plays into the volumes with notes on the handwritten title pages authenticating the texts: "Read to my Father 1826—A Correct Copy by me Ad. O'K."[3] She further notes on each title page that the work was "Never Legally Printed." Adelaide's copy makes complete an incomplete work. Why did she and her father choose to create this copy twenty-eight years after the original edition was published? Who and what was it intended for?

While Adelaide does not specify her purpose or audience in the text, her efforts to assure readers of the textual authenticity of the plays strongly suggests that she and her father were working to secure his legacy. Without the fixity of print, the five works would exist for the public as they had been performed and as they had been represented in pirated editions. As O'Keeffe had lamented in his recently published *Recollections*, these unauthorized editions were "full of the most glaring errors."[4] While Adelaide's unique print-manuscript hybrid edition of her father's complete works could not be mass-produced and would not have the same far-reaching audiences as the original, incomplete version, it nonetheless ensured that versions of the texts approved by her father existed in a fixed form. Created at the same moment that O'Keeffe was publishing his personal *Recollections*, Adelaide's copy of the *Dramatic Works* reveals her father's wish to have a hand in crafting his own posthumous legacy.

O'Keeffe's *Recollections* and Adelaide's copy of his *Dramatic Works* attest to the challenges facing dramatists in the final quarter of the eighteenth century. O'Keeffe's most recent biographer, Frederick Link, calls the *Recollections* "on the whole a disappointing work" because "much of it is trivial and reveals little or nothing about the interior life of its author."[5] Link's search for the author's interiority draws more from our narrative about the development of the novel than from the concerns and interests of eighteenth- and early nineteenth-century theatrical biographers. O'Keeffe's autobiography reveals the concerns of a late eighteenth-century playwright. At this point in his life, these concerns were largely financial. His narrative documents his theatrical earnings, which managers he chose to work with, and whether he was able to assert any control over his works after their premiers. He discusses how he is treated in the theaters and reveals much of the logic behind

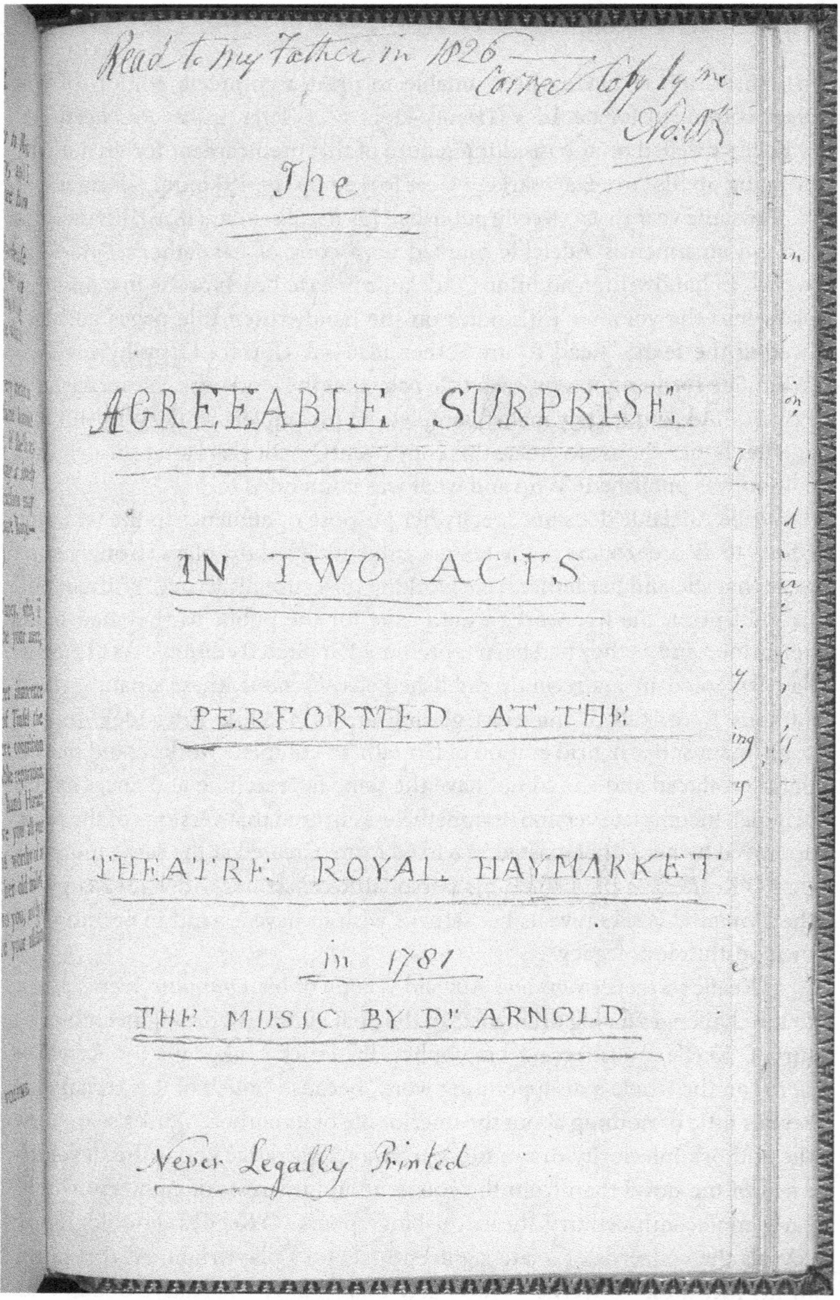

Read to my Father in 1826 —— Correct copy by me A.O.K

The

AGREEABLE SURPRISE

IN TWO ACTS

PERFORMED AT THE

THEATRE ROYAL HAYMARKET

in 1781

THE MUSIC BY D.ᵣ ARNOLD

Never Legally Printed

Fig. 5. Handwritten title page for *The Agreeable Surprise* in John O'Keeffe's *The Dramatic Works*. Adelaide O'Keeffe's annotated copy held in Victoria and Albert Museum, National Art Library, Dyce 8vo 7030. © Victoria and Albert Museum, London.

his choices of whom to sell his copyrights to. His autobiography and his daughter's copy of his plays highlight O'Keeffe's continued preoccupation with dramatic literary property and his feelings of powerlessness as Colman held the author's works hostage, even from the author himself, in a moment of financial need.[6]

The story of Macklin demanding compensation for repeat performances of his work, of Foote leveraging his celebrity for control over his literary works, and of Wilkinson coming to respect literary property was not, unfortunately, one of sustained authorial triumph. These assertive actor-playwrights did not begin a march toward the development of dramatic literary property law that was free from roadblocks and entirely beneficial for future authors. As I argue in chapter 3, a look at the last quarter of the eighteenth century suggests that it was not dramatic authors who benefited from Macklin's pioneering strategy of withholding plays from print, but instead theater managers. Managers saw in Macklin's example the potential for having exclusive performance rights over their repertories—a swing away from the practices of much of the eighteenth century and back toward the practices of Restoration theaters. Managers' adoption of this strategy was often to the detriment of the authors. By the final quarter of the century, dramatists who did not have the benefit of managing their own theater had to contend not only with a competitive theatrical marketplace, but also with managers' desire for their printing rights. With the decline in play publication, many dramatists found it more difficult to develop literary reputations or to assert control over the circulation of their works in any medium. This chapter compares the careers of two of the most commercially successful dramatists of the late eighteenth century, Elizabeth Inchbald and John O'Keeffe, arguing that for dramatists who did not write to create parts for themselves, printing their plays became an act of defiance and self-empowerment in a theatrical culture that was increasingly defined by exclusivity of performance and inaccessibility of play texts.

Inchbald and O'Keeffe experienced and reacted to the new theatrical trend of buying copyrights in vastly different ways and with tellingly different outcomes. The two are fitting figures for comparison, for, in many ways, their situations were quite similar. Their playwriting careers were roughly contemporary: Inchbald premiered her works on the London stage from 1784 to 1805, while O'Keeffe's works premiered between 1778 and 1796. Both playwrights acted early in their careers, but neither ever worked as a theater manager. Both were prolific: Milhous and Hume count both among only five playwrights to make a living by writing plays during the eighteenth century.[7] Moreover, both Inchbald and O'Keeffe worked almost exclusively with the

Colmans at the Haymarket and Thomas Harris at Covent Garden. Yet their publishing choices, their financial security, and their literary reputations could not look more different. Inchbald developed literary celebrity through both print and performance, using her reputation and name to negotiate lucrative performance and publishing contracts, and parlaying a print reputation into an editorial career that vested her with critical authority and further established her reputation in the literary world. She was able to do this, I argue, because she largely rejected the practice of selling her copyright to the theaters, choosing instead to print her popular works. O'Keeffe, by contrast, began selling his copyrights to the theaters early in his career—a choice that left him powerless to control the circulation of some of his most popular works and less able to fashion his own literary celebrity. Aware of his mistakes by the end of his life, O'Keeffe fashioned his celebrity in a different way: he created an image of himself as the poor, exploited author. He held himself up as an object lesson in what happens when an author gives up the right to print their own works. If Macklin, Foote, and Inchbald performed ownership of their works, O'Keeffe performed and publicized his lack of ownership.

A MULTIPLICITY OF *LOVERS' VOWS*: AUTHORIAL CELEBRITY AS A COMMODITY

In 1798, Elizabeth Inchbald found herself in the middle of a paper war about competing editions of her most recent play, *Lovers' Vows*. At the center of this paper war was her name and the value of her identity as a celebrity author, which were connected to questions of literary value and ownership. I begin with this incident in the middle of her career, for it illustrates the effects of her authorial choices in increasing the value of her professional identity.

A reader picking up the latest issue of the *London Chronicle* on October 16–18, 1798, would find two back-to-back advertisements for print editions of *Lovers' Vows*, both "this day . . . published." Inchbald's play by that name, an adaptation of August Friedrich von Kotzebue's *Das Kind der Liebe*, had premiered at Covent Garden five days earlier, on October 11, to great success. It was performed forty-two nights in its first season, earning Inchbald £400 from performance.[8] It is not surprising that publishers would want to profit from the huge popularity of the show, issuing editions quickly. What is surprising, though, is that while both editions use the title *Lovers' Vows* and refer to the Covent Garden performance, neither of the advertisements is for Inchbald's play. Instead, they are for two rival translations of Kotzebue's work: one, entitled *Lovers' Vows, or, the Child of Love*, is by Stephen Porter, and the other, entitled *The Natural Son, or Lovers' Vows*, by Anne Plumptre.

While Inchbald's play is most remembered today for its appearance in Jane Austen's *Mansfield Park*, it was incredibly popular in its own moment, performed more nights in its first season than any of Inchbald's other plays. And it started a paper war, with the Covent Garden production and Inchbald's name at the center. In the advertisements for their editions, both Porter and Plumptre situate their versions in relation to Inchbald's Covent Garden version. Porter calls his work a "complete translation" of Kotzebue's play, which is "now performing, with unbounded applause, at the Theatre Royal, Covent Garden, under the Title of Lovers' Vows." He takes advantage of the name recognition of Inchbald's play to sell his own translation, but he also strives to establish his play as a distinct literary work: he explains that he finished the translation before Inchbald's premier and that his version was originally intended for performance at the rival Drury Lane Theatre. He encourages the theatrical public to buy his version by inviting them to compare and judge the two: "The Public will now be able to judge whether his Translation, or that of Mrs. Inchbald, possesses the greatest portion of merit, and which of them is best calculated for representation." In the preface to his edition, dated October 16, he appears yet more defensive, declaring that he had begun the work well before Inchbald's play premiered and that "I cannot think but I have the same right to publish the Play, as Mrs. Inchbald." He insists, moreover, that his aim was to change as little as possible, in order "to dress Kotzebue in an English dress; and the public will now be able to judge whether he is more beautiful in the garb I have decked him in, or in the disguise in which he has been represented at Covent Garden Theatre."[9]

Plumptre, meanwhile, proceeds with greater confidence: rather than inviting the public to compare her version with Inchbald's, she promises to "enumerate," in the preface, "the omissions and alterations in the English representation." She too sells her version as the most authentic to Kotzebue's original text, defining "authenticity" by the closeness of the translation. She assures her readers that she is working from the only original German edition, that her work is a "perfect facsimile," and that it is "without any abridgement or mutilation whatever." Her assertions of authenticity are, of course, implicitly critical of Inchbald's stage version, and Plumptre sets her version apart from that "mutilated" adaptation by framing her work as a literary text rather than performance text: along with the preface, she includes a life of Kotzebue and a "Dissertation upon his Writings." Porter's advertisement invokes Inchbald's name much more explicitly, inviting comparison between the two versions; but Plumptre's advertisement, although careful not to name the Covent Garden playwright or challenge her explicitly, is nevertheless the more critical, undermining the Covent Garden adaptation through an appeal to literary authenticity and textual authority.

In the preface to her printed edition, though, Plumptre does invoke Inchbald. Like Porter, she explains that she had been writing the translation with an eye to the stage when she heard that Inchbald was already doing so for Covent Garden. In a seeming compliment, Plumptre writes, "Satisfied, therefore, that the Work was in much more able Hands, she totally relinquished her Design."[10] Yet Plumptre was not truly satisfied at all. Having attended the premier at Covent Garden, she found herself "surprized at the Extent of the Alterations and Omissions," and decided to print her own version. While she "readily admits" that the alterations may have been for the sake of stagecraft, she nonetheless finds herself anxious, she writes, to show Kotzebue to the public "in his own native garb." So she lists key differences between Kotzebue's play and Inchbald's adaptation in her preface, before presenting her own version of the text. Plumptre positions herself as a faithful translator, aimed at conveying Kotzebue directly to English audiences.

What is fascinating about both versions is that they were released just days after the premier of Inchbald's adaptation, and they explicitly capitalize on that play's popularity. Plumptre's title page calls her edition the "original" of the work "now performing" at Covent Garden. "Covent Garden" is printed in capital letters, and a buyer who was quickly scanning the page might mistake the work for Inchbald's. Both editions even include the dramatis personae for the Covent Garden performance, linking themselves to that version at the same moment they declare their difference from it. By doing so, these editions position the Covent Garden performance as a work by Kotzebue rather than as a work by Inchbald; if the Covent Garden performance is fundamentally a performance of Kotzebue, all translators might reasonably claim a relationship to that performance and benefit from its popularity. Both translators view Inchbald as a competitor whose version beat their own to the stage. Even as Porter and Plumptre compete with Inchbald, though, they use her name throughout their editions, constantly positioning their own versions in relation to hers. The competing *Lovers' Vows* illustrate the extent to which the name "Mrs. Inchbald" had become a profitable brand.

Yet if Porter and Plumptre viewed Inchbald's version as just one available translation of Kotzebue, neither Inchbald nor Covent Garden manager Thomas Harris saw the work in that way. Harris reacted to these competing editions by treating Inchbald's celebrity name itself as a sort of property. On October 15, Harris placed a notice in the *Morning Chronicle*:

> In consequence of the approbation which the above Play has received from the town, various translations, or pretended translations of the work from which it was taken, have been offered for publication to some eminent Booksellers, who honourably declining such purchase, have given information to the Manager of the attempted imposition. The public are therefore respectfully acquainted, that the Play as now performing at this Theatre, was re-written from a literal translation, sold to the Proprietor by an agent of the German author; and has been adapted to the English stage by considerable alterations in plot and incidents. The piece will not be published till the twentieth night of its representation, when it will be submitted to the reader, with the name of Mrs. Inchbald prefixed to the Publication.[11]

Rather than deny alterations to Kotzebue's text, Harris touts the "considerable alterations in plot and incidents" in Inchbald's version. If Porter and Plumptre, by their own accounts, best conveyed the authenticity of Kotzebue's work, then Inchbald's alone carried the authenticity of Inchbald. The changes to the text by such a well-regarded dramatist added value rather than detracted from it, and readers could be sure that they were getting the authentic Covent Garden text only when they saw Inchbald's name "prefixed to the Publication." By fiercely objecting to rival editions by authors who invoked both Covent Garden and Inchbald to sell their works, Harris was claiming something akin to a modern publicity right: only Inchbald had the right to prefix her valuable name to a print edition.[12]

Since it would be Inchbald who would profit from the print edition of her play and not Harris (she sold her copyright to her usual publisher, George Robinson, for £150), we can surmise that Harris was not worried about the rival editions detracting from sales of Inchbald's print edition. Instead, he was likely protecting and even increasing the performance value of the work. By participating in a paper war with the rival editors while the play was still running at Covent Garden, he was generating interest in the play. By announcing the intentional delay in publication, he was signaling to audiences that they would not have access to the Inchbald version except in the theater for the first few weeks. Harris must have negotiated with Inchbald to delay the publication—a practice not uncommon among managers. By highlighting Inchbald's substantial alterations, he was announcing to rival theaters and their potential audiences that he alone possessed the true performance text.

Inchbald, too, knew the value of her name, and in her edition, which was released on December 1, she called herself the author rather than translator of the text. The title page describes the play as "From the German of Kotzebue. By Mrs. Inchbald." This alone is significant. Paulina Kewes argues that eighteenth-century adaptors often either refrained from putting their names on title pages or "conspicuously cited the name of the original author alongside their own, thereby reinforcing the impression that theirs was merely a cut-and-paste job."[13] Kewes links this to a devaluation of playwriting in the eighteenth century, especially when the plays were adaptations or translations. However, while Inchbald does include Kotzebue's name alongside her own, hers features more prominently, in larger type, and as the author rather than translator. Nor does she devalue the labor of writing from a source text. Indeed, she advertises her originality by condemning "mere verbal translation."[14] Inchbald was very clear about the creative labor that went into her play and the artistic value of translations. In negotiating a contract with Harris for the production of her next play, *The Wise Man of the East*, based on Kotzebue's *Das Schreibepult, oder Die Gefahren der Jugend*, Inchbald wrote to the manager, "I beg leave to mention that this play has given me equal trouble of invention that any one wholly my own ever did."[15] She used this as justification for asking for significant remuneration beyond the ninth night, should the play run longer; when Harris made a counteroffer, she complained to her friend Frances Phillips that she was not paid as well as if the play were one of her originals.[16] For Inchbald, the creative labor of adaptation was as significant as that of original invention and deserved to be rewarded at the same rate. Moreover, she understood that the theaters were profiting not simply from the material or from the celebrity of Kotzebue, but from the attachment of *her* name to it.

Inchbald's and Plumptre's subsequent additions to the paper war addressed questions of literary value and ownership. Did an adaptation's value lie in its faithfulness to the source text? Its stage success? Who had the "right" to publish translations? Plumptre responded to Harris's newspaper notice with a biting letter in the *Morning Chronicle*, in which she took great offense to Harris's suggestion that "every Translation of the Work in question, which may be presented to the Public by any other person than the Manager of Covent-garden Theatre, must be a PRETENSION or an IMPOSITION!!!"[17] Much of her response addresses her right to publish an alternate version of the text. While she compliments Inchbald's ability to adapt the work to the English stage, she insists that her version is the best fit for reading. In publishing her own version of the text a month and a half later, Inchbald counterattacks Porter's and Plumptre's comments about the inauthenticity of her work without even acknowledging their versions. Instead of responding to them directly, she frames her comments in relation to audience reception, establishing that her version has been as well received in England as Kotzebue's had been in Germany. She writes, "I could trouble my reader with many pages to disclose the motives which induced me to alter," employing paralipsis to tell her readers about why she will not enumerate her motives for changing certain elements of the play—a jab at Plumptre's enumeration Inchbald's alterations. After a paragraph alluding to the changes she made, Inchbald explains that she will not say more about these because she has too much respect for her readers and audiences, who will undoubtedly understand why significant revision was necessary. In describing her process of adapting the literal translation she was given, Inchbald notes how "tedious and vapid . . . most literal translations are"—another indirect remark about Plumptre's faithfulness to the source text—and she assures her readers that she would never "suffer my respect for Kotzebue to interfere with my profound respect for the judgment of a British audience."[18] Inchbald situates literary authority with British theatrical publics, identifying the work that succeeds onstage as the most authentic text. Lisa Freeman argues that Inchbald was "the foremost theorist of theatrical production and representation in her period."[19] Her great strength was understanding what worked onstage, and her print publication was very much tied to the work's value in performance. Despite their insistence on faithfulness to the source texts, Porter and Plumptre understood this too, for it was only after the work was a success at Covent Garden that they released their versions.

The *Lovers' Vows* paper war, and the ways that Porter, Plumptre, Harris, and Inchbald framed their versions of Kotzebue's work, all point to one key fact: Inchbald's name had become a valuable commodity. Her print version of the play, not Porter's or Plumptre's, went through nine editions in just over a month.[20] Annibel Jenkins writes that "the publication of Plumptre's version in the same year suggests that the rage for Kotzebue was dominating the current 'charts.'"[21] But Kotzebue's work had been performed and published in Germany seven years earlier, and it was not until the work was performed in England under Inchbald's name that rival publications emerged. Inchbald had developed literary celebrity that made her name a valuable addition to the works of a dramatist who was himself already well regarded. It is for this reason that Harris consistently commissioned her to translate foreign works for his theater. And it is for this reason that she would, several years later, be commissioned to write prefaces to *The British Theatre*. The attachment of Inchbald's name added her literary celebrity and authority to these works. By the time she adapted *Lovers' Vows*, she had created a marketable persona—not as an actress or stage celebrity, but as a celebrity author in print. How did she fashion herself this way? How did she establish such power and agency for herself as a woman writer during a period that has typically been said to devalue playwriting?

PERFORMING AUTHORIAL RIGHTS: INCHBALD'S PLAY PUBLICATION

Inchbald's success and literary reputation is all the more impressive when considering what she was up against as a woman writer. Thirteen years earlier, a review of her first full-length play, *I'll Tell You What* (1785), in the *English Review* had warned Inchbald not to seek literary fame or longevity. At the same time, it revealed the reviewer's deep anxiety that she might do just that. The piece admonishes reviewers who lavish too much praise on Inchbald. The reviewer worries that she will be placed alongside *men* of letters: "We also confess ourselves to have been displeased with the highflown and absurd compliments which have been paid, in this case, to the authoress. . . . We have known some of her silly admirers boldly place her upon a level with Sheridan." Her gender is reinforced through the term "authoress," and her positive critics are reduced to "silly admirers."[22] The critic is anxious about what he sees as a real potential for her to develop lasting fame, insisting in his review that she will not: "Those masterly draughts of character . . . that give immortality at once to the author, and to the creature of his brain, we may seek in Mrs. Inchbald; but we shall seek in vain."[23] The reviewer does not explicitly criticize Inchbald for printing the work, yet that is precisely what he is reacting to. The review was not written after the stage premier in 1785, but more than a year later, after she published the work.[24] He distinguishes between literary success and stage success, allowing her the latter, but advising her not to "vainly pretend to rival men of elegance and parts." If she disavows literary pretensions, he argues, "she will live to the stage," or maintain stage success, greater than that of Frederick Pilon or O'Keeffe, with which she should be content. The reviewer is happy to allow her success in the theaters but reacts very strongly to the idea that she might have literary aspirations. The print publication of her work, with her name placed prominently on the title page, signaled to the reviewer that Inchbald might view herself as a literary author. The reviewer was right to connect printing to reputation. For it was with this first publication that Inchbald began to create a name for herself in print that would ultimately situate her as a literary authority. The choice to print her play was a defining moment for Inchbald—a fact that the reviewer's anxiety attests to.

Misty Anderson calls Inchbald's career "the most commercially successful career of any woman dramatist in the late eighteenth century."[25] John Russell Stephens goes further yet, comparing her not just to women, but all dramatists, and attributing her success to her own negotiating skills: "Of the more prominent patent theatre authors at the turn of the century, it was probably Mrs. Inchbald who asserted most strongly the right of the author to fair and adequate remuneration for the labour involved in every species of dramatic composition."[26] Inchbald's correspondence with theater managers certainly backs up these claims: she writes with an assertive voice and a clear sense of her worth, and her negotiations deserve greater attention, especially within the context of changing payment systems and changing valuations of dramatic texts and dramatic literary property. Scholarship fails to recognize the extent to which her professional success stemmed from her consistent printing of her drama; this is unsurprising, given that few recognize the extent and impact of nonpublication in the late eighteenth century. Unlike Macklin and Foote, Inchbald chose to decouple her acting and writing careers, developing her professional persona not onstage, but in print.

Inchbald printed the majority of her staged works soon after their premiers. Of her nineteen performed plays, including mainpieces and afterpieces, Inchbald printed fifteen—most with the publishing house G.G. and J. Robinson, selling them her copyright directly.[27] With two exceptions, all of her printed plays appeared the same year as their premiers.[28] This was after managers had begun buying copyrights in order to keep authors' works out of print. Colman began buying O'Keeffe's copyrights, for example, five years before Inchbald's first piece was accepted. Her consistent publication, then, is an anomaly. It appears that the only plays for which she was paid by the theater for her copyrights were *The Midnight Hour* (1787) and *Animal Magnetism* (1788), both staged at Covent Garden. Moreover, given that *The Midnight Hour* was published by the Robinsons in 1787, it seems likely that the fee paid by the theater—£31 10s.—was only to delay the publication, not prevent it entirely.[29] Covent Garden brought out this afterpiece so late in the season (May 22) that Harris likely wanted to maintain interest in it for the beginning of the next season, allowing it to be published in November of that year.

Inchbald established a precedent for herself when she published *I'll Tell You What*. To a certain extent, this may have been accidental. According to James Boaden, her earliest biographer, Inchbald offered the printing rights for that play to Colman, and he declined to purchase it, leaving her free to publish. It may be that so early in Inchbald's career, Colman did not see the copyright of a barely tested author as a valuable investment.[30] Boaden does not elaborate on Colman's reasons for refusing the copyright, or, for that matter, Inchbald's reasons for offering it to him in the first place. Inchbald must have seen that other authors were being paid by the theater for their copyrights, and perhaps she felt obligated to offer the right of refusal to the manager. Whatever her reasons, in the year between the play's premier at the Haymarket and when she published it with the Robinsons, two things occurred that, I argue, caused her to print the play and made her value the existence of a fixed, publicly available text. One was the unauthorized performance of spurious texts around the country; the other was Colman's reticence to allow Inchbald to perform her own unprinted work for her actor benefit night at Covent Garden.

In the year between when the play was first performed, on August 4, 1785, and when the Robinsons published it, at least two theaters outside of London performed the work without permission.[31] A letter from Dublin dated October 20, 1785, and extracted in the London papers, reports that the play was to be "brought forward" at the Theatre Royal, Dublin.[32] A report on December 29 of the same year confirms that the play had been performed in Dublin but had not been successful.[33] The play had not been printed in any form, legitimate or spurious, during this time, so it seems likely that a Dublin manager had either sent shorthand writers to see the play, reconstructed it from actors' parts, or gotten someone at the Haymarket to make a copy. Boaden's biography also points to an early performance of the play in Bath. Boaden describes what he perceived to be Inchbald's generosity when she "sent her MS. *herself* for the use of the Bath manager," John Palmer.[34] As proof of this generosity, Boaden includes a letter, dated December 10, 1785, from Palmer's assistant Charles Bonnor to Inchbald thanking her for sending them a manuscript copy and assuring her that he has used it to correct all of the "striking inelegancies of the pirates."[35] Palmer had apparently gotten a pirated manuscript copy of the play, and the theater was either preparing to stage it or had already done so; it seems likely that Inchbald was aware of this and thus sent them the correct play.[36] Bonnor writes, "I have got it into such a state as I trust will answer every end to Mr. P., without discrediting you," suggesting that Inchbald had included a letter complaining about the inaccuracies of Palmer's text.[37] Bonnor's response emphasizes that he aimed to create a workable play text for Bath audiences, and thus he would combine Inchbald's original text with alterations to make it more stageable. The Bath theater did not copy Inchbald's manuscript verbatim, but created its own version. Inchbald's willingness to send country managers copies of her plays is not as altruistic as Boaden suggests, but a deliberate choice to control her authorial reputation: if a work was to be performed under her name, she wanted it to be her version rather than a spurious text. Printing her work would increase the likelihood of country theaters performing an authentic text, as they would be able to acquire it more easily.

In addition to wishing to protect her authorial reputation, Inchbald printed her play to solidify her own rights to reuse her play text. At this point in her career, she was still acting as well as writing. After acting at the Haymarket for the summer season in 1785, she moved to Covent Garden for the 1785–86 season. For her benefit night in May, she wished to perform *I'll Tell You What*. As Boaden tells the story, she wrote to Colman's treasurer about using the play and received a response from Colman himself. Colman told her that he would grant her permission to use the work, but emphasized that his permission was, indeed, required and that he would grant it for one night only.[38] When advertisements for Inchbald's May 20 benefit night appeared in the papers, they included the notes, "FOR THAT NIGHT ONLY" and "(By PERMISSION of Mr. COLMAN)."[39] Visually, Colman's name is as large as Inchbald's, making the work appear to be as much his property as hers.

Colman's and Inchbald's conflicting views on the terms of use arose from a clash between custom and law. Colman wrote to Inchbald, "Your right to your own property I never disputed; but knew that, were your play even in print, neither of the theatres could in honour represent it, without my concurrence, during the present season."[40] Colman does not invoke law, as his argument has no legal basis. Instead, he appeals to common practice of theater managers. As Hume writes, even after the divided repertory had broken down, "There appears to have been an informal agreement between [managers] to respect exclusivity for the first two years after a new show was staged."[41] Colman suggests in this letter that the custom should be respected regardless of whether the play was in print—an observation that must be responding to Inchbald's sense of her legal property rights. Boaden writes, "We have already said that Mr. Colman would not buy the copy-right of 'I'll tell you what;' and having thus a right to publish it, she knew that a play when printed could be acted any where; she accordingly thought this might be done for her benefit with her farce at Covent-Garden Theatre, and that without any favour in the business."[42] While Inchbald ultimately did perform the piece for her Covent Garden benefit night with Colman's blessing, their varying stances on whether or not Inchbald needed Colman's permission tell us that the use of unprinted plays was not operating under set law or even set customs, but was a negotiation between competing interests. Colman upheld a theatrical custom practiced by the managers to protect their own interests. Inchbald wished to be able to use her play, the property of which was still her own, in any way she thought fit. There was no reason, legally, why she could not bring the play to another theater; the problem was that managers were still using the power of the patents to exert control over playwrights. Inchbald seems to have understood that printing the work put it into the public domain for performance, and thus into a domain to which she had access. By printing *I'll Tell You What* later that year, she limited the control of the Haymarket manager over her works, empowering herself in the process.

One other incident early in her authorial career taught her exactly what was at stake in printing her plays. As I briefly mention in the previous chapter, Tate Wilkinson performed her unprinted *Such Things Are* for his April 10, 1787, benefit night in York, touting her explicit permission on his playbill. How he came by that permission, though, is complex, and she likely granted it for the same reason she sent the Bath theater a manuscript copy of *I'll Tell You What*: to ensure that the play produced under her name was the legitimate version. In 1787 Wilkinson and Inchbald, who was formerly an actress in his Yorkshire company, got into what he called one of their rare arguments. According to Wilkinson, Inchbald believed that he was planning to perform her new, yet-unprinted *Such Things Are*. Moreover, she believed that he was doing so without possessing a legitimate copy. Inchbald was not upset about a property violation, but because she believed he was putting on his own recreation of her play, "a flimsy disgraceful imposture" that her name would nevertheless be associated with.[43] Her response, as Wilkinson recalls it, is vituperative:

> She judged from my being in London when her new play was acted, that I had made a jumble of my own from the seeing it, and dished it up for the public. She wrote me word "*she wished he own play* to be acted at York, instead of some contemptible jargon under *that* title: Would pay her thanks to *any* person for wresting her fawn from a pretended short-hand writer."—Also added, "that . . . she would [disown], by a public advertisement, whatever I might hereafter *steal*."[44]

Wilkinson's description of Inchbald's reaction is probably quite accurate: when need be, she was assertive in her correspondence with her former manager.[45]

Inchbald would not have been in this situation had her work been in print. And her work would have been in print by this point had not Covent Garden manager Thomas Harris intercepted and bought the right to print from Inchbald's publishers, the Robinsons, to whom she had already sold the copyright. Inchbald and Wilkinson's conflict occurred, then, because Harris, against Inchbald's wishes, prevented the play from appearing in print. Less than two weeks after the play's premiere, Harris, realizing the performance value of the work, bought the copyright from the Robinsons before they printed it, thus ensuring that Covent Garden alone would offer audiences the play for the foreseeable future.[46] She was now put in a position where she had to worry about the transmission of her popular work. Her response demonstrates just how effective she was in controlling her work and authorial reputation even after the property rights were out of her hands. On March 16, 1787, Inchbald wrote a letter to Wilkinson, preserved in the Beinecke Rare Book and Manuscript Library, promising him a copy of *Such Things Are*:

> Mr. Harris has just been with me and he desires me to give his compliments to you & you are very welcome to a Correct Copy of "Such Things Are." It was his intention he says to have confined this permission to Mr. Palmer of Bath & Mr. Barrett of Norwich to whom he sent Copies with the strictest injunction not to let any other copy be taken—but some friend of yours has represented to him how much more for the credit of the piece it is that you should have a good than an imperfect Copy, especially as you attended the piece so often in town.[47]

Her final sentence is layered with meaning. On the surface, it reads as a compliment, suggesting to Wilkinson that because he had seen the play so often, she is confident that he will do it justice if he is given a correct copy. Underlying that compliment, however, lies her anxiety that he had seen the play so often that even without a copy he would create his own version. Without the play yet in print, Inchbald was put in the difficult position of having to police country performances if she wished her plays to be "gotten up" properly. She then had to negotiate between the London manager and country managers like John Palmer of Bath, Giles Barrett of Norwich, and Wilkinson to ensure correct transmission of her text.[48]

Inchbald and Wilkinson's dispute over the production of *Such Things Are* highlights the two interests that were at odds under a system in which performance was not protected: property and authenticity. While Harris, as a theater manager and copyright holder, was concerned to limit production of the authentic play, Inchbald, as the playwright, did not want her play circulated in any form but the authentic. When Harris sent copies to Bath and Norwich, he did so with the "strictest injunction" not to let copies be made. Inchbald, alternately, was glad for authentic copies to circulate, for, as Wilkinson writes, "*She wished her own play* to be acted at York, instead of some contemptible jargon under *that* title."[49]

Throughout her career, Inchbald maintained artistic and professional independence by limiting the power that managers had over her works. By continuing to print nearly all her works after this, she created agency for herself by taking control of her plays out of the hands of a powerful manager. As Ellen Donkin argues, moreover, she created negotiating power for herself by not working exclusively with a single manager, but instead alternating between working with Colman at the Haymarket and Harris at Covent Garden. Inchbald "capitalized on an old rivalry," Donkin argues, and "played these two managers off one another for the duration of her career."[50] If one manager proved unwilling to work with her on her terms, she could submit her works to the other, not feeling indebted or tied to a single house. When, for example, Harris required that Inchbald turn her play *The Child of Nature* into an afterpiece and paid her only a flat fee of £55 36s. for the work, she did not work with him again for three years.[51] When George Colman the Younger accused Inchbald of ingratitude toward his father, suggesting that the crime was especially cruel since she was "originally encouraged, and brought forward, as an authoress, by that very man," she responded by forcefully claiming her authorial success as her own: "In thus acknowledging my obligations to Mr. Colman, the elder, let it be understood, that they amounted to no more than those usual attentions which every manager of a theatre is supposed to confer, when he first selects a novice in dramatic writing, as worthy of being introduced, on his stage, to the public."[52] Colman's assistance, Inchbald made very clear, was what was expected of a manager, and not a gift bestowed on her. Her response to Colman, furthermore, sets her relationship with his father apart from the relationships fostered by Garrick earlier in the century: Garrick regularly helped new women playwrights stage their work, and "he took pleasure in their public demonstrations of gratitude."[53] He positioned himself as their mentor, claiming much of the responsibility and reward for their success.

Inchbald's negotiating skills and professional independence, paired with the popularity of her plays, resulted in compensation well above the average. By Milhous and Hume's calculations, 60 percent of mainpiece plays between 1776 and 1794 earned their authors less than £200 from benefit nights. While Inchbald's author benefits varied widely, she earned a phenomenal £601 for *Such Things Are* (1787) and the same for *Everyone Has his Fault* (1793). After payment systems changed in 1794, she continued to earn significant sums, including £400 for *Wives as they Were, and Maids as they Are* (1797), £400 for *Lovers' Vows* (1798), £500 for *Wise Man of the East* (1799), and reportedly £600 for *To Marry or Not to Marry* (1805).[54] Her assertiveness sometimes earned her additional income. For instance, Boaden recounts that as *Every-*

one Has his Fault approached twenty nights, Inchbald asked for a fourth benefit. Harris apparently "reproached" her for this request but nevertheless sent her additional money, possibly £100.[55] While her high payments before 1794 are largely the result of successful runs and profitable third, sixth, and ninth nights, many of her later payments result from preperformance negotiations.

"SHE WAS ACTRESS ENOUGH TO PERFORM THE AUTHORESS PROPERLY": PERFORMING LITERARY AUTHORSHIP

Describing the evening when Inchbald revealed herself, onstage, to be the author of her first farce, *A Mogul Tale* (1784), Boaden writes that "she was actress enough to perform the authoress properly."[56] Choosing at first to remain anonymous, Inchbald, who had also performed in the play, revealed herself as the author on the penultimate night of performance, well after the play had proven a success. As the audience cheered her, she "enjoy[ed] the sensation she had excited with seeming humility, but proud delight."[57] Boaden describes authorship as a performance, explaining Inchbald's behavior onstage not as a spontaneous emotional reaction, but as an appropriate, planned presentation of herself in this new role. What is especially interesting about this brief moment in Boaden's biography is that he introduces her new authorial career through her acting career, coding authorship as a performance. The relationship between these two threads of her career is intriguing, and indeed much recent scholarship on Inchbald has focused on the relationship between her acting and writing.[58] Yet Inchbald's career develops in a substantially different way than those of many eighteenth-century actor-playwrights. While Macklin, Foote, Garrick, Charles Mathews, George Alexander Stevens, and Kitty Clive, to name a few, wrote to create parts for themselves, this does not seem to have been Inchbald's primary motivation for writing. She did not always perform in her own plays, and she stopped acting in 1789, five years after the performance of her first play and sixteen years before the premier of her last. She did not become an author to further her stage celebrity, nor did she use her stage celebrity to control the production of her works. The literary celebrity that she would eventually develop was largely distinct from her acting career. What mattered for her lifetime reputation and posthumous fame was how, as Boaden noted, she performed the author. These performances were largely in print.

While Inchbald did not write to serve her acting career, there are some important links between the two roles. Although she did not tend to take the largest parts or monopolize her parts, she did sometimes act in her own plays. The popularity of her writing could certainly serve her as an actress, such as when she performed *I'll Tell You What* for her actor benefit night at Covent Garden. With the huge success of her first few plays, it became clear that she was more likely to be in demand as a writer than actor, and on at least one occasion she held out her writing as a carrot to negotiate an acting contract. In 1786, after she had offered *Such Things Are* to Harris at Covent Garden, but not yet delivered the script to him, she used the play to try to negotiate a seven-year acting contract. According to Boaden, she had begun "to consider herself of the family of the sure-cards."[59] In other words, she understood that she had crossed from being an untried playwright who was at the mercy of the managers to a successful playwright whose works were in demand. She tried to use this position of power to strengthen her place in the theatrical company, which was less sure than her appeal as a writer. Ultimately, her attempt was unsuccessful, as Harris threatened to fire her entirely from the company before the two reached a compromise. Nevertheless, the attempt shows that she was aiming to play one role off the other. Perhaps she was unsuccessful in doing this because, unlike Macklin's or Foote's, her plays did not depend on her performance of a particular part. In negotiating with Harris, she seems to have been less interested in using her plays to make her a star than in establishing a steady salary and financial security as an actor between the release of her plays. If anything, her acting, for a time, subsidized her writing: based on the fact that she continued to work as a salaried performer at Covent Garden, but performed fewer nights than actresses at similar pay rates and fewer nights than she had earlier in her career, Donkin convincingly argues that "Inchbald's salary as an actress had been transformed into a subsidy for her playwriting."[60] For a time, Inchbald essentially became a playwright "in residence," as both Harris and Colman were "coming to terms with the fact that she was more valuable to them as a first-string playwright than as a second-string actress."[61] Her acting career is sometimes dismissed, with Inchbald being characterized as a beautiful, but mid-level, actress with a stutter, never destined for the greatness of Jordan or Siddons. But, as both Donkin and Nora Nachumi recognize, this acting career got her into the theaters, taught her stagecraft, and kept her close to the managers. It played a crucial role, in other words, in her professional success as a dramatist. Yet while acting and writing worked together to develop her professional success, they are largely decoupled in producing her celebrity. She was not known, as Macklin and Foote had been, for the characters she acted in her own plays. Her greatest celebrity was as an "authoress": Mrs. Inchbald.

On the printed page, Inchbald was confident and elegant in her simplicity. The title pages to her printed texts are clean, with plenty of white space and only the essential information: the play's title, the place of performance, the author's name, and the publisher. Her name nearly always appeared on her title pages as the author, even when she was translating a French or German work. Rarely did she include an advertisement or preface, not offering justifications for translating work or defending herself against critics. The works stood on their own merit. Her name began to appear in increasingly prominent positions in newspapers. While her name had appeared in performance announcements for years, it had long been buried in lists of actors. As her writing career took off, her name began to take up more space on playbills and in advertisements for the printed editions of her plays.

Inchbald's name functioned so successfully not only because of her authorial skill, but also because of her careful management of her reputation. Inchbald rejected sexual advances, and even fought off aggressive advances, avoiding scandal. Ben Robertson notes the mature choice of her self-presentation: she was never "Elizabeth" or "Lizzie," but always "Mrs. Inchbald."[62] Moreover, because she was never a star actress, she did not acquire a nickname, like Macklin's "Mr. Shylock," Dorothy Jordan's "Little Pickle," or Mary Robinson's "Perdita," that merged her public character with a stage character. Without such interferences, the name "Mrs. Inchbald" was free to represent her corpus of works. When she retired as an actress in 1789, the corpus was no longer linked to her physical body, but was entirely textual.

Inchbald's later literary authority, writing prefaces to *The British Theatre* (1806–8) and selecting the pieces to be included in *A Collection of Farces and Other Afterpieces* (1809), was possible only because she had developed a reputation as a literary author. The publishing house of Longman, Hurst, Rees, and Orme, which had published her final play, *To Marry or Not to Marry* (1805) after her friend and publisher George Robinson died in 1801, commissioned Inchbald in 1806 to write brief remarks to each play in their new *British Theatre* series. Inchbald had not written literary criticism prior to this, and rarely did she even publish prefaces to her own plays. Longman's faith in Inchbald must have come from her literary ability and from the respect she had acquired as an author. In fact, Boaden, who is critical of Inchbald writing prefaces (because he believed that she had "genius," but not the "learning" necessary for critical judgment), understands why, from a marketing point of view, Longman would have chosen Inchbald for the job. He writes, "She gave her *name* to the book; and that was certainly worth the sixty guineas, which seem to have been the consideration paid for it."[63] Her print publication of her own works garnered her respect as a literary author in her own time and has made authentic editions of her works more accessible to subsequent readers. Inchbald was only able to develop a reputation as a literary author and authority because she resisted the trend of withholding her plays from print or selling her copyrights to theater managers and instead consistently printed her works, with her name attached and with a publisher she trusted to accurately convey her texts.

Inchbald's authorial choices, especially her publication of plays, can be held up among the more effective strategies for late eighteenth-century dramatists wishing to gain some power over the circulation of their works. Even Boaden recognized the extent to which she had created agency for herself as an author in his 1833 *Memoirs of Mrs. Inchbald*. Despite an occasionally vexed relationship with Inchbald's success, Boaden holds Inchbald up as a model of an empowered dramatist during a pivotal moment in the history of the theater. His biography has long been a key source of information in Inchbald scholarship. Yet rarely is the biography considered critically, as a text in which the perspective and the author's interpretation of events reveals important information about theatrical culture at the moment of its publication. The timing of its undertaking makes it especially revealing: Boaden signed a contract to write the biography in July 1832, the month after the Select Committee on Dramatic Literature held a set of hearings related to the theaters and to the treatment of dramatists. The biography is influenced by this public discourse. While this influence sometimes causes Boaden to misunderstand Inchbald's choices, his retrospective view through the lens of dramatic literary property debates also demonstrates that at a moment when dramatic authors felt exploited, Inchbald looked, more than ever, like an author who had figured out how to work effectively within an unfavorable system.

Throughout the biography, as Boaden describes Inchbald's earnings, negotiations, and working conditions, he occasionally steps out of the period of study into the present moment, using her experience to comment on the current state of dramatic authorship. In one of the most explicit examples of this, he introduces Inchbald's 1799 letter to Harris negotiating terms for the performance of *The Wise Man of the East* by writing, "As we are anxious to obtain for *living* authors something equivalent to their labours, we lay with pleasure before them Mrs. Inchbald's proposals to Mr. Harris."[64] Boaden was also a dramatist, though far less successful than Inchbald. His shared experience as a playwright made him sympathetic (at times) to the difficulties of writing for the stage.[65] Thus, he highlights her assertive demands and self-worth as contributors to her fairer remuneration. As he holds Inchbald up as an example of a well-paid and fairly treated playwright, Boaden comments on changing managerial policies, using the biography as an opportunity to encourage fairer treatment of current playwrights. Describing Inchbald's payment for *Lovers' Vows*, Boaden writes, "Harris seems now to have adopted the less liberal style of paying for an altered play differently from an original one. Alas! what strictly *can* be original?"[66] Inchbald had made a substantial £400 for the performance of this play, although the play would have earned more under the older author-benefit system.[67] Boaden understands how valuable the work was, and he suggests that she should have earned more. Even though he believes that her work was undervalued in this instance, his commentary suggests, on the whole, that dramatists were treated better in her time than they were in 1833, when he published the biography. When writing that Inchbald chose to submit *Wives as they Were, and Maids as they Are* (1797) to Covent Garden, he comments that she tended to prefer submitting her works to Harris because "he *paid* for them liberally and at sight. Mr. Harris would have thought himself *disgraced* by such conduct as the present times seem to consider fashionable."[68] Through narrating Inchbald's authorial choices, Boaden comments on the treatment of nineteenth-century playwrights, implicitly suggesting that fairer treatment would encourage talent of her caliber.

"POOR O'KEEFFE": THE CONDITION OF THE AUTHOR WITHOUT PUBLISHING RIGHTS

While Boaden could praise not only Inchbald's talent as an author, but also her success in managing her career, the same could not be said of her contemporary, John O'Keeffe. By 1833, the year of his death, O'Keeffe was generally viewed as a starving artist—exploited, underpaid, and stripped of the agency to print his own works. Retrospectively, O'Keeffe was pitied. Describing a moment in which Inchbald sent O'Keeffe a guinea, Boaden referred to the latter as "poor O'Keeffe."[69] Haymarket manager David Edward Morris would hold O'Keeffe up as an underpaid dramatist of days past in the Select Committee hearings.[70] Dramatist Richard Brinsley Peake described the "illiberality" of Colman's treatment of O'Keeffe in his 1841 *Memoirs of the Colman Family*.[71] Yet for most of his working career, O'Keeffe was not seen as a dramatist to be pitied. He found near-immediate success in his London playwriting career, writing some of the most popular works of the century. Even before premiering in London, O'Keeffe wrote for, acted in, and sang in Irish theaters for over a decade. The first play he submitted to a London theater, in December 1777, was *Tony Lumpkin in Town*, a farcical sequel to Oliver Goldsmith's *She Stoops to Conquer*.[72] Colman accepted it almost immediately, and it premiered at the Haymarket in July 1778 with fair success: the play was performed six times in its first season and remained in the Haymarket repertory.[73] With *Tony Lumpkin*, he had proven himself with Colman and found a manager who was eager to work with him.

O'Keeffe was one of the most popular and successful dramatists of the late eighteenth century. He staged over fifty works in London between 1778 and 1798.[74] Of the twelve most frequently performed afterpieces from 1776 to 1800, five were O'Keeffe's: *The Agreeable Surprise* (1781) was performed 200 times, *The Son-in-Law* (1779) 197 times, *The Poor Soldier* (1783) 165 times, *Peeping Tom* (1784) 152 times, and *The Farmer* (1787) 130 times. He is the only dramatist to have more than one afterpiece in the top twelve.[75] As Frederick Link calculates, "His ten most successful plays received nearly twelve hundred performances before 1801 in London alone."[76] David O'Shaughnessy has argued that "O'Keeffe has a claim to be the most unjustly neglected playwright of the 1780s and the 1790s, having a number of significant theatrical successes, both commercially and critically."[77] It seems that one of his real strengths was in satiating audiences' desire for novelty through the afterpiece: O'Keeffe excelled in a genre where novelty was valued and demanded. Charles Beecher Hogan notes that while many of the most popular mainpieces during the period were older repertory staples, there was a high demand for new afterpieces.[78] O'Keeffe produced new farces and comic operas at a steady pace, often doing so by adding twists and variations to existing plots and characters. His plays were constantly on the London stages throughout the final quarter of the century. Yet by the early nineteenth century, his contemporaries were referring to him as "poor O'Keeffe." As both O'Shaughnessy and Link note, apart from *Wild Oats* (1791), his works have not survived into the twenty-first century. Both of these facts have their roots in his publication choices and in how he fashioned himself as a dramatist.

The timing of O'Keeffe's London premiere was crucial in establishing his success, but also in limiting his control over his works. He began submitting works to Colman just as Colman was taking over management of the Haymarket from Samuel Foote. Link argues that this worked in O'Keeffe's favor, since Colman was looking for new plays and playwrights to supply material for his summer theater—especially after Foote's death in 1777.[79] But, in a less fortunate turn for O'Keeffe, this was also the moment when Colman was thinking most seriously about what works would be unique to the Haymarket repertory. What would differentiate the Haymarket and its offerings from the popular winter theaters? Colman had managed the well-established Covent Garden Theatre from 1767 to 1774, but the new position of managing a summer theater that had previously been sustained by Foote's works made him eager to build a unique repertory. This is the precise moment when he began keeping his own works out of print. It was also right as he was prosecuting the printer John Wheble for publishing Foote's unprinted works, which Colman had purchased and which he wished to retain for exclusive performance at the Haymarket.[80] The concurrence of Colman's new scheme of buying copyrights for the Haymarket with the start of O'Keeffe's London playwriting career meant that some of O'Keeffe's most popular and enduring works would remain out of print for decades. Moreover, because O'Keeffe was at this point still a relatively unknown author, Colman paid for the performance and copyrights to O'Keeffe's works at shockingly low rates for what would become such popular pieces.

O'Keeffe recounts the performance of his first few works by the Haymarket in his *Recollections* (1826), explaining how Colman came to own the copyrights. After the performance of *Tony Lumpkin in Town* in 1778, in March 1779 O'Keeffe returned to Dublin, where he and his family still resided. He stayed in Dublin for the summer but sent Colman a new farce, *The Son-in-Law*, which was performed sixteen times that summer at the Haymarket. Colman traveled to Dublin that winter, paid O'Keeffe £60 from the author benefit night, and asked O'Keeffe to sell him the copyright, which he did for an additional £40.[81] O'Keeffe read about the success of his play in the London newspapers, and he saw his farce staged in Dublin the same summer it premiered in London.[82] But without been having present himself at the London performances, he may not have realized just what a success his play had been. When Colman asked to buy the copyright, O'Keeffe responded out of gratitude rather than making a decision to suit his own best interests. He recounts that Colman asked him to sell him the copyright,

> instead of disposing it to a bookseller; as in the latter case, he said, the winter houses would hack it out, and take from his *nut-shell* (as he termed the Haymarket Theatre) that novelty which was necessary to attract an audience in the hot summers. Bound to Mr. Colman through gratitude for having produced my first play, which else I feared might never have come before a London public, and not thinking it prudent to object to the proposal of a London manager, who had it in his power to shut out my future works for ever from notice, I consented, and he gave me 40l. for my copy-right.[83]

His description of this moment is striking in its difference from the way Inchbald imagined her relationship with the London managers, including Colman. O'Keeffe calls himself "bound" to Colman through gratitude.[84] He fears that if he does not oblige the manager, his works will not be staged in London again. Inchbald knew the value of her works well enough to know that disagreements with managers would not stop them from performing her plays, and she did not let gratitude dictate her professional decisions. O'Keeffe, by contrast, continued to leave himself beholden to managers, even after he had established a reputation as a popular dramatist in London. In 1786, for instance, after the bookseller George Kearsley would not pay O'Keeffe as much as he wanted for the copyright to *Love in a Camp*, O'Keeffe sold it to Harris instead, even though Harris was offering less than Kearsley. His reasoning came from advice he had received, "never to quarrel with a manager."[85] O'Keeffe apparently felt the need, even after the town had developed an appetite for his plays, to gratify managers.

Because of the precedent O'Keeffe had set with *The Son-in-Law*, he ended up selling the copyrights to his next few pieces directly to Colman as well. O'Keeffe sold him the copyright to his next farce, *The Dead Alive* (1781), for £40 "at [Colman's] request."[86] The same summer, the Haymarket also brought out *The Agreeable Surprise*, with Colman again paying £40 for the copyright. With two such popular new works occupying the Haymarket, as well as the regular reperformance of *The Son-in-Law*, O'Keeffe had a clearer sense by the end of the summer of his value to the theater world.[87] He even recounts with pleasure that Macklin was present for the first performance of *The Agreeable Surprise* and "was heard to say 'The Agreeable Surprise' is the best farce in the English language, except 'The Son-in-Law.'"[88] Yet the pattern he established early on with Colman meant that the copyrights to these three plays, as well as *The Young Quaker* (1783) and *Peeping Tom* (1784), were to remain in the Haymarket's exclusive repertory, existing only in performance, for decades.

Although many appeared in unauthorized or Irish editions, O'Keeffe published relatively few of his plays.[89] Of the eight O'Keeffe plays for which Milhous and Hume have information in *The Publication of Plays in London, 1660–1800*, seven copyrights were sold directly to the theaters—three to the Haymarket and four to Covent Garden. These figures only include the plays for which we have information about how much he was paid; in addition to these seven, he sold at least ten more of his copyrights directly to the theaters.[90] He did not often negotiate substantial payment for his copyrights. Nor did he earn much from performance when he negotiated upfront payments rather than earning his salary from author benefit nights. The one instance in which he was offered a very substantial sum upfront—600 guin-eas for *The Banditti* at Covent Garden—was not the result of his own nego-tiations, but his musical collaborator Samuel Arnold's.[91] In proportion to the frequency of performance he was one of the most underpaid authors for his early afterpieces: *The Agreeable Surprise* and *The Son-in-Law* earned him only £100 apiece, including payments for performance and print rights, yet each was performed about two hundred times in London alone before the end of the century. While Macklin made a single farce support him over and over again, O'Keeffe was often paid little for his works and was only able to earn a living because he was so prolific.[92] As Link puts it, O'Keeffe was not an "acute businessman."[93]

O'Keeffe's copyright situation meant that his plays earned phenomenal amounts for the Haymarket Theatre for decades, with little payment to the author; that he could not grant permission to actors wishing to use his plays for their benefit nights at other theaters; and that he was unable to make a name for himself in print as a literary dramatist. George Colman the Elder and later Colman the Younger were voraciously protective of O'Keeffe's works, treating O'Keeffe's works in much the same way Macklin had treated his own *Love à la Mode*. When O'Keeffe's friend William Lewis wished to perform *The Young Quaker* (1783) for his benefit night at Covent Garden the winter after it premiered at the Haymarket, Colman forbade it. O'Keeffe lamented this decision, but he did not, it seems, argue with Colman's decision.[94] The most significant dramatic literary property case of the late eighteenth cen-tury, *Coleman v. Wathen* (1793), revolved around O'Keeffe's *The Agreeable Surprise*.[95] Twelve years after the afterpiece had premiered in London, Col-man still viewed the work as property valuable enough to take a rival theater to court over. The one exception that Colman made in terms of sharing his O'Keeffe scripts was with the Irish theaters. Not viewing Ireland as direct competition, both Colman and Harris allowed O'Keeffe to send a manuscript copy of his plays to Richard Daly in Dublin for an additional sum.[96]

In one rare instance, Colman was compelled to allow a winter theater to perform one of his O'Keeffe properties, and he deeply resented the situa-tion. During the 1781–82 season, Lady Hertford, wife of the Lord Chamber-lain, Francis Seymour-Conway, requested that *The Son-in-Law*, by that point two years old, be performed at Covent Garden for six nights. Lady Hert-ford asked this of Harris, who then asked O'Keeffe to request it of Colman. O'Keeffe writes, "I, knowing how ill he would take it, declined." However, the composer, Samuel Arnold, made the request, and O'Keeffe reports that "Mr. Colman very unwillingly complied, urging how unreasonable it was to deprive his little theatre of attraction, when the heat of the weather and empty town required every pull to get an audience at all."[97] After *The Son-in-Law* had run at Covent Garden for six nights, Lady Hertford requested six nights of *The Agreeable Surprise* and then another two nights. O'Keeffe writes,

> This vexed Mr. Colman exceedingly, yet he consented. . . . and these two pieces, which had produced to me only 100l. each, filled Covent-garden theatre fourteen nights in the dull season, and propped a tragedy. I made no comment; but Mr. Colman regretted to Dr. Arnold, and many of his other friends, that he had not stipulated with Covent-garden for a night for me.[98]

In recounting this incident, O'Keeffe expresses his deference and allegiance to Colman. Even while he highlights that the plays had only made him £100 apiece, he does not describe Colman's vexation as greed. Instead, he paints both himself and Colman as being taken advantage of and emphasizes Colman's goodness in regretting that he had not asked Covent Garden to pay O'Keeffe a benefit night. Colman himself, of course, never paid O'Keeffe further benefits for the plays that ran for decades. Yet O'Keeffe valued the personal relationship with Colman highly enough to disregard poor treatment professionally.[99]

If O'Keeffe had little control over how his plays circulated in performance, he also did little to control his reputation in print. For the first half of his writing career, he made very few of his works available in printed editions. In many cases, this was because he had sold the copyright to the theaters and was no longer able to print. In other cases, he seems simply to have chosen not to print his plays. Perhaps this was because many of his works were shorter pieces—afterpieces, farces, comic operas, and other entertainments. It is possible that he did not see them as worthy of being printed and read, although many playwrights, including Inchbald, did print their shorter works. Looking at the publication record of O'Keeffe's works from when he began writing for the London theaters in the late 1770s through to when he published his collected works in 1798, the vast majority of print publications are of the songs and music in his plays rather than of the plays themselves.[100] The title pages to the many publications of "Songs, Airs, &c." or "Songs, Choruses, &c." for his various plays rarely featured O'Keeffe's name. Buyers would likely have known these were O'Keeffe's works. Yet as textual artifacts, they represent his works not as literary plays, but theatrical entertainments.

When O'Keeffe decided to sell his copyright to *The Prisoner at Large* to a bookseller rather than a manager in 1788, his decision to print was itself an event. Both the author and publisher recognized it as such. O'Keeffe wrote a dedication to the actor John Edwin, emphasizing that this was his first occasion to thank Edwin in print, "having hitherto disposed of my Right in my Copies, to the Proprietors of the Theatres."[101] The publisher, Robinson, celebrated the occasion by creating a title page that represented the author through his substantial corpus. After the author's name, the title page lists sixteen of his previous works: displayed in a large block of text, in all-caps, this corpus is typographically striking. The block paragraph ends with "&c. &c. &c.," giving the impression that the page cannot possibly represent the full body of works of such a prolific author. As O'Keeffe continued to print some of his plays over the next few years—including *The Little Hunchback* (1789), *The World in a Village* (1793), and *The London Hermit* (1793) with Debrett and *Sprigs of Laurel* (1793) with Longman—the publishers imitated Robinson's title page, highlighting O'Keeffe's body of work. These title pages create the image of a prolific author who has contributed a great deal to the public's entertainment. They suggest that he could have made a name for himself in print. But the lists of titles also remind readers of all of O'Keeffe's unprinted, inaccessible texts.

By the mid-1790s, O'Keeffe was no longer writing new work for the stage, and he was not in good shape financially. This is the point at which his reputation began to shift. No longer was he seen as an active playwright, whose works were anticipated and puffed. Nor had he become, as Inchbald had by the time she stopped writing for the stage, an established and respected literary author. His financial situation was well known. Moreover, he had been going blind for decades—a fact well known to the public.[102] At this moment, he shifts from being the prolific author of some of the century's most-performed works to being "poor O'Keeffe." His new reputation emerged at least in part from his own efforts. At this point, as he was trying to raise money for himself and his children, he turned to print, deciding to publish a four-volume edition of his dramatic works. His attempt to publish his complete works showed him just how much an obstacle selling his copyrights twenty years earlier had created. He discovered how long a manager might hold onto a copyright and the complete lack of recourse for the author without a statute law protecting an author's dramatic literary property. As a result, he began holding himself up as an object lesson in what happens when a dramatist sells his copyrights to managers rather than printers. He allowed himself to become "poor O'Keeffe" in order to publicize the mistake he had made in "disposing" of his copyrights. In his published writings from

1798 forward—from the subscription advertisement for his complete works to his 1826 *Recollections*—O'Keeffe fashioned himself as an exploited author. And his self-fashioning stuck, shaping his reputation in the years to come.

From the moment he advertised his *Dramatic Works* until Adelaide filled in a copy with manuscript additions of his five missing plays, O'Keeffe repeatedly publicized the omissions. On November 21, 1797, the *Oracle and Public Advertiser* advertised "Proposals for Publishing by Subscription the DRAMATIC WORKS of JOHN O'KEEFFE." The four-volume work would be printed and delivered to subscribers in June 1798, with the promise that O'Keeffe would personally sign each copy. The advertisement lists the works to be included in each volume, and a note at the bottom reads,

> The Copy-Right of the Pieces marked thus*, were purchased by the Proprietor of the Theatre Royal, Covent-Garden, who has liberally consented to this publication. Mr. O'Keeffe is not at present empowered to print his five remaining Pieces, viz. The Young Quaker, Peeping Tom, The Son in Law, The Dead Alive, and The Agreeable Surprize, having disposed of the Copy Right to the late Patentee of the Haymarket Theatre.[103]

O'Keeffe contrasts the behaviors of the two managers, thanking Harris and highlighting his liberality, by marking each of the eleven works that Harris had bought and was now allowing O'Keeffe to print with an asterisk. Colman the Younger, alternately, who had refused permission to print the five Haymarket pieces, is not even acknowledged. Instead, he mentions Colman's late father, who had originally purchased the pieces. O'Keeffe notes that he is not "empowered" to print the pieces, having "disposed" of the copyrights. Selling his copyrights to that theater is recoded as "disposal"—a loss for the author.

When the *Dramatic Works* appeared the next year, the publication was again framed in terms of what it did not include. The paratextual material is brief, including only a page and a half dedication to the Prince of Wales, a list of subscribers, a table of contents, and an "Address Prefatory" that focuses entirely on the copyright issue. The address, quoted at length in the first pages of this chapter, lists the works that are missing, explaining that "an inconsiderate disposal of the Copy Right of his Pieces . . . prevents their appearance in this Collection." The address repeats the terminology of "disposal" from the newspaper advertisement, adding that the choice was not well thought out by the green author. The sentence is glossed with an especially telling footnote: "Had they been sold to a Bookseller, and consequently then Published, the AUTHOR would, by the laws respecting literary property, have had a right to print them at the expiration of fourteen years, a term now long elapsed." In other words, O'Keeffe was not just lamenting his own disempowerment. He understood and was drawing attention to the fact that any rights he might have over the work depended on a statute law that offered protection (and copyright term limits) that kicked in only once the work was in print. Indeed, according to Peake, O'Keeffe had consulted the copyright lawyer Thomas Erskine, asking "whether, in point of law, the detention of literary property after the term prescribed by act of Parliament was justifiable."[104] Erskine's reply, according to Peake, "left O'Keeffe without any hopes." The new practice of "selling copyrights" to managers was a misnomer, for the work was only copyrighted when it was printed. What dramatists were selling was the right to print, and since the managers were buying this right in order not to print the works, dramatists were fundamentally transferring their common-law rights in the work indefinitely. Colman, as Gerland argues, had established a common-law performance copyright, or a perpetual right to exclusive performance of the works until they were printed. Beneficial as this was for the manager, though, it was incredibly disempowering for the author, who could not benefit from the reversion of their rights after a fourteen-year term. It is for this reason that O'Keeffe began to think of his works as "locked up" in manuscript.

Twenty-eight years later, when O'Keeffe published his *Recollections*, he created a narrative of his professional choices that highlighted how he "disposed" of his copyrights. The narrative is tinged with feelings of regret. He explains how Colman came to own the copyrights to five of his works, but he also treats the readers as if they already understand the situation. When he mentions that he could not give the actor William Lewis permission to perform *The Young Quaker* at Covent Garden, for instance, he writes, "this being one of my five Haymarket pieces locked up in MS," as if readers would already understand that those pieces were being protected by the Colmans. Theatrical publics would, indeed, likely have already understood the situation, since *The Agreeable Surprise* had been at the center of *Coleman v. Wathen*, and O'Keeffe had already announced in his *Dramatic Works* that the plays were "locked up." In other instances, he discusses the monetary and aesthetic implications for the author who cannot control the printing and performance of his works:

And here, in justice to myself, it may not be amiss to take some little notice of the great injury done to the reputation of a dramatic author, (and none other can be injured in the same way,) by the circulation of spurious printed copies of his plays through the world. My five Haymarket-pieces locked up in MS. have been repeatedly printed and published surreptitiously, (as well as those of other authors,) and are full of the most glaring errors. I heard read to me, by my brother, these my early productions, in which were passages and expressions that never came from my pen.

He links the production of spurious editions with the withholding of the plays from print. These spurious editions are mistaken as real because an authoritative version does not exist. As spurious printed texts circulated, so too did unauthorized performances. O'Keeffe regretted that everyone but him seemed to make money from the repeat performance of his plays. Describing his two-act opera *The Wicklow Mountains* (1796), he writes,

> I was told by many of my Irish friends, that this opera was a great favourite all over Ireland, and fully as attractive as any thing of mine, particularly in Dublin, where my "Gold Mine" sent much gold to the treasury of the theatre. During the whole of my dramatic career, including a period of thirty-five years, I never received a shilling from any theatre in the world, except Covent-Garden, the Haymarket, the Dublin theatre, (under Daly,) and my one night at Drury-Lane.[105]

Even as O'Keeffe takes control of his self-representation through his *Recollections*, the image he creates is one of disempowerment. He lacks control over the print production of his works, resulting in inaccessible texts and spurious texts full of errors, and he lacks the ability to make substantial money from repeated performances of his hugely popular works.

O'Keeffe closes his *Recollections* with a chapter beginning, "For thirty-three years I had supported myself and children, hired amanuenses, servants, &c. by the labours of my pen." It is clear in this moment that the autobiography, for O'Keeffe, is a celebratory record of a playwright who was, for a time, able to subsist entirely by his writing—a rare feat. It is as if the work is responding to an unstated question: how does one make a living in the theaters? O'Keeffe's *Recollections* is similar to Boaden's biography of Inchbald in their focus on the dramatists' professional lives. In the final chapter, though, O'Keeffe turns once again to the professional decision that differentiated him from Inchbald—a decision that marred his authorial reputation and undermined his successful career: selling his copyrights to the theaters. To secure his finances, he explains, he decided to publish his complete works and discovered that he could not do so. At this point, though, decades after the fact, O'Keeffe writes about the situation differently. While he once again credits Harris's generosity (this time also thanking the booksellers who allowed him to reprint his works), he surmises that Colman would also have allowed him to print his works had the Haymarket been in a stronger financial situation in 1797: "I am *now* thoroughly convinced that the Haymarket would have done so likewise, could the nature of that property and the circumstances of that theatre then have admitted of it."[106] Why he granted forgiveness at this moment is unclear, although it seems likely to stem from the passage of time and his gratitude to Colman the Elder. Yet the next sentence, with its mixture of forgiveness, generosity, and resentment, reveals the continued complexity of O'Keeffe's feelings about the Haymarket's print suppression of his works:

> But as the London public cannot see the "Agreeable Surprise," "Son-in-law," "Dead Alive," "Peeping Tom," and "Young Quaker" in type, let them repair to the Haymarket Theatre, where they were first brought out for me by the elder George Colman, and see them for their own diversion, and the treasurer's great amusement, in reckoning the cash, which, I trust, they still bring to the coffers of my ever kind and very good friend George Colman the younger.[107]

It is as if O'Keeffe has accepted, with exhaustion, that the five works will exist only in performance and only on the boards of the Haymarket. Defeated, he encourages the public to go see his works at the Haymarket, noting that the public amusement will be matched by the treasurer's amusement, as the struggling author watches from afar. O'Keeffe's autobiography was ultimately not just the memories of a well-known member of the theatrical community, but also a record of the iniquities in payment and copyright systems. The work served as a political statement in the decades when frustration and anger were building in theatrical communities around the issue of dramatic literary property.

Contributing to O'Keeffe's self-fashioning as an exploited author was a literal performance of his destitution. In June 1800, Covent Garden held a benefit performance for the retired author. At the end of the second act of his play *The Lie of the Day* (1796), O'Keeffe came onstage to deliver a "Poetical Address." The newspapers record the event as a moving and pitiful spectacle:

> At the end of the second Act Mr. O'Keeffe, who has long been deprived of sight, was led on the Stage by Mr. Lewis, and the *spectacle* was mournfully interesting. [His] Address was delivered with simplicity and feeling, and with some attempt at pleasantry, which however, his own sensibility interrupted, and which indeed hardly accorded with the sympathy of the Audience, who seemed throughout the recitation to be deeply affected.

> To the credit of his feelings, Lewis, who we understand first introduced
> Mr. O'Keeffe into the Theatrical World, was obliged to leave the Stage.
> On the whole perhaps a more affecting scene of natural pathos never was
> exhibited upon Theatrical boards.[108]

The blind author, hailed in the review as "the Father of *Modern Comedy*,"
was led onstage to speak to an audience aware of his financial hardship; his
friend, the comic actor William Lewis, was moved to tears as he walked
O'Keeffe on and off the stage.[109] While O'Keeffe did not mention his property rights in this performance, the audience would likely have known about
the Haymarket pieces, especially since he had published his *Dramatic Works*
two years earlier. As he staged his ailing body, O'Keeffe literally performed
the hardships that dramatists at the turn of the century were facing.

O'Keeffe's self-fashioning endured beyond his lifetime. Peake's description of O'Keeffe's attempt to publish his *Dramatic Works* mirrors O'Keeffe's
own prefatory address nearly exactly.[110] Like O'Keeffe, Peake begins by citing
Harris's generosity, then explains that Colman wanted the plays solely for his
summer theater, and finally notes that if he had printed them, the copyright
would have already expired. O'Keeffe was cited in the 1832 Select Committee hearings as an example of an underpaid author whose copyrights were
bought by the theater. The real print legacy O'Keeffe left was not a series
of published plays or even a complete works that featured his most popular afterpieces. Instead, he left behind a series of words that memorialized
the failures of copyright and remuneration systems. He turned himself into
"poor O'Keeffe" so that others might push for change.

Two years before the end of the century, O'Keeffe's and Inchbald's careers
could not have looked more different. In 1798, Inchbald was enjoying the
huge success of *Lovers' Vows*. Her popularity was creating competitors who
were trying to sell their own adaptations using her name. She would use the
success of *Lovers' Vows* to negotiate the terms for her next adaptation. And
she would continue to support herself for years to come. O'Keeffe meanwhile, was struggling to print his own complete works, ultimately failing to
include all his most popular plays in the four-volume collection, and failing to make much of a profit from the endeavor. While Inchbald would be
recognized as an arbiter of taste, invited to remark on and select dramatic
works in multiple series, O'Keeffe would live out his life in relative solitude,
depending on charity and on a pension from Covent Garden. The charity
benefit on June 12, 1800, at Covent Garden referred to him as "The Unfor-
tunate Author of many successful Dramatic Pieces."[111] While his works
continued to be successful, the author himself struggled: the productions

of his pen had been decoupled from his fame and from his livelihood. During O'Keeffe's and Inchbald's active years in the theater, especially the 1780s, his works had been the more frequently performed. But her legacy was in a stronger position. For she had made her plays available not just to contemporary audiences, but also to readers. In doing so, she also left behind a fuller archive, making possible the feminist recovery work of the 1980s to early 2000s.

For playwrights like Inchbald and O'Keeffe, who did not strive to be star actors or wish to perform for the entirety of their careers, print publication served important functions. It gave them some control over their reputations and over the circulation of their works in at least one medium. It could release their works from the snare of managers, who might try to hoard and control their plays for decades. Nonpublication had worked for Macklin because he used his unprinted afterpiece as a negotiation tool, earning performance fees from multiple theaters and using the popular afterpiece to secure acting contracts. Nonpublication had worked for Foote because he consistently acted in his own plays, making his presence integral to their performance. When he secured a patent for the Haymarket, moreover, he found himself with a venue in which he could repeatedly profit from the exclusive performance of his unprinted plays. But for many dramatists, Inchbald and O'Keeffe included, but also early nineteenth-century playwrights like Thomas Morton and Douglas Jerrold, nonpublication did not guarantee control over the performance of their work. Instead, as nonpublication became the practice of managers, it often resulted in even less power for playwrights, who had now lost the valuable ability, first granted to playwrights during the Restoration era, to print their plays. With this, their ability to craft an authorial reputation and control the appearance of their work in print was also limited. The lack of dramatic literary property law was, ultimately, not a problem that could be fixed through subterfuge and clever tactics. Even common-law performance copyright offered less protection to dramatists than to managers. Dramatists needed legal protection for the performance of their works—protection that existed whether or not the dramatist chose to print her plays. Such protection would begin to arrive, after decades of struggle, in 1833.

Epilogue

Performing Ownership before Parliament
Literary Property and the "Decline of Drama"

I have argued in this book that eighteenth-century playwrights valued drama by valuing performance. This argument overturns narratives that suggest that the eighteenth century saw a decline in the quality and the cultural valuation of drama. In spite of the qualities that made it difficult to regulate and reward legally—its unfixity, its evanescence, the multiplicity of authorship involved in stage production—performance was drama's primary mode of publication. It was the medium that generated profit in a hugely popular theater industry. It was the medium that helped develop modern celebrity. Playwrights wrote *for* performance. Thus, to create value and to protect that value, playwrights turned to the medium itself, embracing its embodiment and its existence in a particular moment. They turned away from print to protect their works in performance. It is telling that many of the most commercially successful and popular playwrights of the period saw neither their authorship as being distinct from the playhouse nor their plays as artistic products that were alienable from the author: as actor-playwrights, Macklin, Foote, Garrick, and others tied their work's value to their performing bodies and celebrity.

The turn away from print was a bold move in an era that has often been studied as an age of print. The figures in this study did not maximize the opportunities afforded by print publication to develop their literary authorship in the ways that their predecessors, such as John Dryden and Aphra Behn, had. Inchbald is an exception, though even her carefully crafted print persona drew heavily on her works' value in performance.[1] What many dramatists did instead was play with dramatic form, altering it in ways that tied their works to their own performing bodies and celebrity presence.

Developments in dramatic form altered the theatrical landscape, producing a nation in which one was likely to see satiric reviews advertised as dishes of chocolate, dramatic medleys like Wilkinson's anthologies of performance, or scenes extracted from plays and repurposed. One-man shows grew in popularity, for these were works that bound the celebrity performer and his words into one creative product. The prevalence of such shows is a testament to the fact that writers and performers alike were seeking control over performance: one-man shows made it difficult to parse out where the value of a work lay. Was it the words spoken, the performance, the presence of the celebrity? George Alexander Stevens, for instance, wrote and performed his popular one-man show *The Lecture on Heads* (1764). As I have written about elsewhere, he used his advertisements for the show to draw parallels between the labor of manufacturing a physical product, the labor of writing a text, and the labor of performing. He also highlighted the authenticity not just of his performance text, but also of his performing body, suggesting that only he could stage the true work.[2] Innovations in dramatic form, especially involving one-man shows, continued into the nineteenth century. Charles Mathews, for example, famously developed the monopolylogue, a scene in which he would perform multiple characters, rapidly shifting among them. Much like Foote's performances, this genre relied on Mathews's skill as a performer and a mimic. Moreover, because Mathews kept the works out of print and improvised in performance, he believed himself to be their sole authentic purveyor. His wife Anne describes his annoyance at print piracies of his work that were "made up of the most contemptible trash."[3] These print piracies enabled unauthorized performances in places "where the real performance was never heard."[4] Mathews publicized his complaint by filing an injunction and by announcing in playbills that no authorized print edition existed. But if he could ultimately do nothing to stop other performances, he could at least rely on the drawing power of his celebrity to maintain interest in his own performances. Theater historians and literary scholars need to take these new dramatic forms, from Foote's *Tea* to Mathews's monopolylogues, seriously instead of repeating the narrative about a decline of drama. Many of the new dramatic works of the period were not traditional five-act plays, and of those that were, many were written by actor-playwrights who composed elements onstage in performance, through their bodies and through improvisation.

The theatrical trends I have outlined in this book—from playwrights' explicit rejection of print, to their performances of ownership, to the multiplicity of dramatic forms that developed in a culture of ephemerality—came to a head in the early nineteenth century. To many figures within the literary community, these trends represented a crisis, and playwrights themselves began making serious claims about a "decline of drama." These claims have been repeated uncritically in scholarship for centuries: such scholarship relies on aesthetic judgments and a devaluation of drama in relation to the new form of the novel.[5] More recently, theater historians have "dismantled the blatant white patriarchalism and cultural snobbery of this history, freighted as it is with fraying assumptions about aesthetic autonomy and 'literariness.'"[6] But how did the narrative of a "decline of drama" develop in the first place? How is it related to the turn away from print and the culture of ephemerality that developed out of property considerations? In the final pages of this book, I turn to that narrative and its deployment in the years leading up to the passage of the Dramatic Literary Property Act (1833), analyzing two important performances of ownership: the last major performance rights case before the passage of the act, *Murray v. Elliston* (1822), which involved the unauthorized performance of Lord Byron's *Marino Faliero*, and the 1832 Select Committee on Dramatic Literature hearings. In both of these moments, dramatists insisted that there had been a decline in drama over the previous decades. In part, what they were reacting to was the culture of ephemerality I have described in this book. At the same time these playwrights were attacking the current state of drama, though, they were doing so in order to establish its value to the nation. By focusing on "drama" as a literary category rather than celebrating the rich and thriving theatrical culture that surrounded them, dramatists worked to establish a play text's value independent of the theater, and in so doing, argue for authorial property in performance. The narrative of a "decline of drama" and its uncritical acceptance by later scholars is misleading. Drama did not decline. It simply responded to the market, not just in the sense of audience demand for spectacle, but also in terms of creating its own value in a way it could maintain and protect when the law failed to do so.

On the surface of things, Lord Byron's complaint against Drury Lane Theatre in 1821 for performing his printed tragedy *Marino Faliero* (1821) would seem to be the inverse of what I have described in this book: here was a playwright who wanted his work to exist solely in print. When Byron published his tragedy with the bookseller John Murray on April 21, 1821, he included a statement in the preface declaring his intention that this play was meant to be read and not staged. Unlike Macklin and Foote, who withheld works from print to protect their value in performance, Byron saw his work's value as residing entirely in print:

> I have no view to the stage; in its present state it is, perhaps, not a very exalted object of ambition; besides I have been too much behind the

scenes to have thought it so at any time. And I cannot conceive any man of irritable feeling putting himself at the mercies of an audience:—the sneering reader, and the loud critic, and the tart review, are scattered and distant calamities; but the trampling of an intelligent or of an ignorant audience on a production which, be it good or bad, has been a mental labour to the writer, is a palpable and immediate grievance.[7]

Byron was rejecting the qualities of performance—its immediacy and liveness—that the figures in this study embraced. He positions drama as better read than staged, because though it might be criticized in print, that criticism is "scattered and distant" in contrast to the "palpable and immediate" response generated in the space of the theater. He denigrates the state of the stage, suggesting that his work is too legitimate to suit audience taste because it follows the dramatic unities and therefore is, ironically, unstageable. In a footnote, he further disparages the theaters by writing that as a member of the subcommittee of Drury Lane Theatre, he attempted, unsuccessfully, to "bring back the legitimate drama." While for Macklin, Foote, Wilkinson, Inchbald, and O'Keeffe, performance was the goal and print was a medium that might support or undermine it, for Byron, the theater was no longer the best venue for the display of "mental labor" that went into writing drama.

Byron may have intended for his work to be read, but theater managers felt differently. Robert William Elliston, manager of Drury Lane, obtained a copy directly from the printer as it was in production, giving his company time to prepare a stage version. He submitted his version to the licenser of plays and advertised a performance for April 25, just four days after it appeared in print.[8] The copyright owner, John Murray, obtained an injunction against the performance. In response, Elliston spoke with Lord Chancellor Eldon directly, obtaining his permission to perform the work for one night on April 25 until the case could be heard. Against Byron's and Murray's wishes, *Marino Faliero* appeared at Drury Lane.

While many eighteenth-century playwrights forewent print publication to control the performance of their works and Byron wanted his work to exist only in print, their problem was fundamentally the same: they could not invoke the law to stop unauthorized performances. Thus, like his predecessors, Byron performed ownership. He did this first through his printed preface. Moreover, on the night of the Drury Lane premiere, Murray printed handbills and had them dropped from the balcony into the pit and boxes at the start of the second act. They read:

> The public are respectfully informed, that the representation of Lord Byron's tragedy, *The Doge of Venice*, this evening, takes place in defiance of the injunction of the Lord Chancellor, which was not applied for until the remonstrance of the publisher, at the earnest desire of the noble author, had failed in protecting that drama from its intrusion on the stage, for which it was never intended.[9]

The legal system had failed Byron and Murray when their injunction was overturned. If they could not stop the performance, though, they could participate in it. As Derek Miller writes, "The question of copyright law thus formed part of the performance itself."[10] By dropping handbills, Murray distracted the audience, redirecting their attention, and making the context of the performance, especially its celebrity author's complaint against the theater, part of the show.

In addition to performing Byron's authorship, Byron and Murray took the case to court. First heard before the Lord Chancellor on April 27, 1821, *Murray v. Elliston* was tried in the Court of King's Bench a year later, in May 1822. It was a generally accepted practice at this point—as it had been more or less since the breakdown of the divided repertory system—that a work in print was fair game for performance. Indeed, in the April hearing before the Lord Chancellor, the attorney general, Sir Robert Gifford, expressed this view: "It had always been understood by the managers of theatres, when an author gave a play to the public, or, in other words, when he published it, that they were at liberty to perform it."[11] Byron's printing of the play was what made his complaint and the ensuing court case exceptional. As the lawyers and judges sought for legal precedent, they kept coming up with cases that involved either unprinted works or works that existed only in pirated editions. Whereas earlier injunctions and cases (such as Colman's case against George Wathen for performance of *The Agreeable Surprise*) were predicated on the deliberate choice the authors and managers had made not to print the work and therefore not to make the work a "gift to the public," Byron and Murray's lawyers were arguing for the right to print a work *and* still control its use in performance. Although Byron was rejecting the stage, his aim to have the right to forbid performances ultimately recognized the power and value of the medium.

Murray v. Elliston raised important questions about the relationship between print and performance, drawing attention to the difficulties in assigning property rights to a work that existed in multiple media. Attorney General Gifford took for granted that dramatic works were meant to be staged: "The object of writing a tragedy being to have it performed."[12] Murray's lawyer, Lancelot Shadwell, countered this idea, not only on the basis that Byron had expressly stated his desire for this work not to be performed, but by pointing to Elliston's own advertisements. Shadwell argued that "in the bill announcing the performance, it was stated that the tragedy was written in a manner not fit for the theatre. Now it could not be supposed, that a poem, which came from the author's pen, not fit for the theatre, implied a poem that was to be performed on the stage."[13] In debating Elliston's right to stage Byron's work without Byron's or Murray's permission, the two sides questioned the fundamental purpose of drama: was drama written to be heard or read?

The case also called into question print's and performance's effects on one another's value. Attorney General Gifford suggested that performance of a play increased rather than damaged print sales. Shadwell, alternately, argued that Elliston's alterations to the work, and elements of the performance itself, might hurt the work, thereby hurting print sales (Murray's copyright) and Byron's authorial reputation. The public "might discover faults in the performers; they might be displeased with the embellishments of the theatre; they might perceive various errors, for which the author was not accountable," and "those very alterations might cause the tragedy to be censured by the public, while the work, if left as it originally stood, might add to the author's fame."[14] For a genre that existed in multiple media, to have legal control over one medium but no control over the other left authors in a vulnerable position.

When the trial was heard in King's Bench a year later in 1822, James Scarlett, arguing on behalf of Murray, challenged the idea that the Statute of Anne could be violated only through a print publication. He argued that "if the statute makes a literary work property, the common law will give the remedy for the invasion of it. The only question is, whether the representation of this piece for profit may not injure the copy-right. If so, the plaintiff is entitled to the judgment of the Court."[15] The value of the copyright, he argued, could be diminished not only by a competing print publication, but also by performance, which might taint the public's view of the work and dissuade audiences from buying a printed copy. Scarlett's argument justified a performance right. Elliston's attorney, John Adolphus, countered with the prevailing ruling (from *Donaldson v. Becket*) that protection under the statute erased common-law rights. He further argued that because Elliston had "altered and abridged" the work, it was not a violation of property. In the latter argument, Adolphus was not just relying on the fact that Elliston had removed scenes. He argued that any stage performance was a significant alteration: "Persons go thither [to the theater], not to read the work, or to hear it read, but to see the combined effect of poetry, scenery, and act-ing. Now of these three things, two are not produced by the author of the work; and the combined effect is just as much a new production, and even more so than the printed abridgment of a work."[16] In pointing to the differ-ences between print and performance, Adolphus invoked the multiplicity of authorship involved in stage production, suggesting that the creative labor of the author contributed to a fraction of the overall effect. The author, then, could not claim sole rights in a performance. Lord Chief Justice Eldon ulti-mately found for Elliston, though whether this was on the basis of his argu-ment about the Statute of Anne or his argument about abridgment is unclear from the ruling. Eldon's decision meant that printed works would continue to be free for use in performance regardless of the author's intentions.

In revolving around a play intended only for print, *Murray v. Elliston* invoked questions about the purpose of drama, the relationship between print and performance, their effects on one another's value, and the creative labor that went into each. Moreover, as Derek Miller argues, *Murray* dem-onstrates that the question of performance rights could not be considered apart from the question of print rights: "These cases could not isolate a per-formance from its written form: the value of a written text—whether that value be articulated as vague notions of literary quality or quantifiable mea-sures of commercial sales—haunted legal battles over performance rights."[17] This particular sort of relationship between the two media emerged pre-cisely because they were protected and rewarded differently, as I have argued in this book. Scholarship that investigates the uses of printed drama during the period tends to focus on the cooperative relationship between print and performance. The Multigraph Collective, for instance, notes that audiences "may have collected [printed play texts] as souvenirs to memorialize their experience, or to clarify their perception of the production. Eighteenth-and nineteenth-century readers thus could expect play texts to evoke per-formance and anchor their memory of it."[18] Yet while the two media could certainly interact productively, they increasingly took on an antagonistic relationship because performance remained unprotected by legal systems. As the country moved toward recognizing the medium of performance as a form of property, print and the literary value of dramatic texts increasingly took center stage.

The limits of the law created an antagonistic relationship between the two media, for without legal protection for performance, print publication could infringe on the value of performance. As I have argued, this brought about a culture of ephemerality, with playwrights strategically embracing the qualities that differentiated performance from print. But while eighteenth-century dramatists embraced performance because of its value, we see this turn away from print recoded in the early nineteenth century as evidence of a decline in drama. As Jane Moody argues, Romantic ideals have shaped our views of the early nineteenth-century theaters:

> Critics implicitly defend the Romantic poet-playwrights for having invented a "mental theatre" consisting of lyrical, experimental tragedies which brilliantly transcend the irrational and capricious desires of mass audiences and the degraded condition of dramatic institutions such as Drury Lane and Covent Garden. The result of this complicity is that Romantic tragedy has remained the unquestioned cultural apex of late Georgian Drama.[19]

But the fact remains that a rich theatrical culture thrived alongside the critically celebrated "mental theatre." The corporeality of Foote's works was set in contrast to the mental theater of Byron, in spite of the fact that both authors were responding to a theater world that limited their authorial control over the text in performance. The "ideological dispute" between staged, often illegitimate, drama and printed mental theater emerged out of the material, economic, and legal contexts of dramatic authorship and theatrical production. This included not only the rise of minor theaters in London (theaters that, because of the restrictions of the patent duopoly, were only allowed to stage illegitimate drama) but also, I argue, the culture of ephemerality that developed out of a legal devaluation of performance.[20] While performance generated immense profit, new payment systems for authors and the continued lack of legal protection for performance meant that those writing for the stage did not fully share in performance's lucrative potential.[21]

But while the "decline of drama" rhetoric that we see develop in a case like Byron's retroactively devalued the eighteenth and early nineteenth century's contributions to a British dramatic canon, it was also used strategically to make a legal argument for protecting performance. The strategic invocation became central to theatrical reform efforts in Parliament in the early 1830s. An essay entitled "The State of the Drama," published in February 1832 in the *New Monthly Magazine and Literary Journal,* succinctly sets up the argument that playwrights would make in Parliament just a few months later. The essay opens by lamenting, "In a literary age, acknowledged to abound with writers endowed with a true poetical spirit, the decline, or rather the extinction of the English Drama seems a paradox as curious as it is lamentable, and deserves, at least, some investigation."[22] The sentence immediately following attributes this decline to the lack of performance rights: "It is capable of being explained by very natural and efficient causes, the chief of which will be found ultimately to be resolved by the unparalleled injustice of the law relative to dramatic copyright." In the five pages that follow, the writer argues that the value of drama has decreased for London managers because so many of their competitors immediately reperform the works they initially paid for and staged. Having no legal recourse to combat the "deterioration of their property from the competition of other managers," these managers pass on the losses to authors by paying them less for their works.[23] Not being adequately paid for their work, "Men of genius have ceased to write for the stage."

Although the writer deals with minutiae of theater operations, often comparing the English system to the French laws, he strives to emphasize the weight of the issue for the general public by focusing on the theater as part of a larger national literary canon. He writes that "the English drama, once the pride of the nation, has dwindled down so as to have ceased even to form a province of its literature."[24] Moreover, he notes that "the fashion of reading the last new play passed away," suggesting that the practice of reading drama is evidence of literary quality. If the decline in the quality of drama were not high-enough stakes, the writer ties drama to nationalist values, insisting that it "exercise[s] a mighty influence on the thoughts, the feelings, and the morals of the nation."[25]

Having made an ambitious argument about a decline in the literary value of drama arising from a legal system that does not protect dramatic literary property and a resulting theatrical economy that does not adequately reward authors, the essay ends by hearkening back three decades to the 1800 charity benefit performance that Covent Garden held for the retired dramatist John O'Keeffe:

> Let not the English public again witness such a spectacle as that of a writer, who had indeed excited the "gaiety of nations," the late Mr. O'Keeffe, being literally obliged to beg his bread at the very period when every manager in the kingdom was being enriched by the performance of his numerous and money-drawing pieces. The degrading exhibition was calculated to excite so powerful an emotion of compassion and indignation, that the liveliest of comedians [Mr. Lewis] in vain endeavoured to suppress his tears when he presented his friend, blind, and infirm, and old, and destitute, to the gaze of the audience.[26]

In 1832, O'Keeffe was still alive, and though his popular works were still being performed, he had long since stopped earning any money from them.

By describing his pathos-inducing benefit performance from three decades earlier—when the aging and blind author had stopped writing new work—the essay creates a pitiable image in order to argue that dramatists must be better compensated and offered fuller copyright protection. In the early 1830s, periodical essays like this one constructed a narrative linking the mistreatment of playwrights to a decline of drama broadly, in order to push for legislative reform.

"The State of the Drama" was published anonymously, but the periodical it appeared in, the *New Monthly Magazine*, was newly edited by member of Parliament and dramatist Edward Bulwer-Lytton, the very man who, three months later, would bring a motion in Parliament to convene a Select Committee on Dramatic Literature.[27] The Select Committee intended to look into a range of issues affecting the performance of drama, including the duopoly created by the patent system, the existence of minor theaters in London, and the lack of copyright protection for performance. The committee's name is telling: it was framed as a committee not on theater or performance, but on "dramatic literature." Just as the Statute of Anne was framed as "An Act for the Encouragement of Learning," the push for performance rights became one about improving drama for the national good. To unquestioningly accept the idea that there was a decline in the quality of drama, as I have argued, ignores the rich innovations in form and the sorts of drama that eluded capture in print. What I am interested in here is how the playwrights orchestrating this parliamentary fight both tapped into and helped to create that narrative and how the narrative emerged in opposition to the culture of ephemerality that the theater world had embraced in the previous century.

The hearings ought to be considered as a culminating performance of ownership—an ensemble performance, carefully managed by the committee members. Bulwer-Lytton used his periodical and place in Parliament as complementary platforms from which to perform the need for dramatic literary property. The *New Monthly Magazine* article foreshadows the approach that Bulwer-Lytton and his colleagues would take in the hearings. Over the course of twelve days, the committee questioned thirty-nine witnesses, including managers, authors, actors, and theater historians.[28] As Katherine Newey argues, "Bulwer and his colleagues posed their questions to witnesses from a set of premises about what they thought a reformed theatre should become."[29] Their leading questions reinforced their belief that the patents ought to be dissolved, that the theaters were currently too large, and that dramatists were hurt, in terms of money and reputation, when their work was performed without their permission. Bratton, meanwhile, examines the hearings as a form of theater history, arguing that the committee strategically interviewed theater historian John Payne Collier in order to focus attention on Renaissance drama rather than the modern stage. Collier's testimony offered a "scholarly exposition of the superiority of England" through a dramatic lineage tracing back to Shakespeare.[30] Bratton argues that Collier's version of theater history operated "at the service of the dramatist's text," allowing the committee to make the case that drama had declined. This was in spite of evidence to the contrary in the form of audience size and the number of theaters successfully operating in London. Moreover, as Miller argues, the language that the committee used throughout centered on "literature" and "literary value," comparing the rights afforded to dramatists to the rights "granted to authors in any other branch of letters." The hearings, Miller argues, "imagined novels as theater's main cultural competitor."[31] This comparison has contributed to parallel "rise of the novel" and "decline of drama" narratives; but it also served a distinct legal purpose. By comparing drama to novels, the committee focused on the printing, textual purity, and literary value of drama. A case for protecting performance was made, then, not by highlighting the value of performance itself, but the value of the authorial text as an independent literary object. Approaching drama this way allowed the committee to isolate the dramatist's contribution from the contributions of actors and managers, offering a solution to Elliston's argument that audiences go to the theater to see "the combined effect of poetry, scenery, and acting."

When the Dramatic Literary Property Act was passed the next year, granting authors or copyright holders perpetual rights in the performance of unprinted drama and twenty-eight years or the author's life for the performance of printed works, a major step was taken in recognizing performance as a valuable medium of publication. Indeed, of the issues investigated by the Select Committee, dramatic literary property was the only one immediately addressed. This was the "first and only Copyright Act," John Russell Stephens has argued, "specifically to try to recognize the special problems of the playwright and the crucial difference between the publication of a literary work and dramatic performance."[32] This law, of course, did not fully solve the problems that dramatists struggled with as they worked to control performance. Policing provincial performances remained a challenge even after the passage of the act, and, as Stephens points out, the law did a better job of protecting theater managers and publishers than authors themselves.[33] The effects and limits of the Dramatic Literary Property Act have been discussed in greater detail elsewhere. This book has aimed, instead, to examine the prehistory of the act, illustrating the effects of new ideas about literary property on the realm they did not address: the theaters. The fact that dramatists could not control the repeat performances of their plays during a century when literary property was increasingly seen as one of the chief benefits and badges of authorship had substantial effects on theatrical cultures. Print publication rates for drama plummeted, as playwrights and managers sought to limit other theaters' access to play texts. Actor-playwrights dominated the theater world, leveraging their stage celebrity as a means to control their work. Literary property law changed the form and nature of drama, shaped the eighteenth-century repertory, and blurred the realms of legitimate and illegitimate drama.

After a century of performing ownership in the theatrical public sphere, working to change public opinion about authorial rights, and staging ownership by staging their own bodies, dramatists began performing proprietary authorship on a new parliamentary stage. The Select Committee hearings were effective in bringing about legal change. The fact that they turned to printed drama and literary value to give force to their argument speaks to an important point: the relationship between print and performance is crucial. A law that protected one medium but not the other created a rift, with the result that eighteenth-century dramatists turned away from print, creating a theatrical culture grounded instead in the evanescence of performance, onstage invention, and celebrity. The nineteenth-century rhetoric of a decline in drama seemingly devalues this culture of ephemerality: in an age of print, a theatrical culture that embraced the embodiment of performance was not fully comprehensible as part of literary culture. But the same rhetoric was used to argue for rewarding performance. The passage of the Dramatic Literary Property Act was not an ending point: there were still many questions to resolve about how it would be enforced and many legal cases that would ensue. But then, neither was it the starting point, as this book has shown. Byron's performances of his literary authorship and Bulwer-Lytton's arguments before Parliament followed on nearly a century of changing discourse and creative, extralegal strategies for owning performance.

Notes

INTRODUCTION

1. Autograph letter signed from Charles Macklin, [London?], to Tate Wilkinson, Theatre Royal, York, May 8, 1773. Folger Shakespeare Library Y.c.5380 (11).

2. John O'Keeffe, *Recollections of the Life of John O'Keeffe, Written by Himself,* 2 vols. (London: Henry Colburn, New Burlington Street, 1826), 2:315.

3. Tate Wilkinson, *The Wandering Patentee; or, a History of the Yorkshire Theatres, from 1770 to the Present Time: Interspersed with Anecdotes Respecting Most of the Performers in the Three Kingdoms, from 1765 to 1795,* 4 vols. (York: printed for the author, by Wilson, Spence, and Mawman, 1795), 3:34.

4. John Bernard, *Retrospections of the Stage,* 2 vols. (London: Henry Colburn and Richard Bentley, 1830), 1:208.

5. O'Keeffe, *Recollections,* 2:305.

6. An Act to Amend the Laws Relating to Dramatic Literary Property was passed on June 10, 1833, and stipulated that "the author of any . . . Dramatic Piece or Entertainment . . . shall have as his own Property the sole Liberty of representing, or causing to be represented, . . . any such Production as aforesaid." An Act to Amend the Laws Relating to Dramatic Literary Property, 1833, 3 & 4 Will. IV, c.15 in *Primary Sources on Copyright (1450–1900),* ed. Lionel Bently and Martin Kretschmer, www.copyrighthistory.org

7. As Marina Abramović's show *The Artist Is Present* suggests, performance art commodifies liveness and the physical presence of the "original" performer. These qualities call into question whether performance art can be recreated and whether reenactments (especially those by someone other than the original performer) count as the work. For more on presence and reperformance, see Amelia Jones, "'The Artist Is Present': Artistic Re-enactments and the Impossibility of Presence," *TDR: The Drama Review* 55, no. 1 (Spring 2011): 16–45.

8. Rebecca Schneider, *Performing Remains: Art and War in Times of Theatrical Reenactment* (New York: Routledge, 2011), 97; Diana Taylor, *The Archive and the Repertoire: Performing Cultural Memory in the Americas* (Durham, NC: Duke University Press, 2003); Emily Hodgson Anderson, *Shakespeare and the Legacy of Loss* (Ann Arbor: University of Michigan Press, 2018).

9. Paulina Kewes argues that by the middle of the eighteenth century, "playwriting no longer possessed the cultural centrality it had attained in the first decade or so of the eighteenth century; its literary pretensions had been virtually abandoned." Kewes, "'[A] Play Which I Presume to Call *Original*': Appropriation, Creative Genius, and Eighteenth-Century Playwriting," *Studies in the Literary Imagination* 34, no. 1 (Spring 2001): 17–47, at 19. As Derek Miller argues, "Copyright history is essential to understanding how we value the arts because copyright mediates between economic

and other discourses of value." Miller, *Copyright and the Value of Performance, 1770–1911* (New York: Cambridge University Press, 2018), 10.

10. Margaret Ezell, *Social Authorship and the Advent of Print* (Baltimore: Johns Hopkins University Press, 1999), 1.

11. In addition to Ezell, see Dustin Griffin, "The Social World of Authorship 1660–1714," in *The Cambridge History of English Literature, 1660–1780*, ed. John Richetti (New York: Cambridge University Press, 2005), 37–60, and Rachael Scarborough King, *Writing to the World: Letters and the Origins of Modern Print Genres* (Baltimore: Johns Hopkins University Press, 2018).

12. Derrida emphasizes in *Archive Fever* that the archive is an expression of state power, and Diana Taylor builds on this idea, arguing that the archive's "western logocentrism" has meant that print has been the medium of the state. Jacques Derrida, "Archive Fever: A Freudian Impression," trans. Eric Prenowitz, *Diacritics* 25, no. 2 (Summer 1995): 9–63; Taylor, *Archive and the Repertoire*, 6.

13. The 1737 Stage Licensing Act limited the performance of legitimate drama to the two royally sanctioned theaters at Drury Lane and Covent Garden. It also required the theaters to submit manuscripts for the performance of new plays to the dramatic censor. By "the regulation of actors' bodies," I am referring to the part of the Stage Licensing Act that deemed all actors working outside the patent theaters "vagrants." This part of the act reinforced and tightened up vagrancy statutes that dated back to Queen Elizabeth's 1598 Acte for the Punishment of Rogues, Vagabonds, and Sturdy Beggars.

14. These two legal systems are central to the development of modern authorship. As Michel Foucault argues, the author function came into being first as authors became subject to punishment for their texts, and following that, as authors were able to participate in systems of ownership. These "juridical and institutional system[s]" are invested in determining the author-text relationship. Foucault, "What Is an Author?," in *Aesthetics, Method, and Epistemology: The Essential Works of Foucault, 1954–1984*, vol. 2, ed. James B. Faubion and trans. Robert Hurley and others (New York: New Press, 1998), 205-22, at 216.

15. See Mark Rose, "The Author as Proprietor: Donaldson v. Becket and the Genealogy of Modern Authorship," *Representations* 23 (Summer 1988): 51–85.

16. An Act for the Encouragement of Learning, by Vesting the Copies of Printed Books in the Authors or Purchasers of such Copies, During the Times therein mentioned, 1710, 8 Anne, c.19, in Bently and Kretschmer, *Primary Sources on Copyright*.

17. Meredith McGill, "Copyright and Intellectual Property: The State of the Discipline," *Book History* 16 (2013): 387–427, at 388.

18. Rose, "The Author as Proprietor."

19. This relationship is the subject of many important studies, from Mark Rose's *Authors and Owners: The Invention of Copyright* (Cambridge, MA: Harvard University Press, 1993) to Brean Hammond's *Professional Imaginative Writing in England, 1670–1740* (Oxford: Clarendon Press, 1997) and Jody Greene's *The Trouble with Ownership: Literary Property and Authorial Liability in England, 1660–1730* (Philadelphia: University of Pennsylvania Press, 2005).

20. Quoted in Jesse Foot, *The Life of Arthur Murphy, Esq.* (London: Printed for J. Faulder by John Nichols and Son, 1811), 344. Foot was in possession of seventy-three pages of Murphy's notes for the case.

21. For more on how the image of the author and ideas about authorial original-ity were used against authors' best interests, see Simon Stern, "Copyright, Originality, and the Public Domain in Eighteenth-Century England," in *Originality and Intellectual Property in the French and English Enlightenment*, ed. Reginald McGinnis (New York: Routledge, 2009), 69–101.

22. Edward Young, *Conjectures on Original Composition. In a Letter to the Author of Sir Charles Grandison* (London: Printed for A. Millar, in The Strand; and R. and J. Dodsley, in Pall-Mall, 1759), 54.

23. Rose, *Authors and Owners*, 7.

24. For more on Hogarth's Engravers' Act, see Ronan Deazley, "Commentary on the Engravers' Act (1735)," in Bently and Kretschmer, *Primary Sources on Copyright*. In addition to copyright for the visual arts, the century also saw cases that dealt with how to copyright music. See Nancy Mace, "Music Copyright in Late Eighteenth and Early Nineteenth Century Britain," in *Research Handbook on the History of Copyright Law*, ed. Isabella Alexander and H. Tomás Gómez-Arostegui (Northampton, MA: Edward Elgar, 2016).

25. In a 2015 essay Mark Sableman asks, "In a world of ubiquitous videos, will performance rights become the next intellectual property frontier?" Sableman points out that questions of performance rights are still unsettled and become more so as new technologies enable performance to circulate in new ways. See Sableman, "Copyright and Performance Rights in an Online Video World," *Licensing Journal* 35, no. 1 (January 2015): 22–25.

26. See, for instance, Ronan Deazley, *Rethinking Copyright: History, Theory, Language* (Northampton, MA: Edward Elgar, 2006); and Rose, *Authors and Owners*.

27. No single term is consistently used across modern scholarship to describe the author's right to control and profit from repeat performance. Nor did eighteenth-century playwrights have a clear way of discussing this concept, which did not yet exist in law. Julie Stone Peters refers to it as "performance copyright." Peters, *Theatre of the Book, 1480–1880: Print, Text, and Performance in Europe* (New York: Oxford University Press, 2000), 77–78. Derek Miller, meanwhile, uses "performance rights" to signify the same concept, noting that prior to 1833, it was not a term of law: "The British 'performance right' prior to 1833 (in practice, really 1842) emanates an aura of proprietary ownership, not property available for exchange." Miller, *Copyright*, 30. Where I use either of these terms, I do so to refer to the concept rather than an actual legal construction. A third term—"play right"—is also used by some, including Jessica Litman and Oliver Gerland, to refer to this concept.

28. Isabella Alexander, "'Neither Bolt nor Chain, Iron Safe nor Private Watchman, Can Prevent the Theft of Words': The Birth of the Performing Right in Britain," in *Privilege and Property: Essays on the History of Copyright*, ed. Ronan Deazley, Martin Kretschmer, and Lionel Bently (Cambridge: Open Book Publishers, 2010), 321–46.

29. Deazley, *Rethinking Copyright*, 153.

30. Jessica Litman, "The Invention of Common Law Play Right," *Berkeley Technology Law Journal* 25, no. 3 (2010): 1382–452.

31. Miller, *Copyright*.

32. McGill, "Copyright and Intellectual Property," 389.

33. Ezell, *Social Authorship*, 1.

34. As Robert D. Hume writes, "Managers saw no reason to take risks" by staging new drama. Hume, "Theatre as Property in Eighteenth-Century London," *Journal for Eighteenth-Century Studies* 31, no. 1 (2008): 17–46, at 19. Kewes echoes this point, writing that a perennial favorite presented less financial risk for the theaters than a new play. Kewes, "[A] Play," 23. During the Garrick years, Drury Lane produced on average only two new full-length plays per season. See Richard W. Schoch, "'A Supplement to Public Laws': Arthur Murphy, David Garrick, and Hamlet, with Alterations," *Theatre Journal* 57, no. 1 (March 2005): 21–32, at 24.

35. On these nights, the author earned all of the profits beyond operating costs. For more on remuneration systems, as well as detailed information about the profits for particular plays, see Judith Milhous and Robert D. Hume, "Playwrights' Remuneration in Eighteenth-Century London," *Harvard Library Bulletin* 10, nos. 2–3 (1999): 3–90, or their more recent collaboration, *The Publication of Plays in London, 1660–1800: Playwrights, Publishers, and the Market* (London: British Library, 2015). The payment system changed in 1794, after which authors were paid £33 6s. 8d. per night for the first nine nights, for a possible £300. The author could earn an additional £100 if the show ran for twenty nights.

36. To illustrate the contrast, in the same season (1771–72) that Elizabeth Griffith earned nothing for her *Wife in the Right* at Covent Garden, Arthur Murphy earned £563 for his *Grecian Daughter* at Drury Lane. Milhous and Hume, "Playwrights' Remuneration," 63.

37. Paulina Kewes, *Authorship and Appropriation: Writing for the Stage in England, 1660–1710* (Oxford: Clarendon Press, 1998).

38. Milhous and Hume, *Publication of Plays*, 116.

39. By midcentury, some authors were printing plays before the first run had finished. Shirley Strum Kenny, "The Publication of Plays," in *The London Theatre World, 1660–1800*, ed. Robert D. Hume (Carbondale: Southern Illinois University Press, 1980), 309-36.

40. Tate Wilkinson, *Memoirs of his Own Life, by Tate Wilkinson, Patentee of the Theatres-Royal, York & Hull*, 4 vols. (York: Printed for the Author, by Wilson, Spence, and Mawman, 1790), 2:230.

41. Charles Beecher Hogan, "One of God Almighty's Unaccountables: Tate Wilkinson of York," in *The Theatrical Manager in Britain and America: Players of a Perilous Game*, ed. Joseph W. Donohue Jr. (Princeton, NJ: Princeton University Press, 1971), 63-86, at 63.

42. Jane Moody, "Playbills under House Arrest: A Reply to Richard Schoch, Victorian Theatricalities Forum," *19: Interdisciplinary Studies in the Long Nineteenth Century* 8 (2009): 1–4, and Michael Ragussis, *Theatrical Nation: Jews and Other Outlandish Englishmen in Georgian Britain* (Philadelphia: University of Pennsylvania Press, 2010), 31.

43. Hume, "Theatre as Property," 38.

44. John Russell Stephens, *The Profession of the Playwright: British Theatre, 1800–1900* (New York: Cambridge University Press, 1992).

45. Julia Fawcett, *Spectacular Disappearances: Celebrity and Privacy, 1696–1801* (Ann Arbor: University of Michigan Press, 2016); Joseph Roach, *Cities of the Dead: Circum-Atlantic Performance* (New York: Columbia University Press, 1996); Emily

Hodgson Anderson, *Eighteenth-Century Authorship and the Play of Fiction: Novels and the Theatre, Haywood to Austen* (New York: Routledge, 2009) and *Shakespeare*; Nora Nachumi, *Acting Like a Lady: British Women Novelists and the Eighteenth-Century Theatre* (New York: AMS Press, 2008); and Ellen Donkin, *Getting into the Act: Women Playwrights in London, 1776–1829* (New York: Routledge, 1995).

46. Stella Tillyard, "Celebrity in 18th-Century London," *History Today* 55 (June 2005): 20–27, at 25. For more on actresses' self-fashioning, see Laura Engel, *Fashioning Celebrity: Eighteenth-Century British Actresses and Strategies for Image-Making* (Columbus: Ohio State University Press, 2011) and Felicity Nussbaum, *Rival Queens: Actresses, Performance, and the Eighteenth-Century British Theater* (Philadelphia: University of Pennsylvania Press, 2010).

47. Allardyce Nicoll writes, "It has been said again and again . . . that the eighteenth century was an age, not of the author, but of the actor." Nicoll, *A History of Early Eighteenth Century Drama, 1700–1750* (Cambridge: Cambridge University Press, 1925), 39.

48. Christopher Balme, "Playbills and the Theatrical Public Sphere," in *Representing the Past: Essays in Performance Historiography*, ed. Charlotte Canning and Thomas Postlewait (Iowa City: University of Iowa Press, 2010), 37-62; Jacky Bratton, *New Readings in Theatre History* (New York: Cambridge University Press, 2003); and Mark Vareschi and Mattie Burkert, "Archives, Numbers, Meaning: The Eighteenth-Century Playbill at Scale," *Theatre Journal* 68, no. 4 (December 2016): 597–613.

49. Balme advocates for "interrogating" the playbill in more methodologically complex ways. He argues that the "playbill constituted a central point of articulation between theatres and their public spheres" ("Playbills," 39).

50. The two most famous actor-playwrights of the century, Colley Cibber and David Garrick, are largely absent from this book. As managers of Drury Lane Theatre and hugely popular actors, Cibber and Garrick did not worry about finding venues in which to perform their works or whether their works would continue to generate profit. Moreover, both were working early enough in the century that they did not have to deal, as managers, with authors trying to control the use of their works. Thus, although both of these figures were giants in the theater world, neither was an active participant in the narrative my book charts.

51. Diana Taylor, "Performance and Intangible Cultural Heritage," in *The Cambridge Companion to Performance Studies*, ed. Tracy C. Davis (New York: Cambridge University Press, 2008), 91-106, at 92.

52. Two of the most frequently quoted articulations of this loss come from the century's most famous actor-playwrights, Colley Cibber and David Garrick. Cibber lamented, "Pity it is, that the momentary Beauties flowing from an harmonious Elocution, cannot like those of Poetry, be their own Record! . . . Could *how Betterton* spoke be as easily known as *what* he spoke." Colley Cibber, *An Apology for the Life of Colley Cibber: With an Historical View of the Stage during His Own Time*, ed. B. R. S. Fone (Mineola, NY: Dover Publications, 2000), 60. Garrick declared, in the preface to *The Clandestine Marriage* (1766), "But he, who struts his Hour upon the Stage, / Can scarce extend his Fame for Half an Age; / Nor Pen nor Pencil can the Actor save, / The Art, and Artist, share one common Grave."

53. Schneider, *Performing Remains*, 97.

54. Hume, "Theatre as Property," 17.

CHAPTER 1

1. Georg C. Lichtenberg qtd. in Philip H. Highfill Jr., Kalman A. Burnim, and Edward A. Langhans, *A Biographical Dictionary of Actors, Actresses, Musicians, Dancers, Managers, and Other Stage Personnel in London, 1660-1800*, 16 vols. (Carbondale: Southern Illinois University Press, 1973-93), 10:9.

2. For more on Macklin's forced retirement from the stage from 1753 to 1759, see Matthew J. Kinservik, "*Love à la Mode* and Macklin's Return to the London Stage in 1759," *Theatre Survey* 37, no. 2 (1996): 1-22.

3. As Judith Milhous and Robert D. Hume note, he was more successful in achieving this than any other playwright of the eighteenth century. "Playwrights' Remuneration," 34-35.

4. Shirley Strum Kenny writes that at the beginning of the eighteenth century, plays were typically published within a month of their premiere. This generally allowed the play to complete its full run before entering print circulation. By mid-century, some authors were printing plays before the first run had finished. Kenny, "The Publication of Plays," 309-36.

5. See William W. Appleton, *Charles Macklin: An Actor's Life* (Cambridge, MA: Harvard University Press, 1960), chap. 5, for a discussion of Macklin's role in the 1743 actor rebellion. Although Macklin acted in solidarity with his fellow actors, the walkout harmed him more than the rest of the company. Fleetwood had seen Macklin as an ally, and as Appleton puts it, "For Macklin to join the rebels seemed to Fleetwood the rankest ingratitude" (62).

6. The Statute of Anne allowed authors, for the first time, to own their works. Before this, only a member of the Stationers' Company could do so.

7. Quoted in Peter Holland, *The Ornament of Action: Text and Performance in Restoration Comedy* (New York: Cambridge University Press, 1979), 65.

8. David A. Brewer, *The Afterlife of Character, 1726-1825* (Philadelphia: University of Pennsylvania Press, 2005), 67.

9. The divided repertory was initially upheld in London but not necessarily respected by strolling companies or Dublin theaters. A role, then, might only have been performed by one performer in London but simultaneously by others outside the metropolis.

10. Holland, *The Ornament of Action*, 66.

11. Judith Milhous and Robert D. Hume, "Theatrical Custom versus Rights: The Performers' Dispute with the Proprietors of Covent Garden in 1800," *Theatre Notebook* 63, no. 2 (2009): 92-125, at 120.

12. Hume, "Theatre as Property," 39-40.

13. For more on this competition, see Leslie Ritchie, "Pox on Both Your Houses: The Battle of the Romeos," *Eighteenth-Century Fiction* 27, nos. 3-4 (Spring–Summer 2015): 373-93, and Chelsea Phillips, "Bodies in Play: Maternity, Repertory, and the Rival *Romeo and Juliet*s, 1748-51," *Theatre Survey* 60, no. 2 (May 2019): 207-36.

14. Kitty Clive, "To the Author of the London Daily Post," *London Daily Post and General Advertiser*, November 19, 1736.

15. "Spectator," "To the Author of the *Daily Gazetteer*," *Daily Gazetteer*, November 4, 1736.

16. Cibber, *Apology*, 106.

17. Thomas Davies, *Memoirs of the Life of David Garrick, Esq. Interspersed with Characters and Anecdotes of His Theatrical Contemporaries*, 2 vols. (London: Printed for the Author and sold at his Shop in Great Russell-street, Covent-Garden, 1780), 1:54.

18. *Universal Museum and Complete Magazine*, August 1765, 392–93, quoted in David Thomas, *Restoration and Georgian England, 1660–1788* (New York: Cambridge University Press, 1989), 350.

19. Berta Joncus, "'In Wit Superior, as in Fighting': Kitty Clive and the Conquest of a Rival Queen," *Huntington Library Quarterly* 74, no. 1 (2011): 23–42, at 28.

20. Manuscript letter from Charles Mathews to George Colman, London, July 10, 1807. Harvard Theatre Collection, MS Thr 357 (100).

21. John Johnstone et al., *A Statement of the Differences Subsisting between the Proprietors and Performers of the Theatre-Royal, Covent-Garden* (London: Printed by J. Davis, Chancery-Lane, for W. Miller, Old Bond-Street, 1800), 62. Coauthors were Joseph George Holman, Alexander Pope, Charles Incledon, Joseph S. Munden, John Fawcett, Thomas Knight, and Henry Erskine Johnston.

22. Quoted in Milhous and Hume, "Theatrical Custom," 114.

23. Harris and the other proprietors' response is recorded in an annotated copy of the actors' complaints submitted to the Lord Chamberlain. A copy, owned by John Genest, is preserved in the Harvard Theatre Collection, TS 313.1.41 (A). Manuscript notes across from page 62.

24. Quoted in Milhous and Hume, "Theatrical Custom," 117.

25. Appleton's narrative emphasizes parts, pointing out that not only had Sheridan angered Macklin by playing Shylock, a part that Macklin saw as his own, but he also hired Theophilus Cibber, whose repertory of parts, which was very similar to Macklin's, was "a perpetual reminder of the fact that his services were not essential to the company." Appleton, *Charles Macklin*, 90.

26. Kinservik, "*Love à la Mode*," 2.

27. Autograph letter from Charles Macklin to George Colman, October 16, 1770, Y.c.5380 (3), Folger Shakespeare Library, Washington, DC.

28. Appleton, *Charles Macklin*, 141.

29. Autograph letter signed from Charles Macklin, Dublin, to George Colman, Piazza Covent Garden, London, February 17, 1773, Y.c.5380 (5), Folger Shakespeare Library, Washington, DC.

30. Smith's venture failed, and he returned to Covent Garden for the 1773–74 season.

31. Charles Macklin to George Colman, February 17, 1773.

32. Charles Macklin to George Colman, February 17, 1773.

33. For a description of Macklin's Macbeth, see Matthew J. Kinservik, "A Sinister *Macbeth*: The Macklin Production of 1773," *Harvard Library Bulletin* 6, no. 1 (1995): 51–76.

34. It is interesting to note that at the time of his death, Macklin owned four copies of Locke's works and letters. The contents of his library are recorded in an extra-illustrated copy of Kirkman's *Memoirs of the Life of Charles Macklin*, preserved in the Harvard Theatre Collection. James Thomas Kirkman, *Memoirs of the Life of Charles Macklin, Esq. Principally Compiled from His Own Papers and Memorandums*, 2 vols. (London: Printed for Lackington, Allen, and Co., 1799). Theatre Collection f TS 943.2, Houghton Library, Harvard University.

35. Although little contemporary commentary on these performances exists, most eighteenth-century critics assumed that Doggett played Shylock as a comic villain. This assumption is based on Doggett's typical comedic roles and on brief commentary by Nicholas Rowe and John Downes. Rowe wrote that he had seen the play "Acted as a Comedy, and the Part of the *Jew* perform'd by an Excellent Comedian." See Nicholas Rowe, *The Works of Mr. William Shakespear*, 6 vols. (London: Printed for Jacob Tonson, 1709), 1:xix.

36. John Henderson, *Letters and Poems, by the Late Mr. John Henderson. With Anecdotes of His Life, by John Ireland* (London: Printed for J. Johnson, 1786), 196.

37. Touchstone [pseud.], "To the Printer of the *Morning Chronicle*," *Morning Chronicle and London Advertiser*, October 23, 1773. Appleton attributes the review to Arthur Murphy.

38. *The Present State of the Stage in Great-Britain and Ireland* (London: Printed for Paul Vaillant, 1753), 40.

39. George Colman and Bonnell Thornton, *The Connoisseur*, no. 1, January 31, 1754, 1.

40. William Cooke, *Memoirs of Charles Macklin, Comedian, with the Dramatic Characters, Manners, Anecdotes, &c. of the Age in which He Lived* (London: Printed for James Asperne, 1804), 92.

41. "Theatrical Intelligence," *London Chronicle and Universal Evening Post*, October 23, 1773, and Davies, *Memoirs*, 1:62.

42. "Old Macklin," *Courier and Evening Gazette*, August 4, 1797.

43. Appleton, *Charles Macklin*, 46.

44. Charles Macklin, Commonplace Book [manuscript], 1778-1790, M.a.9, Folger Shakespeare Library, 7.

45. William Rufus Chetwood, *A General History of the Stage, from Its Origin in Greece Down to the Present Time* (London: Printed for W. Owen, 1749), 188–89.

46. John Locke, *Two Treatises of Government by John Locke*, ed. Thomas I. Cook (New York: Hafner, 1947), 135–36.

47. Chetwood, *General History*, 189.

48. William Shakespeare, *The Merchant of Venice*, ed. Jay Halio (New York: Oxford University Press, 2008), 3.2.114–16.

49. Chetwood, *General History*, 190.

50. James Henry Leigh, *The New Rosciad, in the Manner of Churchill: Containing a Judicious, Humorous and Critical Description of our Present Dramatic Characters* (London: Printed for E. Macklew, 1785), 10.

51. Cooke, *Memoirs of Charles Macklin*, 1:134. Character-based judgments of actors were not unusual in the eighteenth century. Actresses, for example, were often judged by the virtue of the women they performed.

52. Quoted in Appleton, *Charles Macklin*, 50.

53. Emily Hodgson Anderson, "Celebrity Shylock," *PMLA* 126, no. 4 (2011): 935–49, at 942.

54. Marvin Carlson, *The Haunted Stage: The Theatre as Memory Machine* (Ann Arbor: University of Michigan Press, 2001).

55. John Gross, *Shylock: A Legend & Its Legacy* (New York: Simon & Schuster, 1992), 119.

56. William Cooke, *Memoirs of Samuel Foote, Esq. with a Collection of Genuine*

Bon-Mots, Anecdotes, Opinions, &c., Mostly Original, 3 vols. (London: Printed for Richard Phillips, 1805), 1:156.

57. Appleton, *Charles Macklin,* 171.

58. Manuscript facsimile reproduced in Kinservik, "A Sinister *Macbeth,*" 53.

59. Kinservik, "A Sinister *Macbeth,*" 56.

60. Appleton, *Charles Macklin,* 170.

61. For more detail on the Macbeth riots, see Appleton, *Charles Macklin,* chap. 10, "Riot and Conspiracy," and Kristina Straub, "The Newspaper 'Trial' of Charles Macklin's Macbeth and the Theatre as Juridical Public Sphere," *Eighteenth-Century Fiction* 27, nos. 3–4 (Spring–Summer 2015): 395–418.

62. Kinservik, "A Sinister *Macbeth,*" 51.

63. "Theatrical Intelligence," *Morning Chronicle,* October 25, 1773.

64. "Criticus," "Morning Post. Monday, Nov. 1, 1773," *Middlesex Journal or Universal Evening Post,* November 2, 1772.

65. In the original prologue to *The Relapse,* for example, John Vanbrugh uses such a metaphor to describe his haste in writing: "'Twas got, conceived, and born in six weeks' space" (3). In *The Dunciad,* Alexander Pope satirizes Cibber's dramatic failures as "embryos" and "abortions" (I.121).

66. Touchstone, "To the Printer."

67. Arthur Murphy, "Advertisement," in Charles Macklin, *Love à la Mode. A Farce. As Performed at the Theatres-Royal, Drury-Lane and Covent-Garden* (London: Printed by John Bell, 1793).

68. Charles Durnford and Edward Hyde East, *Reports of Cases Argued and Determined in the Court of King's Bench,* 8 vols. (Dublin: Printed for L. White, P. Byrne, and W. Jones, 1793–1800), 5:245.

69. Roger L'Estrange, *Considerations and Proposals in Order to the Regulation of the Press* (London: Printed by A. C., 1663), 1.

70. Barbara A. Mowat, "The Theatre and Literary Culture," in *A New History of Early English Drama,* ed. John D. Cox and David Scott Kastan (New York: Columbia University Press, 1997), 213-30, at 217.

71. See Jane Milling, "'Abominable, Impious, Prophane, Lewd, Immoral': Prosecuting the Actors in Early Eighteenth-Century London," *Theatre Notebook* 61, no. 3 (2007): 132–43.

72. Philip Dormer Stanhope, Fourth Earl of Chesterfield, *Miscellaneous Works of the Late Philip Dormer Stanhope, Earl of Chesterfield: Consisting of Letters to his Friends, never before printed, and Various other Articles,* 3 vols. (Dublin: printed for Messrs. W. Watson, Whitestone, Sleater, Chamberlaine, Potts . . . , 1777), 2:231.

73. Gerald Eades Bentley, *The Profession of Dramatist in Shakespeare's Time, 1590–1642* (Princeton, NJ: Princeton University Press, 1971), 198. See also Stephen Orgel, "What Is a Text?," in *Staging the Renaissance: Reinterpretations of Elizabethan and Jacobean Drama,* ed. David Scott Kastan and Peter Stallybrass (New York: Routledge, 1991), 83-87.

74. W. B. Worthen, "Intoxicating Rhythms: Or, Shakespeare, Literary Drama, and Performance (Studies)," *Shakespeare Quarterly* 62, no. 3 (2011): 309–39.

75. Rose, *Authors and Owners,* 114.

76. Milhous and Hume, "Playwrights' Remuneration," 35.

77. The conditions of theatrical ownership often affect print publication trends.

Before 1642, when the Crown did not mandate a separation of repertory, theater companies sometimes kept plays out of print to ensure their exclusive performance. See Joseph Loewenstein, "The Script in the Marketplace," *Representations* 12 (Fall 1985): 101–14.

78. Peters, *Theatre of the Book*, 77.

79. Charles Macklin and D. Hussey, "Fair Copy Draft Bill introduced in the Court of Chancery in Ireland in *Macklin* v. *Robert Owenson*," Autograph Papers of Charles Macklin [manuscript], Y.d.515, Folger Shakespeare Library.

80. He may also have written clauses into contracts that would fine managers for future use of the play. When Henry Mossop hired Macklin for the 1763–64 season at Smock Alley, the contract stipulated that "the sole property of his Pieces were to remain in him, that they were not to be acted without his consent; and that his Farces were not to be played at Benefits, under the penalty of 500£." See Kirkman, *Memoirs*, 1:441.

81. O'Keeffe, *Recollections*, 1:315–16.

82. Macklin and Hussey, "Fair Copy."

83. Milhous and Hume, "Playwrights' Remuneration," 34.

84. Milhous and Hume, "Playwrights' Remuneration," 34. Macklin's contract with Drury Lane reads, "to have for his performing in the said plays [*The Merchant of Venice* and *The Refusal*] and Farce [*Love à la Mode*] a Fifth part of the profits of the first five nights after deducting sixty-three pounds for the charges of each night during the said five nights—and the sixth night to be for the Benefit of Mr. Macklin, he paying the usual charges of sixty-three pounds." Quoted in Kinservik, "*Love à la Mode*," 9.

85. Milhous and Hume, "Playwrights' Remuneration," 29, 39.

86. Cooke, *Memoirs of Charles Macklin*, 234.

87. Shirley Strum Kenny, *The Performers and Their Plays* (New York: Garland Publishing, 1982), xxxi.

88. It is interesting to note that the same year Wilkinson refused to help Garrick hurt Macklin's property, he did exactly that to Samuel Foote. In November 1760, while Foote was performing in his own play, *The Minor*, at Drury Lane, Wilkinson began performing Foote's parts in that play at Covent Garden, in direct opposition to Foote's performances. For more on this rivalry, see chapter 2.

89. Wilkinson, *Memoirs*, 2:261.

90. Wilkinson, *Memoirs*, 2:264.

91. For more on this and other print piracies, see W. Matthews, "The Piracies of Macklin's *Love à-la-Mode*," *Review of English Studies* 10, no. 39 (July 1934): 311–18, and Miller, *Copyright*.

92. Charles Ambler, *Reports of Cases Argued and Determined in the High Court of Chancery, with Some Few in Other Courts*, 2nd ed., ed. John Elijah Blunt, 2 vols. (London: Joseph Butterworth and Son, 1828), 2:695.

93. Ambler, *Reports of Cases*, 2:694.

94. Charles Macklin to Tate Wilkinson, April 22, 1769, Correspondence of Alexander Dyce and others preserved in the Dyce Collection, MSL/1869/64/103–104, National Art Library, Victoria and Albert Museum, London.

95. Wilkinson, *Memoirs*, 4:9.

96. Macklin and Hussey, "Fair Copy."

97. Quoted in Kirkman, *Memoirs*, 2:35.

98. Kirkman, *Memoirs*, 2:33.

99. Wilkinson, *Memoirs*, 4:10.

100. Charles Dibdin, *A Complete History of the English Stage*, 5 vols. (London: Printed for the Author, 1797–1800), 5:149.

101. Even with today's more robust copyright system, social norms still prove more effective in certain contexts, as Dotan Oliar and Christopher Sprigman argue about joke-stealing in stand-up comedy. Their description sounds right out of the eighteenth century: norms "are enforced with sanctions that start with simple bad-mouthing and may escalate from refusals to work with an offending comedian up to threats of, and even actual, physical violence"—something Macklin certainly threatened. Oliar and Sprigman, "There's No Free Laugh (Anymore): The Emergence of Intellectual Property Norms and the Transformation of Stand-Up Comedy," *Virginia Law Review* 94, no. 8 (December 2008): 1787–867, at 1791.

102. Letter from Charles Macklin to James Whitley, preserved in Kirkman's *Memoirs*.

103. See Balme, "Playbills." Indeed, it was sometimes through the circulation of playbills that Macklin discovered and retained evidence of unauthorized performances.

104. Appleton, *Charles Macklin*, 122.

CHAPTER 2

1. *General Advertiser*, April 24, 1747.

2. *General Advertiser*, May 2, 1747.

3. *General Advertiser*, May 15, 1747.

4. *General Advertiser*, June 1, 1747.

5. Arthur H. Scouten, *The London Stage, 1660–1800*, Part 3: *1729–1747*, 2 vols. (Carbondale: Southern Illinois University Press, 1961).

6. See, for instance, Matthew J. Kinservik, *Disciplining Satire: The Censorship of Satiric Comedy on the Eighteenth-Century London Stage* (Lewisburg, PA: Bucknell University Press, 2002) and Jane Moody, *Illegitimate Theatre in London, 1770–1840* (New York: Cambridge University Press, 2000).

7. Moody, *Illegitimate Theatre in London*, 18.

8. "Literary Property," *Morning Chronicle*, February 8, 1774.

9. Peggy Phelan, *Unmarked: The Politics of Performance* (New York: Routledge, 1993).

10. Taylor, *Archive and the Repertoire*, 20–21. See also Schneider, *Performing Remains*.

11. Macklin ran performances from February 6 to July 3, 1744. Appleton, *Charles Macklin*, 68–69.

12. For more on the act, see Kinservik, *Disciplining Satire*; Vincent J. Leisenfeld, *The Licensing Act of 1737* (Madison: University of Wisconsin Press, 1984); and L. W. Connolly, *The Censorship of English Drama, 1737–1824* (San Marino, CA: Huntington Library, 1976).

13. Thomas Lockwood, "Great Off-Stage Performances by James Lacy," *British Journal for Eighteenth-Century Studies* 7 no. 2 (September 1984): 199–210. As Jane

Moody writes, "legitimacy" is a concept encompassing comedy, tragedy, and other spoken drama. The idea is outlined in the Licensing Act; however, the term was not used regularly until the 1790s. Moody, *Illegitimate Theatre in London*, 51.

14. Moody, *Illegitimate Theatre in London*, 18.

15. Cooke, *Memoirs of Samuel Foote*, 3:114.

16. Kinservik, *Disciplining Satire*, 155.

17. *Report from the Select Committee on Dramatic Literature: with the Minutes of Evidence* (London: Ordered by the House of Commons, to be Printed, 1832), 158.

18. For more on pantomime and its perceived threat to legitimate theatrical culture, see John O'Brien, *Harlequin Britain: Pantomime and Entertainment, 1690–1760* (Baltimore: Johns Hopkins University Press, 2004). Daniel O'Quinn also discusses nontraditional dramatic forms in *Entertaining Crisis in the Atlantic Imperium, 1770–1790* (Baltimore: Johns Hopkins University Press, 2011).

19. Moody, *Illegitimate Theatre in London*, 12.

20. Mary Megie Belden, *The Dramatic Work of Samuel Foote* (Hamden, CT: Archon Books, 1969), 8–9.

21. Cooke, *Memoirs of Samuel Foote*, 1:50–52.

22. Simon Trefman, *Sam. Foote, Comedian, 1720–1777* (New York: New York University Press, 1971), 29.

23. George Winchester Stone Jr., ed., *The London Stage, 1660–1800* (Carbondale: Southern Illinois University Press, 1962), 4:728.

24. Stone, *The London Stage*, 4:691.

25. The Multigraph Collective, *Interacting with Print: Elements of Reading in the Era of Print Saturation* (Chicago: University of Chicago Press, 2018), 275.

26. Heather Davis-Fisch, *Loss and Cultural Remains in Performance: The Ghosts of the Franklin Expedition* (New York: Palgrave Macmillan, 2012), 16.

27. Wilkinson, *Wandering Patentee*, 4:243.

28. Wilkinson, *Wandering Patentee*, 4:249.

29. Walpole's copies of Foote's play texts are preserved in the Lewis Walpole Library. A few examples of Walpole's marginalia include a note on *The Commissary*, calling the character of Zachary Fungus a "burlesque of Glover, author of Leonides" (LWL 49 1810 v.7) and a note on *The Mayor of Garret* identifying Matthew Mug as being "meant for the Duke of Newcastle" (LWL 49 1810 v.5).

30. Kinservik, *Disciplining Satire*, 146–47.

31. Benjamin Victor, *The History of the Theatres of London, from the Year 1760 to the Present Time* (London: printed for T. Becket, in the Strand, 1771), 190.

32. George Carey, *Momus, a Poem; or a Critical Examination into the Merits of the Performers, and Comic Pieces, at the Theatre Royal in the Hay-Market* (London: printed for the Author, and sold by J. Almon, 1767), 18.

33. Kinservik, *Disciplining Satire*, 185.

34. Up to this point, Foote did not submit any of the plays that he premiered at the Haymarket.

35. Belden, *Dramatic Work*, 74.

36. Quoted in Belden, *Dramatic Work*, 78.

37. Kinservik, *Disciplining Satire*, 146.

38. Kinservik, *Disciplining Satire*, 147.

39. Samuel Foote, *The Orators* (London: printed for J. Coote, G. Kearsley, and T. Davies, 1762), 28.

40. Highfill, Burnim, and Langhans, *Biographical Dictionary*, 13:349–50.

41. The Cock Lane Ghost incident was a purported haunting in a house in Cock Lane that attracted mass interest. Samuel Johnson, whom Foote had originally intended to take off in the play, was part of the commission investigating the case.

42. Foote, *The Orators*, 37.

43. Foote, *The Orators*, 51.

44. Foote, *The Orators*, 47.

45. Foote, *The Orators*, 47.

46. Foote, *The Orators*, 48.

47. Foote, *The Orators*, 48.

48. Samuel Foote, *The Trial of Samuel Foote, Esq. For a Libel on Peter Paragraph. Performed at the Theatre-Royal in the Haymarket, 1763. Written by Mr. Foote. Printed from his own Hand-writing*, in Wilkinson, *Wandering Patentee*, 4:251–60, at 259–60.

49. Foote, *The Trial*, 260.

50. Cooke, *Memoirs of Samuel Foote*, 1:122.

51. For a review of the first performance, see "Sketch of Mr. Foote's Lectures on Oratory, delivering at the Little Theatre in the Haymarket," *London Magazine, or, Gentleman's Monthly Intelligencer* 31 (May 1762): 258–59.

52. Cooke, *Memoirs of Samuel Foote*, 1:121–22.

53. "Anecdote of Mr. Foote, being an Extract of a Letter from Dublin," *London Magazine, or, Gentleman's Monthly Intelligencer* 32 (March 1763): 135–36.

54. Kinservik, *Disciplining Satire*, 152–53. Kinservik notes that it is unclear whether he paid Faulkner. It is also worth noting that because this was in Dublin, it was outside the reach of the Licensing Act.

55. Chesterfield, *Miscellaneous Works*, 1:322.

56. Chesterfield, *Miscellaneous Works*, 1:322.

57. Kinservik, *Disciplining Satire*, 152.

58. See Matthew J. Kinservik, "Dialectics of Print and Performance after 1737," in *The Oxford Handbook of the Georgian Theatre, 1737–1832*, ed. Julia Swindells and David Francis Taylor (New York: Oxford University Press, 2014), 123-39.

59. Chesterfield, *Miscellaneous Works*, 2:231.

60. Greene, *The Trouble with Ownership*, 25. Loewenstein refers to the "authoriality of the press" in explaining the capaciousness of "authorship" in the seventeenth century. Joseph F. Loewenstein, "Legal Proofs and Corrected Readings: Press-Agency and the New Bibliography," in *The Production of English Renaissance Culture*, ed. David Lee Miller, Sharon O'Dair, and Harold Weber (Ithaca, NY: Cornell University Press, 1994), 93-122, at 93.

61. Chesterfield, *Miscellaneous Works*, 2:230. In many cases actors did self-censor or refuse to play parts that were morally objectionable. Kitty Clive, for instance, refused a lead role in Fielding's *The Wedding Day* (1743) because of obscenity and immorality. Kinservik, *Disciplining Satire*, 114.

62. *The Change of Crowns: A Tragi-Comedy by the Honourable Edward Howard*, edited from the manuscript prompt copy by Frederick S. Boas (London: Oxford University Press, 1949).

63. Judith Milhous and Robert D. Hume, *A Register of English Theatrical Documents, 1660–1737*, 2 vols. (Carbondale: Southern Illinois University Press, 1991), 1:100.

64. Milhous and Hume, *Register*, 1:229.

65. Milling, "Abominable, Impious," 133.

66. Foote, *The Trial*, 258.

67. Oliar and Sprigman, "There's No Free Laugh," 1801.

68. This April 10, 1767, letter from O'Brien to Garrick is preserved in the David Garrick Papers from the Thomas Rackett Collection, James Marshall and Marie-Louise Osborn Collection, Beinecke Rare Book and Manuscript Library, Yale University.

69. Henry Fielding, "Proceedings at the Court of Criticism, Thursday, April 28," *Jacobite's Journal*, April 30, 1748, 2.

70. Nora Johnson, *The Actor as Playwright in Early Modern Drama* (New York: Cambridge University Press, 2003), 4.

71. Douglas A. Brooks, *From Playhouse to Printing House: Drama and Authorship in Early Modern England* (New York: Cambridge University Press, 2000), 23.

72. Tiffany Stern, *Rehearsal from Shakespeare to Sheridan* (Oxford: Clarendon Press, 2000), 288.

73. Kewes, "[A] Play," 24.

74. I borrow the phrase "authorial singularity" from Douglas Brooks, *Playhouse to Printing House*, who uses it to describe a space in which a single author claims control over a work. Scholars of early modern drama debate to what extent we can identify and talk about a singular "author" who creates a play text. Stephen Orgel, David Kastan, John Cox, and Jeffrey Masten respond to constructions of "authorial univocality" (Jeffrey Masten, *Textual Intercourse: Collaboration, Authorship, and Sexualities in Renaissance Drama* [New York: Cambridge University Press, 1997], 15) by emphasizing the "radically collaborative" nature of drama, not only as it is produced onstage, but also in its print forms (Cox and Kastan, *New History*, 2). Yet, increasingly, dramatic authors wished to emphasize their singular genius. Ben Jonson's printed edition of his works offers a strong example of this. I suggest that what Jonson was trying to do in print, Foote was trying to do in performance. See Orgel, "What Is a Text?"

75. Kewes's essay does not mention Foote. It is unclear why, when she lists the few eighteenth-century playwrights whose plays were released in a collected edition, she omits Foote, whose plays were twice published in collections during his lifetime.

76. Jane Moody, "Stolen Identities: Character, Mimicry and the Invention of Samuel Foote," in *Theatre and Celebrity in Britain, 1660–2000*, ed. Mary Luckhurst and Jane Moody (New York: Palgrave Macmillan, 2005), 65-89, at 65.

77. Leo Braudy, *The Frenzy of Renown: Fame & Its History* (New York: Vintage Books, 1997), 3–4; Joseph Roach, "Public Intimacy: The Prior History of 'It,'" in Luckhurst and Moody, *Theatre and Celebrity*, 15-30, at 16.

78. Tillyard, "Celebrity in 18th-Century London," 25.

79. Janine Barchas and Kristina Straub, "Curating *Will & Jane*," *Eighteenth-Century Life* 40, no. 2 (April 2016): 1–35.

80. Taylor, *Archive and the Repertoire*, and Roach, *Cities of the Dead*.

81. Ritchie, "Pox."

82. Roach, *Cities of the Dead*, 6. See also Sharon Marcus, *The Drama of Celebrity* (Princeton, NJ: Princeton University Press, 2019). Marcus argues that celebrity is the joint construction of the individual, the public, and the media.

83. Laura Engel emphasizes the constructed, artistic nature of celebrity in *Fashioning Celebrity*. As Engel notes, many actresses, from Kitty Clive to Frances Abington and Sarah Siddons, were particularly adept at developing celebrity personae to further their careers.

84. Braudy, *The Frenzy of Renown*, 397.

85. Moody, "Stolen Identities," 68.

86. Moody, "Stolen Identities," 68.

87. Foote, *The Trial*, 253.

88. Foote, *The Trial*, 253–54.

89. Foote, *The Trial*, 254.

90. John Henley, "Foote a Fool," *General Advertiser*, April 21, 1747.

91. Foote, "To the Orator, and Mr. T.B.," *General Advertiser*, April 22, 1747.

92. Foote, *The Trial*, 254.

93. Foote, *The Trial*, 254.

94. Ritchie uses the phrase "gestural thefts" to describe nonparodic mimicry ("Pox," 376).

95. "Part of a Letter from Paris," *Gazetteer and New Daily Advertiser*, May 11, 1767.

96. "The Inspector No. 249," *London Daily Advertiser*, December 18, 1751.

97. Carey, *Momus*, 10.

98. Moody, "Stolen Identities," 71. Laura Engel makes a similar argument about Mary Wells's imitations of Sarah Siddons, writing that Wells's mimicry "exposes the constructed mechanisms behind Siddons's claims to authenticity." Engel, *Fashioning Celebrity*, 7.

99. "To the Printer, &c.," *Whitehall Evening Post*, April 5–8, 1755.

100. Foote, *The Trial*, 260.

101. Samuel Foote, *The Roman and English Comedy Consider'd and Compar'd. With Remarks on The Suspicious Husband. And an Examen into the Merit of the present Comic Actors* (London: printed for T. Waller in Fleet-Street, 1747), 19–20.

102. Carey, *Momus*, 10.

103. Foote, *Roman and English Comedy*, 22.

104. Wilkinson described Foote's reaction to being mimicked: "This surely is a striking instance how little we allow for the feelings of others, and how soon in general we are touched, galled, mortified, and enraged ourselves; that Mr. Foote should have felt himself hurt by my sallies of mimicry is not only strange; but that he should be so weak as confess it, still more extraordinary." Wilkinson, *Memoirs*, 2:175.

105. Samuel Foote, *The Englishman in Paris. A Comedy, in Two Acts. As it is performed at the Theatre-Royal in Covent-Garden* (London: Printed for Paul Vaillant, facing Southampton-Street, in the Strand, 1753).

106. The printed edition was advertised on February 14, 1754, less than a week after the play premiered at Drury Lane on February 9 (*Whitehall Evening Post*, February 14, 1754).

107. *The London Stage* reports that December 5, 1763, was "Mr. Foote's Night" at Drury Lane (Stone, *The London Stage*, 4:1024). This phrasing suggests that this

was an actor benefit night. However, because advertisements for the night do not announce that it is his benefit night, it is more likely that he was receiving an author benefit for this afterpiece on the fifth night of its performance.

108. *Memoirs of the Life and Writings of Samuel Foote, Esq.; the English Aristophanes: to which are added the Bon Mots, Repartees, and Good Things said by that great Wit and Excentrical Genius* (London: printed for J. Bew, Paternoster-Row, 1777), 22–23.

109. *Memoirs of the Life and Writings*, 29.

110. *The Devil upon Two Sticks* was not performed at Drury Lane or Covent Garden until 1780, three years after Foote's death. *The Maid of Bath* was not performed at one of the winter theaters until 1787, in spite of a spurious 1775 printing of the play. *The Nabob* was not performed at a winter theater until 1786 and *The Cozeners* until 1792. Within London at least, the Haymarket held a monopoly on performances of Foote's most popular plays.

111. One way he did this was by writing and producing a new play that featured himself in a key role nearly every summer at the Haymarket.

112. *Morning Chronicle*, January 17, 1777.

113. Charles Churchill, *The Rosciad* (London: Printed for the Author, and sold by W. Flexney, near Gray's-Inn-Gate, Holborn, 1761), lines 297–300. Wilkinson insists in his *Memoirs* that Churchill changed his mind about this after seeing Wilkinson perform Bayes for his benefit night on August 20, 1764, at the Haymarket. He writes, "My imitation of Holland . . . had such a sudden effect, that Mr. Churchill who sat in a balcony with the late Lucy Cooper, after laughing to a very violent degree, most vociferously encored the speech, which was echoed by the whole voice of the theatre, and complied with by me of course with great pleasure. Mr. Churchill said, that he was convinced I was not a mimic's mimic, for the imitations were palpably my own" (3:258).

114. Wilkinson, *Memoirs*, 1:32.

115. Wilkinson, *Memoirs*, 1:126.

116. Wilkinson, *Memoirs*, 1:147.

117. Wilkinson, *Memoirs*, 2:82.

118. Wilkinson, *Memoirs*, 2:83.

119. Playbills: Drury Lane, Covent Garden, Dublin, Edinburgh, Glasgow, and others, 1748–1778, Folio 767 P69B W65, Lewis Walpole Library, Yale University.

120. Lady Pentweazle was a character from Foote's *Taste*.

121. Wilkinson, *Memoirs*, 2:171.

122. Cooke, *Memoirs of Samuel Foote*, 1:99–100.

123. Wilkinson, *Memoirs*, 2:184.

124. Samuel Foote, *The Minor*, in *Plays by Samuel Foote and Arthur Murphy*, ed. George Taylor (New York: Cambridge University Press, 1984), 55.

125. Foote, *The Minor*, 55.

126. He tells Sir William Wealthy, "Wednesday, at Mrs. Gammut's, near Hanover Square, there, there I shall make a meal upon the Mingotti, for her ladyship is in the opera interest, but however, I shall revenge her cause upon her rival Mattei, Sunday evening, at Lady Sustinuto's concert" (Foote, *The Minor*, 56).

127. Foote, *The Minor*, 54–55.

128. Foote, *The Trial*, 257.

129. Foote, *The Minor*, 49.

130. Wilkinson, *Memoirs*, 2:235.

131. *Read's Weekly Journal*, November 22, 1760.

132. Wilkinson, *Memoirs*, 3:20.

133. *Whitehall Evening Post*, November 25–27, 1760. An obituary for Wilkinson also focuses on his layered mimicry: "As an imitator he was once high in repute. . . . He not only mimicked the actors who were distinguished about forty years ago on the London stage, but Foote's manner of imitating them." See "Died," *Monthly Register and Encyclopedian Magazine* 3, no. 18 (October 1803): 328–29.

134. Haymarket playbill for August 24, 1763, preserved in York Minster Library, "A Collection of Playbills for Theatres Mainly in Yorkshire, 1787–88."

135. Davies, *Memoirs*, 2:259–60.

CHAPTER 3

1. Wilkinson, *Memoirs*, 2:230.

2. The actor-playwright George Alexander Stevens attempted the same strategy. See Jane Wessel, "'My Other Folks' Heads': Reproducible Identities and Literary Property on the Eighteenth-Century Stage," *Eighteenth-Century Studies* 53, no. 2 (Winter 2020): 279–97.

3. Milhous and Hume, "Playwrights' Remuneration," 34.

4. Macklin's original proposals and his letter to Colman are preserved in the British Library, Miscellaneous English Autograph Letters, Egerton MS 2334.

5. *Morning Chronicle*, February 4, 1778.

6. O'Keeffe, *Recollections*, 1:400.

7. Wheble printed *The Maid of Bath* and *The Cozeners* and advertised an edition of *The Devil upon Two Sticks*.

8. *Morning Chronicle*, February 4, 1778.

9. See chapter 1.

10. *The Spanish Barber* was the eighth most-performed mainpiece between 1776 and 1800. Hogan, *The London Stage*, 5:clxxii.

11. Robert W. Jones suggests that Sheridan's withholding of *The School for Scandal* was not only because he feared "that a printed text would enable rival productions," but also because he "was an inveterate reviser of his work, adjusting his text frequently without ever completing a final version." See Jones, "Texts, Tools, and Things: An Approach to Manuscripts of Richard Brinsley Sheridan's *The School for Scandal*," *Review of English Studies* 66, no. 276 (September 2015): 723–43, at 724.

12. *Morning Chronicle and London Advertiser*, May 17, 1777.

13. Bernard, *Retrospections of the Stage*, 1:208.

14. Bernard, *Retrospections of the Stage*, 1:187. Bernard writes that Sheridan "took a fortnight to get up the play, and drilled all the servants and underlings himself."

15. Bernard, *Retrospections of the Stage*, 1:208.

16. That is, he compiled individual parts from various actors, and "with these materials for a groundwork, my general knowledge of the play, collected in rehearsing and performing in it above forty times, enabled me in a week to construct a comedy in five acts, called, in imitation of the original, 'The School for Scandal.'" Bernard, *Retrospections of the Stage*, 1:209.

17. Bernard, *Retrospections of the Stage*, 1:208.

18. Peters, *Theatre of the Book*, 77–78; Stephens, *Profession of the Playwright*, 86–87.

19. Quoted in *The Dramatic Works of Richard Brinsley Sheridan*, ed. Cecil Price, 2 vols. (Oxford: At the Clarendon Press, 1973), 1:215.

20. O'Keeffe, *Recollections*, 1:400, 2:6.

21. O'Keeffe, *Recollections*, 1:400.

22. Milhous and Hume, "Playwrights' Remuneration," 41.

23. Milhous and Hume, *Publication of Plays*, 116.

24. Kewes, *Authorship and Appropriation*.

25. Kewes, "[A] Play."

26. Hogan, *The London Stage*, 5:clxxi.

27. *Gazetteer and New Daily Advertiser*, May 3, 1777.

28. *Gazetteer and New Daily Advertiser*, May 3, 1777.

29. *Hibernian Journal* (Dublin), April 21–23, 1777.

30. "Law Report. King's Bench," *Morning Herald*, February 25, 1793.

31. Durnford and East, *Reports of Cases*, 5:245.

32. Durnford and East, *Reports of Cases*, 5:245.

33. Durnford and East, *Reports of Cases*, 5:245.

34. Oliver Gerland, "The Haymarket Theatre and Literary Property: Constructing Common Law Playright, 1770–1833," *Theatre Notebook* 69, no. 2 (2015): 74–96, at 83.

35. Durnford and East, *Reports of Cases*, 5:245.

36. Durnford and East, *Reports of Cases*, 5:245; "Law Intelligence. Court of King's Bench. Saturday, May 5. Colman versus Wathen," *Lloyd's Evening Post*, May 6, 1793; "Law Intelligence. Court of King's Bench. Saturday, May 4, 1793. *Colman* v. *Wathen*," *Morning Chronicle*, May 6, 1793.

37. "Law Intelligence. Court of King's Bench. Saturday, May 5. Colman versus Wathen," *Lloyd's Evening Post*, May 6, 1793.

38. Gerland, "Haymarket Theatre," 74.

39. Litman, "Invention of Common Law Play Right," 1389.

40. See Stern, "Copyright, Originality."

CHAPTER 4

1. Wilkinson, *Memoirs*, 2:230.

2. Hogan, *The London Stage*, 5:clxxi.

3. Wilkinson, *Memoirs*, 2:230.

4. Wilkinson, *Memoirs*, 2:230. See also Sheridan, *Dramatic Works*, 1:216.

5. Wilkinson, *Wandering Patentee*, 1:237.

6. Annibel Jenkins, *I'll Tell You What: The Life of Elizabeth Inchbald* (Lexington: University Press of Kentucky, 2003), 41.

7. Moody, "Playbills under House Arrest," 1. Charles Beecher Hogan calculates that by 1800, there were 150 provincial theaters in Great Britain, 17 of which had royal patents. Hogan, "God Almighty's Unaccountables," 63.

8. Wilkinson writes in his *Memoirs* that he has acted in "almost every principal theatre in the three kingdoms," listing twenty-seven theaters before an "&c." (1:1–2).

9. As Wilkinson's playbill collection reveals (and as Charles Beecher Hogan notes), there was a fairly consistent pattern to Wilkinson's circuit: from February to May, the company would perform in York; June and July in Leeds; part of August back in York; August to September in Pontefract; September in Wakefield; October in Doncaster; and October to January in Hull. Hogan, "God Almighty's Unaccountables," n. 58.

10. See Betsy Bolton, "Theorizing Audience and Spectatorial Agency," in Swindells and Taylor, *Oxford Handbook of the Georgian Theatre*, 31-52, at 37, and Chris Morash and Shaun Richards, *Mapping Irish Theatre: Theories of Space and Place* (New York: Cambridge University Press, 2013), 18. I am building, of course, on Benedict Anderson's *Imagined Communities* (New York: Verso, 2003).

11. Taylor, *Archive and the Repertoire*, xviii.

12. Wilkinson, *Memoirs*, 1:xiii.

13. Highfill, Burnim, and Langhans, *Biographical Dictionary*, 16:105. Hogan has gone as far as to suggest that "Tate Wilkinson was possibly the greatest mimic who ever lived." Hogan, "God Almighty's Unaccountables," 75.

14. Highfill, Burnim, and Langhans, *A Biographical Dictionary*, 16:99.

15. Bratton, *New Readings*, 115.

16. The quotation comes from an 1827 summary of Mathews's performance. No script of the performance itself exists. See *Sketches of Mr. Mathews' Celebrated Lecture on Character, Manners, and Peculiarities, Entitled The Home Circuit* (London: published by J. Limbird, 1827), 27.

17. *Sketches of Mr. Mathews'*, 27. While this is how Mathews understood his theatrical lineage, not all of these actors actually knew each other. For example, Betterton died before Garrick was born.

18. John Downes, *Roscius Anglicanus, or an Historical Review of the Stage* (London: Printed and sold by H. Playford, 1708), 21. For more on the continuity of performance, see Holland, *The Ornament of Action*, 66–67.

19. Richard Schoch discusses the way that Downes imagines theater history as a "living archive" in *Writing the History of the British Stage, 1660–1900* (New York: Cambridge University Press, 2016), 140.

20. Taylor, "Performance," 92.

21. Taylor, "Performance," 92.

22. Bratton, *New Readings*, 5–6.

23. Jones, "The Artist Is Present," 20.

24. Churchill, *The Rosciad*, lines 35–36.

25. Wilkinson, *Memoirs*, 2:98.

26. This language, which is repeated on many of Wilkinson's playbills, comes from a May 19, [1764] performance in York. The playbill is preserved in the York Minster Library.

27. See William W. West, "Intertheatricality," in *Early Modern Theatricality*, ed. Henry S. Turner (New York: Oxford University Press, 2013), 151-72, at 152. West's argument suggests that even when full plays were performed, the boundaries of the "play" as a single unit were flexible because of the ways audience understanding was shaped by the many intertheatrical references within the play. Wilkinson goes further, often not giving his audiences an entire play at all, but instead, only textual segments and intertheatrical references.

28. Bratton also discusses intertheatricality in *New Readings*.

29. Wilkinson, *Memoirs*, 3:27.

30. Audience unfamiliarity with the objects of mimicry often generated interest, as Wilkinson's mimicry gave them a sort of access to celebrity actors they might not otherwise see. His advertising likely played a large part in generating anticipation. Just as Foote had made sure audiences knew in advance whom he was mimicking, Wilkinson did the same with his playbills. At times, however, his mimicry of London actors alienated audiences. His first performance of *Tea* in York (in 1763), for instance, was not well received. He writes that it was "the opinion of every body, I only sneered at the York audience." *Memoirs*, 3:148.

31. Wilkinson, *Memoirs*, 1:vii.

32. Marvin Carlson writes about the relationship between theater and memory in *The Haunted Stage*. He argues that the reuse of sets, music, actors, or parts activates audience memory of the original and shapes how the audience understands the current performance. Hogan notes that Wilkinson's Yorkshire audiences would have "very rarely, if ever" visited London. See Hogan, "God Almighty's Unaccountables," 64.

33. Bernard, *Retrospections of the Stage*, 1:151–52.

34. Wilkinson, *Wandering Patentee*, 1:viii–ix.

35. Hogan, "God Almighty's Unaccountables," 77.

36. When he performed in London, he continued to mimic Foote. When Harris invited him to perform at Covent Garden in 1778, the year after Foote's death, for instance, Wilkinson records that he was nearly perfect in his imitation of Foote as Major Sturgeon. Wilkinson, *Wandering Patentee*, 1:281–82.

37. Leslie Ritchie, "'The Spouters' Revenge: Apprentice Actors and the Imitation of London's Theatrical Celebrities," *Eighteenth Century: Theory and Interpretation* 53, no. 1 (Spring 2012): 41–71, at 50.

38. Rosenfeld discusses the reforms that Wilkinson instituted as he worked to dignify his country theaters and make acting in the provinces a polite profession. Sybil Rosenfeld, *The York Theatre* (London: Society for Theatre Research, 2001).

39. Wilkinson, *Memoirs*, 4:63–64.

40. Wilkinson, *Memoirs*, 4:66–67.

41. Wilkinson, *Memoirs*, 4:67.

42. Wilkinson, *Memoirs*, 4:68–69.

43. *The Theatrical Register containing Candid and Impartial Strictures on the Various Performances at the Theatre-Royal, York* (York: Printed by Lucas Lund, in Low-Ousegate, 1788), 68. Anne Mathews records that "Tate had a most extravagant, nay, childish fondness for spangled and embroidered clothes." *Memoirs of Charles Mathews, Comedian*, 4 vols. (London: Richard Bentley, New Burlington Street, Publisher in Ordinary to Her Majesty, 1838), 1:386.

44. Rosenfeld, *The York Theatre*, 52.

45. A near-complete collection of Wilkinson's Yorkshire playbills from 1766 to 1803 is preserved in the York Minster Library. When I cite his playbills, I am referring to this collection, unless otherwise noted.

46. Wilkinson records in *The Wandering Patentee* that he had obtained a copy of the play while he was in London earlier that year. He does not say how he got the copy, whether it was with Sheridan's blessing, or how correct it was. However, because he boasts, both on the playbill and in *The Wandering Patentee*, of the "simili-

tude" between the London and York productions, it seems likely that he was using a correct copy. *Wandering Patentee*, 1:302–3.

47. This had premiered at Drury Lane late in the season, on May 18, 1782. The author benefit nights continued into the next season. See Milhous and Hume, "Playwrights' Remuneration," 66.

48. Charles Macklin to Tate Wilkinson, April 22, 1769, Correspondence of Alexander Dyce and others preserved in the Dyce Collection, MSL/1869/64/103–104, National Art Library, Victoria and Albert Museum, London.

49. Macklin would have been particularly attuned to the case because his own case against the printers Richardson and Urquhart was being delayed until a ruling was reached in *Millar v. Taylor*.

50. Charles Macklin to Tate Wilkinson, July 27, 1772, Correspondence of Alexander Dyce and others preserved in the Dyce Collection, MSL/1869/64/103–104, National Art Library, Victoria and Albert Museum, London.

51. "Tate Wilkinson to Charles Macklin," September 30, 1772, Lewis Walpole Library, Yale University.

52. Macklin to Wilkinson, July 27, 1772.

53. Wilkinson uses the phrase "borrow, beg, or buy" referring to Harris's attempt to obtain a copy of *The Follies of a Day* from the Paris theater. The play's success, Wilkinson writes on a May 10, 1785, playbill, "induced Mr. Harris . . . to use every Endeavour to procure a Copy. . . . Unable to borrow, beg, or buy it, a Translation has at length been stolen, and performed in London." In pointing out Harris's own theft of a play text, Wilkinson may have been commenting on Harris's tendency to make his own plays inaccessible to country theaters, forcing them into piracy.

54. "Theatrical Intelligence," *Morning Post*, April 10, 1776.

55. While Wilkinson's alterations (and particularly his choice to advertise the work as a derivative) satisfied Harris, it would not have worked with all copyright holders. Macklin, for instance, thought that textual alteration did nothing to mitigate what he saw as a crime. In a letter to James Whitley, who had defended his performances of *Love à la Mode* on the grounds that the texts were not exactly the same, Macklin wrote, "By this kind of reasoning, and justice—if you had stolen, or had received my horse that had been stolen by another, and then you had lamed him, cut off one of his ears . . . you think you might effectually plead that the horse was not mine, as he was so nicely and artfully disguised, so lame, and so very much altered for the worse." Kirkman, *Memoirs*, 2:39–40.

56. *Morning Chronicle and London Advertiser*, March 1, 1777.

57. Price writes, "The outcome, then, of Harris's policy of restriction was that he preserved the authentic version at Covent Garden until 1794, but that the comic opera was known to most people outside London through seeing Wilkinson's feeble version or reading the equally poor adaptations, Ryder's *The Governess* and Vandermere's *The Duenna*." Price in Sheridan, *Dramatic Works*, 1:216.

58. William Kenrick, *Introduction to the School of Shakespeare; Held, on Wednesday Evenings, In the Apollo, at the Devil Tavern, Temple Bar* (London: printed for the Author, and sold by the Booksellers, 1774), 13.

59. See C. S. Rogers and Betty Rizzo, "Kenrick, William (1729/30–1779)," in *Oxford Dictionary of National Biography* (Oxford University Press, 2004; online edition, January 2008).

60. Kenrick, *School of Shakespeare*, v.

61. Kenrick, *School of Shakespeare*, 3.

62. Kenrick, *School of Shakespeare*, 15.

63. A review of the first performance called it an "almost *new line* of performance," suggesting that although the lecture format was not new, the way Kenrick was employing it was. "*For the* London Evening Post. School of Shakespeare," *London Evening Post*, January 18–20, 1774.

64. Wilkinson refers to the performance as "this fête, or compilement, call it which you please" in *Wandering Patentee*, 2:108.

65. Note on the playbill for a May 4, 1782, performance of "A New Theatrical Fete" in York.

66. *Julius Caesar* was performed often in London in the early eighteenth century, but was performed only sixteen times in the last four decades.

67. In a note on his May 4, 1782, bill, Wilkinson explains that "the Pieces are disposed in such Order as not to occasion more Delay betwixt each Division than is usual on the Representation of any Tragedy or Comedy." Length was clearly an issue, as were scene changes and casting.

68. The "favourite" or "principal" scene from *Love à la Mode* focused on Sir Archy, while Wilkinson's excerpts of Foote's *Diversions* and *Taste* featured Lady Pentweazle prominently.

69. Wilkinson, *Wandering Patentee*, 1:16–17.

70. Letter from Henry Woodward to Tate Wilkinson, March 26, 1771, in Wilkinson, *Memoirs*, 4:258–60.

71. Wilkinson uses the term "catalogue" in this way often in his *Wandering Patentee*, writing, for instance, "by not having any change of performers that year, my catalogue of plays and farces were very extensive" (4:44).

72. Garrick wrote this in a letter to the actor John Moody, describing a recent Dublin performance of *The Jubilee*. The letter, dated June 6, 1771, is in a Scrapbook of David Garrick, W.b.472, held in the Folger Shakespeare Library, Washington, DC.

73. Wilkinson calls it "the only time I ever exercised my pen on such an occasion." *Memoirs*, 2:230.

CHAPTER 5

1. John O'Keeffe, *The Dramatic Works of John O'Keeffe, Esq. Published Under the Gracious Patronage of His Royal Highness the Prince of Wales. Prepared for the Press by the Author*, 4 vols. (London: Printed for the Author, by T. Woodfall, 1798).

2. O'Keeffe, *Recollections*, 2:53.

3. O'Keeffe, *Dramatic Works*. Annotated copy held in Victoria and Albert Museum, National Art Library, Dyce 8vo 7030 1798. The note on *The Young Quaker* varies a bit, reading "Genuine Copy ~~by me Adelaide O'Keeffe~~ 1826," with "Read to My Father in 1826, and pronounced by Him, quite correct Ad OK" on the facing page.

4. O'Keeffe, *Recollections*, 2:305.

5. Frederick Link, "Introduction," *The Plays of John O'Keeffe* (New York: Garland, 1981), vii.

6. O'Keeffe describes publishing his *Dramatic Works* as an effort to ensure his and his daughter's financial future. *Recollections*, 2:365.

7. Milhous and Hume, *Publication of Plays*, 205.

8. Milhous and Hume, "Playwrights' Remuneration," 73.

9. Stephen Porter, *Lovers' Vows, or, the Child of Love. A Play, in Five Acts. Translated from the German of Augustus von Kotzebue: with a Brief Biography of the Author* (London: Printed for J. Parsons, Paternoster-Row, 1798), i–ii.

10. Anne Plumptre, *The Natural Son; a Play, in five Acts, by Augustus von Kotzebue, Poet Laureat and Director of the Imperial Theatre at Vienna. Being the Original of Lovers' Vows, now Performing, with Universal Applause, at the Theatre Royal, Covent Garden. Translated from the German by Anne Plumptre, (Author of the Rector's Son, Antoinette, &c.) who has prefixed a Preface, Explaining the Alterations in the Representation; and has also annexed A Life of Kotzebue* (London: Printed for R. Phillips, 1798), ii.

11. "Theatre Royal, Covent Garden. Lovers' Vows," *Morning Chronicle*, October 15, 1798.

12. The right of publicity, which prevents the unauthorized use of someone else's name or likeness for commercial profit, exists on a state-by-state basis in the United States and not at all in the United Kingdom, though other laws, including trademark and privacy laws, can sometimes be used for similar purposes.

13. Kewes, "[A] Play," 22.

14. Elizabeth Inchbald, *Lovers' Vows. A Play, in Five Acts* (London: Printed for G.G. and J. Robinson, Pater-noster-row, 1798), ii.

15. Qtd. in James Boaden, *Memoirs of Mrs. Inchbald: including her Familiar Correspondence with the Most Distinguished Persons of her Time. To Which are Added The Massacre, and A Case of Conscience; Now First Published from her Autograph Copies*, 2 vols. (London: Richard Bentley, New Burlington Street, 1833), 2:25.

16. Inchbald asked for £100 each on the third, sixth, and ninth nights, and £20 per night for each night it was performed after that, up to a total of thirty nights. Boaden, *Memoirs of Mrs. Inchbald*, 2:24–25.

17. Anne Plumptre, "Lovers' Vows. To the Editor of the Morning Chronicle," *Morning Chronicle*, October 16, 1798.

18. Inchbald, *Lovers' Vows*, i–ii.

19. Lisa Freeman, "On the Art of Dramatic Probability: Elizabeth Inchbald's *Remarks for the British Theatre*," *Theatre Survey* 62, no. 2 (May 2021): 163–81, at 165.

20. Ben P. Robertson, *Elizabeth Inchbald's Reputation: A Publishing and Reception History* (London: Pickering & Chatto, 2013), 115.

21. Jenkins, *I'll Tell You What*, 428.

22. "Article XI. I'll Tell You What; a Comedy, in Five Acts; as it is performed at the Theatre-Royal, Hay-Market," *English review, or, An Abstract of English and Foreign Literature* 8 (November 1786): 374–80, at 378.

23. "Article XI," 379.

24. The Robinsons published two editions of the play in 1786, the first in July. Because this review does not appear until November, the reviewer is likely responding to the second edition.

25. Misty G. Anderson, "Women Playwrights," in *The Cambridge Companion to*

British Theatre, 1730–1830, ed. Jane Moody and Daniel O'Quinn (New York: Cambridge University Press, 2007), 145-58, at 153.

26. Stephens, *Profession of the Playwright*, 27–28.

27. The four performed plays that she did not print were *A Mogul Tale* (1784), *All on a Summer's Day* (1787), *Animal Magnetism* (1788), and *Hue and Cry* (1791). Some of these were printed in unauthorized editions.

28. *I'll Tell you What* (1785) was not printed until 1786, and *Such Things Are* (1787) was delayed by Harris, who bought the copyright from the Robinsons after Inchbald had sold it to them.

29. Milhous and Hume, "Playwrights' Remuneration," 88.

30. While the play does not appear to have made Inchbald a phenomenal amount of money from performance, as her later plays would, it earned her a decent sum and cemented her reputation. Boaden writes that Inchbald earned £300 from three benefit nights. Her own records, preserved in the Folger Shakespeare Library, suggest that she earned £243 (£94 from the third night, £96 from the sixth, and £53 from the ninth). Milhous and Hume have no entry for this play in "Playwrights' Remuneration." It is unclear where the gap of nearly £60 comes from if not from copyright. It is possible that Colman gave Inchbald an additional payment for a successful first run (the play ran for twenty nights in the first season) or that Boaden is simply incorrect.

31. The print edition of the play was advertised on July 22–25, 1786, in the *London Chronicle* as "this Day was published" by G.G.J. and J. Robinson.

32. "Extract of a letter from Dublin, Oct. 20," *Morning Chronicle and London Advertiser*, October 25, 1785.

33. *Morning Post and Daily Advertiser*, December 29, 1785.

34. Boaden, *Memoirs of Mrs. Inchbald*, 1:225.

35. Qtd. in Boaden, *Memoirs of Mrs. Inchbald*, 1:226.

36. John Palmer, manager of the Theatre Royal, Bath, was not the same John Palmer who acted in *I'll Tell You What* at the Haymarket.

37. Boaden does not include Inchbald's letters to Bonnor.

38. Boaden, *Memoirs of Mrs. Inchbald*, 1:224-25.

39. *Morning Post and Daily Advertiser*, Wednesday, May 3, 1786.

40. This letter is held at the National Art Library in the Victoria and Albert Museum, Forster MS 116. It is also quoted in Boaden, *Memoirs of Mrs. Inchbald*, 1:225.

41. Hume, "Theatre as Property," 40.

42. Boaden, *Memoirs of Mrs. Inchbald*, 1:224.

43. Wilkinson, *Wandering Patentee*, 3:34.

44. Wilkinson, *Wandering Patentee*, 2:59-60.

45. A letter from Inchbald to Wilkinson, preserved in the Folger Shakespeare Library, captures her forceful nature beautifully. In it, she asserts her rights as a member of his acting company ("You much forget that I am articled and will stay with you just as long as I please, therefore don't affront me") and insists that he give her better parts. Elizabeth Inchbald to Tate Wilkinson, [1780], Autograph letters signed from Mrs. Inchbald to various people, Y.c.1376 (10), Folger Shakespeare Library, Washington, DC.

46. A notice in the *World and Fashionable Advertiser* on February 19, 1787,

remarks, "Robinson, the bookseller, who had purchased Mrs. Inchbald's play for the sum of 200 guineas—has ceded his bargain to Mr. Harris—and therefore, 'Such Things Are' to be seen in future upon the stage at Covent Garden only."

47. Elizabeth Inchbald to Tate Wilkinson, March 16, [1787], Osborn Manuscripts, File 7864, Beinecke Rare Books Room, Yale University.

48. This story is more complex yet, for an actress in Wilkinson's company, Mrs. Belfille, got a legitimate manuscript copy from the Norwich manager before Wilkinson received one from Inchbald. Both Belfille and Wilkinson wished to perform the play for their own benefit nights at York. Wilkinson's playbill, then, is not only asserting the authenticity of the work, but suggesting that the author gives her blessing for Wilkinson rather than Belfille to perform it on his night, which he did: *"This Comedy is to be acted for Mr. Wilkinson, not only by permission, but by the express desire of Mr. Harris and Mrs. Inchbald; as the author's own letter to Mr. W can testify."*

49. Wilkinson, *Wandering Patentee*, 2:60.

50. Donkin, *Getting into the Act*, 120.

51. Donkin, *Getting into the Act*, 123.

52. Colman's public letter to Inchbald and her response were published as the preface to his *Heir at Law* in the *British Theatre* series. Elizabeth Inchbald, *Remarks for the British Theatre (1806–1809)*, ed. Cecilia Macheski (Delmar, NY: Scholars' Facsimiles & Reprints, 1990).

53. Donkin, *Getting into the Act*, 26.

54. These figures come from Milhous and Hume's "Playwrights' Remuneration," with the exception of the figure for *To Marry or Not to Marry*, which comes from Boaden.

55. Boaden, *Memoirs of Mrs. Inchbald*, 1:310.

56. Boaden, *Memoirs of Mrs. Inchbald*, 1:223.

57. Boaden, *Memoirs of Mrs. Inchbald*, 1:223.

58. See, for instance, Anderson, *Eighteenth-Century Authorship*; Nachumi, *Acting Like a Lady*; and Donkin, *Getting into the Act*.

59. Boaden, *Memoirs of Mrs. Inchbald*, 1:238.

60. Donkin, *Getting into the Act*, 125–26.

61. Donkin, *Getting into the Act*, 126.

62. Robertson, *Elizabeth Inchbald's Reputation*, 11.

63. Boaden, *Memoirs of Mrs. Inchbald*, 2:87.

64. Boaden, *Memoirs of Mrs. Inchbald*, 2:24.

65. Amanda Weldy Boyd argues that Boaden tacks his own legacy to his subject's. By inserting himself into the narrative, even briefly, Boaden reminds readers that he is a player in and not just an observer of the theater world. Boyd, *Staging Memory and Materiality in Eighteenth-Century Theatrical Biography* (New York: Anthem Press, 2017).

66. Boaden, *Memoirs of Mrs. Inchbald*, 2:22.

67. Milhous and Hume estimate that under the pre-1794 remuneration system, the work would have earned Inchbald £570. "Playwrights' Remuneration," 73.

68. Boaden, *Memoirs of Mrs. Inchbald*, 2:8.

69. Boaden, *Memoirs of Mrs. Inchbald*, 2:37.

70. *Report from the Select Committee*, 150–51.

71. Richard Brinsley Peake, *Memoirs of the Colman Family, Including their Correspondence with the Most Distinguished Personages of their Time*, 2 vols. (London: Richard Bentley, 1841), 2:280.

72. O'Keeffe had staged a version of this three years earlier in Dublin.

73. Hogan, *The London Stage* Part 5.

74. Link, "Introduction," lix.

75. Hogan, *The London Stage*, 5:clxxii.

76. Link, "Introduction," lix.

77. David O'Shaughnessy, "'Rip'ning Buds in Freedom's Field': Staging Irish Improvement in the 1780s," *Journal for Eighteenth-Century Studies* 38, no. 4 (2015): 541–54, at 545.

78. Hogan, *The London Stage*, 5:clxxii.

79. Link, "Introduction," xix–xx.

80. See chapter 3 for a discussion of Colman's injunctions against Wheble.

81. O'Keeffe, *Recollections*, 1:400.

82. O'Keeffe, *Recollections*, 1:399.

83. O'Keeffe, *Recollections*, 1:400. The term "nut-shell" had connotations of small size and little value, either or both of which O'Keeffe might have been invoking. "Nutshell, n. and adj.," *Oxford English Dictionary Online*, June 2017.

84. It was not the case that O'Keeffe simply did not wish to print his works. In fact, O'Keeffe did print *Tony Lumpkin* in 1780. On the title page, he advertised the play as being by J. O'Keeffe, author of *The Son-in-Law*, demonstrating his understanding that popularity onstage could sell his works in print. He dedicated Tony Lumpkin to Colman, expressing his gratitude to the manager for staging his first work and "promoting" his second. John O'Keeffe, *Tony Lumpkin in Town* (London: Printed for T. Cadell in the Strand, 1780).

85. O'Keeffe, *Recollections*, 2:110.

86. O'Keeffe, *Recollections*, 2:2.

87. *The Dead Alive* was performed fourteen times its first season and *The Agreeable Surprise* seven times, even though it did not open until September. Hogan, *The London Stage*, 5:368.

88. O'Keeffe, *Recollections*, 2:4–5.

89. Link argues that he did not sell one of his copyrights to a bookseller until 1788, when he sold *The Prisoner at Large* to Robinson. Link, "Introduction," xliv.

90. Milhous and Hume do not include information for *Peeping Tom* and *The Young Quaker*, which he sold to the Haymarket. From the list of plays he includes on the subscription advertisement for his *Dramatic Works*, we also know that he sold the copyrights for the following eight plays to Covent Garden: *The Castle of Andalusia*, *The Poor Soldier*, *Modern Antiques*, *The Positive Man*, *Love in a Camp*, *The Highland Reel*, *Fontainebleau*, and *Sprigs of Laurel*. "Mr. O'Keeffe's Dramatic Works," *Oracle and Public Advertiser*, November 21, 1797. A few of these works were published before 1798 in individual editions, so Harris must have granted permission to print before this point.

91. O'Keeffe writes that when Harris approached him to write an opera for Covent Garden and asked him, "What am I to give you for this opera; your nights, and copyright?" Arnold quickly replied with the sum of six hundred guineas. O'Keeffe, *Recollections*, 2:12.

92. A small handful of his many works made him substantial sums. He earned £369 for *The Castle of Andalusia* at Covent Garden (1782), 300 guineas for the performance and copyright of *The Poor Soldier* at Covent Garden (1783), 480 guineas for *Fontainebleau* at Covent Garden (1784), 350 guineas for the performance and copyright of *The Toy* at Covent Garden (1789), and 450 guineas for the performance and copyright of *Wild Oats* at Covent Garden (1793).

93. Link, "Introduction," xxxi.

94. O'Keeffe, *Recollections*, 2:53. On the copy annotated by Adelaide O'Keeffe, she writes in a note, dictated by her father, that "William Lewis the Actor regretted very Much I had not brought out this Comedy at Covent Garden where he was engaged, that he might have acted Young Sadboy—John O'K." O'Keeffe, *The Dramatic Works*, Victoria and Albert Museum, National Art Library, Dyce 8vo 7030.

95. See chapter 3 for a discussion of *Coleman v. Wathen* (1793).

96. O'Keeffe records which plays he sent to Daly throughout his *Recollections*. Daly sent O'Keeffe and Harris £100 apiece for a copy of *The Castle of Andalusia*, and he sent O'Keeffe £50 for *The Young Quaker* (and "Mr. Colman consented I should accept it," 2:52), fifty guineas for *The Poor Soldier* (which O'Keeffe sent "with his [Harris's] consent"; O'Keeffe, however, gave the money to Harris out of a sense that he should have that profit, 2:71), and £50 for *The Farmer*, again with Harris's consent (2:129). When Colman allowed O'Keeffe to send Daly *The Young Quaker*, he expressed "in a handsome letter his pleasure at any occasion of making a return to me for the great advantages he said his theatre had derived from my productions, the profits of his house being so inadequate to the recompense I deserved" (2:52–53).

97. O'Keeffe, *Recollections*, 2:13.

98. O'Keeffe, *Recollections*, 2:14.

99. O'Keeffe emphasizes his personal relationship with Colman, and the gratitude he felt to Colman not only for accepting his first plays, but also for his friendship, in his *Recollections*. He describes spending time at Colman's house after he moved to London and Colman's fondness for his children. *Recollections*, 2:6–7.

100. Of his early works, O'Keeffe published *Tony Lumpkin in Town*, *The Birthday*, and an account of his pantomime *Omai* with Cadell. Many of his works appeared in pirated editions, most coming out of Ireland.

101. John O'Keeffe, *The Prisoner at Large: A Comedy. In Two Acts* (London: Printed for G.G.J. and J. Robinson, Paternoster-Row, 1788).

102. O'Keeffe began going blind in the late 1770s, and *The Agreeable Surprise* was the last play he wrote out by hand himself. His daughter Adelaide was his amanuensis for most of his career.

103. "Mr. O'Keeffe's Dramatic Works," *Oracle and Public Advertiser*, November 21, 1797.

104. Peake, *Memoirs of the Colman Family*, 2:280.

105. O'Keeffe, *Recollections*, 2:349.

106. O'Keeffe, *Recollections*, 2:365.

107. O'Keeffe, *Recollections*, 2:365–66.

108. "The Theatre," *True Briton*, June 13, 1800.

109. "The Theatre," *True Briton*, June 13, 1800.

110. Peake, *Memoirs of the Colman Family*, 2:280.

111. *Morning Post and Gazetteer*, May 30, 1800.

EPILOGUE

1. As Lisa Freeman argues, the *British Theatre* series that Inchbald wrote prefaces for was "meant to reflect not the history of English drama so much as the likes and tastes that regulated the contemporary playhouse repertoire." Freeman, "On the Art," 164.

2. Wessel, "My Other Folks' Heads."

3. Anne Mathews, *The Life and Correspondence of Charles Mathews, the Elder, Comedian*, ed. Edmund Yates (London: Routledge, Warne, and Routledge, 1860), 219.

4. Mathews, *Life and Correspondence*, 219.

5. J. Paul Hunter writes that while the actors of the period were greats, "the men and women who wrote for those talented actors were not." He describes drama of the period as the "foothills of literary history" and repeats the phrase "the decline of drama." Hunter, "The World as Stage and Closet," in *British Theatre and the Other Arts, 1660-1800*, ed. Shirley Strum Kenny (Washington, DC: Folger Shakespeare Library, 1984), 271-87, at 271. Laura Brown has argued that "the rise of the novel defines the decline of the drama." Brown, *English Dramatic Form, 1660-1760: An Essay in Generic History* (New Haven: Yale University Press, 1981), 184. J. W. Saunders, meanwhile, argues that "the decline of drama in the eighteenth century may be attributed, directly, to the growth of an entertainment industry which thought of plays, exclusively, as a commodity to be sold." Saunders, *The Profession of English Letters* (New York: Routledge, 1964), 147.

6. David Francis Taylor, "Introduction," in *The Oxford Handbook of the Georgian Theatre, 1737-1832*, ed. Julia Swindells and David Francis Taylor (New York: Oxford University Press, 2014), 1-7, at 2.

7. Lord Byron, *Marino Faliero, Doge of Venice. An Historical Tragedy, in Five Acts. With Notes* (London: John Murray, 1821), xvii–xviii.

8. Miller, *Copyright*, 46.

9. "The Drama," *Literary Chronicle and Weekly Review* 3, no. 102 (April 28, 1821): 270.

10. Miller, *Copyright*, 48.

11. "Mr. Elliston for the Representation of Marino Faliero. Court of Chancery, April 27," in *The Edinburgh Annual Register, for 1821* (Edinburgh: Printed by James Ballantyne and Co., 1823), 78.

12. "Mr. Elliston," 78.

13. The advertisement notes that "those who have perused 'Marino Faliero,' will have anticipated the necessity of considerable curtailments, aware that conversations or soliloquies, however beautiful and interesting in the closet, will frequently tire in public recital." "Mr. Elliston," 79.

14. "Mr. Elliston," 80, 79.

15. Richard Vaughan Barnewall and Edward Hall Alderson, *Reports of Cases Argued and Determined in the Court of King's Bench. With Tables of the Names of the Cases and the Principal Matters*, vol. 5 (London: Printed by A. Strahan, 1822), 659.

16. Barnewall and Alderson, *Reports of Cases*, 660.

17. Miller, *Copyright*, 63.

18. Multigraph Collective, *Interacting with Print*, 279-80.

19. Moody, *Illegitimate Theatre in London*, 2.

20. Moody writes that "illegitimate drama," in contrast to the traditional five-act comedies and tragedies performed at the patent houses, was made up of "melodrama, burlesque, [and] extravaganza" (*Illegitimate Theatre in London*, 6).

21. For more on the changes in payment systems, see Milhous and Hume, "Playwrights' Remuneration," 21.

22. "The State of the Drama," *New Monthly Magazine and Literary Journal*, February 1832, 131.

23. "State of the Drama," 131.

24. "State of the Drama," 132.

25. "State of the Drama," 133.

26. "State of the Drama," 135.

27. Edward Bulwer-Lytton took that name in 1843. Prior to that, he was known as Edward Lytton Bulwer.

28. Katherine Newey, "The 1832 Select Committee," in Swindells and Taylor, *Oxford Handbook of the Georgian Theatre*.

29. Newey, "The 1832 Select Committee," 151.

30. Bratton, *New Readings*, 82.

31. Miller, *Copyright*, 60.

32. Stephens, *Profession of the Playwright*, 91.

33. Stephens, *Profession of the Playwright*, 93.

Bibliography

An Act to Amend the Laws Relating to Dramatic Literary Property, 1833, 3 & 4 Will. IV, c.15. In *Primary Sources on Copyright (1450–1900)*, edited Lionel Bently and Martin Kretschmer, www.copyrighthistory.org

An Act for the Encouragement of Learning, by Vesting the Copies of Printed Books in the Authors or Purchasers of such Copies, During the Times therein mentioned, 1710, 8 Anne, c.19. In *Primary Sources on Copyright (1450–1900)*, Edited by Lionel Bently and Martin Kretschmer, www.copyrighthistory.org

Alexander, Isabella. "'Neither Bolt nor Chain, Iron Safe nor Private Watchman, Can Prevent the Theft of Words': The Birth of the Performing Right in Britain." In *Privilege and Property: Essays on the History of Copyright*, edited by Ronan Deazley, Martin Kretschmer, and Lionel Bently. Cambridge: Open Book Publishers, 2010.

Ambler, Charles. *Reports of Cases Argued and Determined in the High Court of Chancery, with Some Few in Other Courts*. 2nd ed. Edited by John Elijah Blunt. 2 vols. London: Joseph Butterworth and Son, 1828.

Anderson, Benedict. *Imagined Communities*. New York: Verso, 2003.

Anderson, Emily Hodgson. "Celebrity Shylock." *PMLA* 126, no. 4 (2011): 935–49.

Anderson, Emily Hodgson. *Eighteenth-Century Authorship and the Play of Fiction: Novels and the Theatre, Haywood to Austen*. New York: Routledge, 2009.

Anderson, Emily Hodgson. *Shakespeare and the Legacy of Loss*. Ann Arbor: University of Michigan Press, 2018.

Anderson, Misty G. "Women Playwrights." In *The Cambridge Companion to British Theatre, 1730–1830*, edited by Jane Moody and Daniel O'Quinn, 145–58. New York: Cambridge University Press, 2007.

"Anecdote of Mr. Foote, being and Extract of a Letter from Dublin." *London Magazine, or, Gentleman's Monthly Intelligencer* 32 (March 1763): 135–36.

Appleton, William W. *Charles Macklin: An Actor's Life*. Cambridge, MA: Harvard University Press, 1960.

Balme, Christopher. "Playbills and the Theatrical Public Sphere." In *Representing the Past: Essays in Performance Historiography*, edited by Charlotte Canning and Thomas Postlewait, 37–62. Iowa City: University of Iowa Press, 2010.

Barchas, Janine, and Kristina Straub. "Curating *Will & Jane*." *Eighteenth-Century Life* 40, no. 2 (April 2016): 1–35.

Barnewall, Richard Vaughan, and Edward Hall Alderson. *Reports of Cases Argued and Determined in the Court of King's Bench. With Tables of the Names of the Cases and the Principal Matters*. Vol. 5. London: Printed by A. Strahan, 1822.

Belden, Mary Megie. *The Dramatic Work of Samuel Foote*. Hamden, CT: Archon Books, 1969.

Bentley, Gerald Eades. *The Profession of Dramatist in Shakespeare's Time, 1590–1642*. Princeton, NJ: Princeton University Press, 1971.

Bernard, John. *Retrospections of the Stage*. 2 vols. London: Henry Colburn & Richard Bentley, 1830.

Boaden, James. *Memoirs of Mrs. Inchbald: including her Familiar Correspondence with the Most Distinguished Persons of her Time. To Which are Added The Massacre, and A Case of Conscience; Now First Published from her Autograph Copies*. 2 vols. London: Richard Bentley, New Burlington Street, 1833.

Bolton, Betsy. "Theorizing Audience and Spectatorial Agency." In *The Oxford Handbook of the Georgian Theatre, 1737–1832*, edited by Julia Swindells and David Francis Taylor, 31–52. New York: Oxford University Press, 2014.

Boyd, Amanda Weldy. *Staging Memory and Materiality in Eighteenth-Century Theatrical Biography*. New York: Anthem Press, 2017.

Bratton, Jacky. *New Readings in Theatre History*. New York: Cambridge University Press, 2003.

Braudy, Leo. *The Frenzy of Renown: Fame & Its History*. New York: Vintage Books, 1997.

Brewer, David A. *The Afterlife of Character, 1726–1825*. Philadelphia: University of Pennsylvania Press, 2005.

Brooks, Douglas A. *From Playhouse to Printing House: Drama and Authorship in Early Modern England*. New York: Cambridge University Press, 2000.

Brown, Laura. *English Dramatic Form, 1660–1760: An Essay in Generic History*. New Haven: Yale University Press, 1981.

Byron, George Gordon, Lord. *Marino Faliero, Doge of Venice. An Historical Tragedy, in Five Acts. With Notes*. London: John Murray, 1821.

Carey, George. *Momus, a Poem; or a Critical Examination into the Merits of the Performers, and Comic Pieces, at the Theatre Royal in the Hay-Market*. London: printed for the Author, and sold by J. Almon, opposite Burlington-House, Piccadilly, and J. Williams, No. 38, next the Mitre Tavern, Fleet-Street, 1767.

Carlson, Marvin. *The Haunted Stage: The Theatre as Memory Machine*. Ann Arbor: University of Michigan Press, 2001.

Chetwood, William Rufus. *A General History of the Stage, from Its Origin in Greece Down to the Present Time*. London: Printed for W. Owen, 1749.

Churchill, Charles. *The Rosciad*. London: Printed for the Author, and sold by W. Flexney, near Gray's-Inn-Gate, Holborn, 1761.

Cibber, Colley. *An Apology for the Life of Colley Cibber: with an Historical View of the Stage during his Own Time*. Edited by B. R. S. Fone. Mineola, NY: Dover Publications, 2000.

"A Collection of Playbills for Theatres mainly in Yorkshire, 1766–1801." 19 vols. Special Collections—Theatre Playbills, York Minster Library, York.

Colman, George, and Bonnell Thornton, *The Connoisseur*, no. 1 (January 31, 1754): 1–6.

Connolly, L. W. *The Censorship of English Drama, 1737–1824*. San Marino, CA: Huntington Library, 1976.

Cooke, William. *Memoirs of Charles Macklin, Comedian, with the Dramatic Characters, Manners, Anecdotes, &c. of the Age in which He Lived*. London: Printed for James Asperne, 1804.

Cooke, William. *Memoirs of Samuel Foote, Esq. with a Collection of his Genuine Bon-Mots, Anecdotes, Opinions, &c. mostly Original. And Three of his Dramatic Pieces,*

Not Published in his Works. 3 vols. London: Printed for Richard Phillips, No. 6, Bridge-Street, Blackfriars, 1805.

Cox, John D., and David Scott Kastan. *A New History of Early English Drama*. New York: Columbia University Press, 1997.

Davies, Thomas. *Memoirs of the Life of David Garrick, Esq. Interspersed with Characters and Anecdotes of His Theatrical Contemporaries. The Whole Forming a History of the Stage, which Includes a Period of Thirty-Six Years*. 2 vols. London: Printed for the Author, and sold at his Shop in Great Russell-street, Covent-Garden, 1780.

Davis-Fisch, Heather. *Loss and Cultural Remains in Performance: The Ghosts of the Franklin Expedition*. New York: Palgrave Macmillan, 2012.

Deazley, Ronan. "Commentary on the Engravers' Act (1735)." In *Primary Sources on Copyright (1450-1900)*, edited by Lionel Bently and Martin Kretschmer (2008), www.copyrighthistory.org

Deazley, Ronan. *Rethinking Copyright: History, Theory, Language*. Northampton, MA: Edward Elgar Publishing, 2006.

Derrida, Jacques. "Archive Fever: A Freudian Impression." Translated by Eric Prenowitz. *Diacritics* 25, no. 2 (Summer 1995): 9–63.

Dibdin, Charles. *A Complete History of the English Stage*. 5 vols. London: Printed for the Author, 1797–1800.

"Died." *Monthly Register and Encyclopedian Magazine* 3, no. 18 (October 1803): 328–29.

Donkin, Ellen. *Getting into the Act: Women Playwrights in London, 1776–1829*. New York: Routledge, 1995.

Downes, John. *Roscius Anglicanus, or an Historical Review of the Stage*. London: Printed and sold by H. Playford, 1708.

Durnford, Charles, and Edward Hyde East. *Reports of Cases Argued and Determined in the Court of King's Bench*. 8 vols. Dublin: Printed for L. White, P. Byrne, and W. Jones, 1793–1800.

Engel, Laura. *Fashioning Celebrity: Eighteenth-Century British Actresses and Strategies for Image-Making*. Columbus: Ohio State University Press, 2011.

Ezell, Margaret. *Social Authorship and the Advent of Print*. Baltimore: Johns Hopkins University Press, 1999.

Fawcett, Julia. *Spectacular Disappearances: Celebrity and Privacy, 1696–1801*. Ann Arbor: University of Michigan Press, 2016.

Fielding, Henry. "Proceedings at the Court of Criticism, Thursday, April 28." *Jacobite's Journal*, April 30, 1748.

Foot, Jesse. *The Life of Arthur Murphy, Esq*. London: Printed for J. Faulder, New Bond Street; by John Nichols and Son, Red Lion Passage, Fleet Street, 1811.

Foote, Samuel. *The Commissary. A Comedy in Three Acts. As it is Performed at the Theatre in the Hay-Market*. London: Printed for P. Vaillant, 1765. 49 1810 7:10, Lewis Walpole Library, Yale University.

Foote, Samuel. *The Englishman in Paris. A Comedy, in Two Acts. As it is performed at the Theatre-Royal in Covent-Garden*. London: Printed for Paul Vaillant, facing Southampton-Street, in the Strand, 1753.

Foote, Samuel. *The Mayor of Garret: a Comedy, in Two Acts. As it is Performed at the Theatre-Royal in Drury-Lane*. London: Printed for P. Vaillant, facing Southampton-Street in the Strand, 1764. 49 1810 5:5, Lewis Walpole Library, Yale University.

Foote, Samuel. *The Minor*. In *Plays by Samuel Foote and Arthur Murphy*. Edited by George Taylor. New York: Cambridge University Press, 1984.

Foote, Samuel. *The Orators. As it is now performing at the New Theatre in the Hay-Market*. London: printed for J. Coote, in Pater-Noster-Row; G. Kearsly, in Ludgate-Street; and T. Davies, in Russel-Street, Covent Garden, 1762.

Foote, Samuel. *The Roman and English Comedy Consider'd and Compar'd. With Remarks on the Suspicious Husband. And an Examen into the Merit of the present Comic Actors*. London: printed for T. Waller in Fleet-Street, 1747.

Foote, Samuel. *The Trial of Samuel Foote, Esq. For a Libel on Peter Paragraph. Performed at the Theatre-Royal in the Haymarket, 1763. Written by Mr. Foote. Printed from his own Hand-writing*. In Tate Wilkinson, *The Wandering Patentee*.

Foucault, Michel. "What Is an Author?" In *Aesthetics, Method, and Epistemology: The Essential Works of Foucault, 1954–1984*, vol. 2, edited by James B. Faubion and translated by Robert Hurley and others, 205–22. New York: New Press, 1998.

Freeman, Lisa. "On the Art of Dramatic Probability: Elizabeth Inchbald's *Remarks for the British Theatre*." *Theatre Survey* 62, no. 2 (May 2021): 163–81.

Gerland, Oliver. "The Haymarket Theatre and Literary Property: Constructing Common Law Playright, 1770–1833." *Theatre Notebook* 69, no. 2 (2015): 74–96.

Greene, Jody. *The Trouble with Ownership: Literary Property and Authorial Liability in England, 1660–1730*. Philadelphia: University of Pennsylvania Press, 2005.

Griffin, Dustin. "The Social World of Authorship 1660–1714." In *The Cambridge History of English Literature, 1660–1780*, edited by John Richetti, 37–60. New York: Cambridge University Press, 2005.

Gross, John. *Shylock: A Legend & Its Legacy*. New York: Simon & Schuster, 1992.

Hammond, Brean. *Professional Imaginative Writing in England, 1670–1740*. Oxford: Clarendon Press, 1997.

Henderson, John. *Letters and Poems, by the Late Mr. John Henderson. With Anecdotes of His Life, by John Ireland*. London: Printed for J. Johnson, 1786.

Highfill, Philip H., Jr., Kalman A. Burnim, and Edward A. Langhans. *A Biographical Dictionary of Actors, Actresses, Musicians, Dancers, Managers, and Other Stage Personnel in London, 1660–1800*. 16 vols. Carbondale: Southern Illinois University Press, 1973-93.

Hogan, Charles Beecher. "One of God Almighty's Unaccountables: Tate Wilkinson of York." In *The Theatrical Manager in Britain and America: Players of a Perilous Game*, edited by Joseph W. Donohue Jr., 63–86. Princeton, NJ: Princeton University Press, 1971.

Holland, Peter. *The Ornament of Action: Text and Performance in Restoration Comedy*. New York: Cambridge University Press, 1979.

Howard, Edward. *The Change of Crowns: A Tragi-Comedy by the Honourable Edward Howard*. Edited by Frederick S. Boas. London: Oxford University Press, 1949.

Hume, Robert D. "Theatre as Property in Eighteenth-Century London." *Journal for Eighteenth-Century Studies* 31, no. 1 (2008): 17–46.

Hunter, J. Paul. "The World as Stage and Closet." In *British Theatre and the Other Arts, 1660–1800*, edited by Shirley Strum Kenny, 271–87. Washington, DC: Folger Shakespeare Library, 1984.

Inchbald, Elizabeth. Autograph Letter Signed to Tate Wilkinson, March 16, [1787]. Osborn Manuscripts, File 7864, Beinecke Rare Books Room, Yale University.

Inchbald, Elizabeth. Autograph letters signed from Mrs. Inchbald to various people [manuscript], 1780–1810. Y.c.1376 (1–14), Folger Shakespeare Library, Washington, D.C.

Inchbald, Elizabeth. *Lovers' Vows. A Play, in Five Acts.* London: Printed for G.G. and J. Robinson, Pater-noster-row, 1798.

Inchbald, Elizabeth. *Remarks for the British Theatre (1806–1809).* Edited by Cecilia Macheski. Delmar, NY: Scholars' Facsimiles & Reprints, 1990.

Jenkins, Annibel. *I'll Tell You What: The Life of Elizabeth Inchbald.* Lexington: University Press of Kentucky, 2003.

Johnson, Nora. *The Actor as Playwright in Early Modern Drama.* New York: Cambridge University Press, 2003.

Johnstone, John, Joseph George Holman, Alexander Pope, Charles Incledon, Joseph S. Munden, John Fawcett, Thomas Knight, and Henry Erskine Johnston. *A Statement of the Differences Subsisting between the Proprietors and Performers of the Theatre-Royal, Covent-Garden.* London: Printed by J. Davis, Chancery-Lane, for W. Miller, Old Bond-Street, 1800.

Joncus, Berta. "'In Wit Superior, as in Fighting': Kitty Clive and the Conquest of a Rival Queen." *Huntington Library Quarterly* 74, no. 1 (2011): 23–42.

Jones, Amelia. "'The Artist Is Present': Artistic Re-enactments and the Impossibility of Presence." *TDR: The Drama Review* 55, no. 1 (Spring 2011): 16–45.

Jones, Robert W. "Texts, Tools, and Things: An Approach to Manuscripts of Richard Brinsley Sheridan's *The School for Scandal*." *Review of English Studies* 66, no. 276 (September 2015): 723–43.

Kahan, Gerald. *George Alexander Stevens and "The Lecture on Heads".* Athens: University of Georgia Press, 1984.

Kenny, Shirley Strum. *The Performers and Their Plays.* New York: Garland Publishing, 1982.

Kenny, Shirley Strum. "The Publication of Plays." In *The London Theatre World, 1660–1800,* edited by Robert D. Hume, 309–36. Carbondale: Southern Illinois University Press, 1980.

Kenrick, William. *Introduction to the School of Shakespeare; Held, on Wednesday Evenings, In the Apollo, at the Devil Tavern, Temple Bar.* London: printed for the Author, and sold by the Booksellers, 1774.

Kewes, Paulina. *Authorship and Appropriation: Writing for the Stage in England, 1660–1710.* Oxford: Clarendon Press, 1998.

Kewes, Paulina. "'[A] Play Which I Presume to Call Original': Appropriation, Creative Genius, and Eighteenth-Century Playwriting." *Studies in the Literary Imagination* 34, no. 1 (Spring 2001): 17–47.

King, Rachael Scarborough. *Writing to the World: Letters and the Origins of Modern Print Genres.* Baltimore: Johns Hopkins University Press, 2018.

Kinservik, Matthew J. "Dialectics of Print and Performance after 1737." In *The Oxford Handbook of the Georgian Theatre, 1737–1832,* edited by Julia Swindells and David Francis Taylor, 123–39. New York: Oxford University Press, 2014.

Kinservik, Matthew J. *Disciplining Satire: The Censorship of Satiric Comedy on the Eighteenth-Century London Stage.* Lewisburg, PA: Bucknell University Press, 2002.

Kinservik, Matthew J. "*Love à la Mode* and Macklin's Return to the London Stage in 1759." *Theatre Survey* 37, no. 2 (1996): 1–22.

Kinservik, Matthew J. "A Sinister *Macbeth*: The Macklin Production of 1773." *Harvard Library Bulletin* 6, no. 1 (1995): 51–76.

Kirkman, James Thomas. *Memoirs of the Life of Charles Macklin, Esq. Principally Compiled from His Own Papers and Memorandums.* 2 vols. London: Printed for Lackington, Allen, and Co., 1799. Theatre Collection f TS 943.2, Houghton Library, Harvard University.

Leigh, Henry James. *The New Rosciad, in the Manner of Churchill: Containing a Judicious, Humorous and Critical Description of our Present Dramatic Characters.* London: Printed for E. Macklew, Bookseller, opposite the Opera-House, Haymarket; and Sold by him, and at Swift's Library, Charles-Street, St. James's-Square, 1785.

Leisenfeld, Vincent J. *The Licensing Act of 1737.* Madison: University of Wisconsin Press, 1984.

L'Estrange, Roger. *Considerations and Proposals in Order to the Regulation of the Press.* London: Printed by A. C., 1663.

Link, Frederick. "Introduction." *The Plays of John O'Keeffe.* New York: Garland, 1981.

Litman, Jessica. "The Invention of Common Law Play Right." *Berkeley Technology Law Journal* 25, no. 3 (2010): 1382–452.

Locke, John. *Two Treatises of Government by John Locke.* Edited by Thomas I. Cook. New York: Hafner, 1947.

Lockwood, Thomas. "Great Off-Stage Performances by James Lacy." *British Journal for Eighteenth-Century Studies* 7, no. 2 (September 1984): 199–210.

Loewenstein, Joseph F. "Legal Proofs and Corrected Readings: Press-Agency and the New Bibliography." In *The Production of English Renaissance Culture*, edited by David Lee Miller, Sharon O'Dair, and Harold Weber, 93–122. Ithaca, NY: Cornell University Press, 1994.

Loewenstein, Joseph F. "The Script in the Marketplace." *Representations* 12 (Fall 1985): 101–14.

The London Stage, 1660-1800: A Calendar of Plays, Entertainments and Afterpieces, Together with Casts, Box-Receipts and Contemporary Comment. Compiled from the Playbills, Newspapers and Theatrical Diaries of the Period. Part 1, 1660-1700, edited by William Van Lennep; part 2, 1700-29, 2 vols., edited by Emmett L. Avery; part 3, 1729–47, 2 vols., edited by Arthur H. Scouten; part 4, 1747-76, 3 vols., edited by George Winchester Stone Jr.; part 5, 1776-1800, 3 vols., edited by Charles Beecher Hogan. Carbondale: Southern Illinois University Press, 1965–68.

Mace, Nancy. "Music Copyright in Late Eighteenth and Early Nineteenth Century Britain." In *Research Handbook on the History of Copyright Law*, edited by Isabella Alexander and H. Tomás Gómez-Arostegui, 139–57. Northampton, MA: Edward Elgar, 2016.

Macklin, Charles. "Autograph letter signed from Charles Macklin, Dublin, to George Colman, Piazza Covent Garden, London [manuscript]," February 17, 1773. Folger Shakespeare Library, Y.c.5380 (5).

Macklin, Charles. "Autograph letter from Charles Macklin to George Colman, London [manuscript]," October 16, 1770. Folger Shakespeare Library, Y.c.5380 (3).

Macklin, Charles. "Autograph letter signed from Charles Macklin, [London?], to Tate Wilkinson, Theatre Royal, York," May 8, 1773. Folger Shakespeare Library, Y.c.5380 (11).

Macklin, Charles. "Commonplace book [manuscript], 1778–1790." Folger Shakespeare Library, M.a.9.

Macklin, Charles. "Letters: to Tate Wilkinson," April 22, 1769. Correspondence of Alexander Dyce and others preserved in the Dyce Collection, MSL/1869/64/103–104, National Art Library, Victoria and Albert Museum, London, UK.

Macklin, Charles. "Letters: to Tate Wilkinson," July 27, 1772. Correspondence of Alexander Dyce and others preserved in the Dyce Collection, MSL/1869/64/103–104, National Art Library, Victoria and Albert Museum, London, UK.

Macklin, Charles. "Proposals to George Colman Esqr. & the other Managers of Covent Garden Theatre." Miscellaneous English Autograph Letters, Egerton MS2334, Archives and Manuscripts, British Library.

Macklin, Charles, and D. Hussey. "Fair Copy Draft Bill introduced in the Court of Chancery in Ireland in *Macklin v. Robert Owenson*." Autograph Papers of Charles Macklin [manuscript], Folger Shakespeare Library, Y.d.515 (1–11).

Marcus, Sharon. *The Drama of Celebrity*. Princeton, NJ: Princeton University Press, 2019.

Masten, Jeffrey. *Textual Intercourse: Collaboration, Authorship, and Sexualities in Renaissance Drama*. New York: Cambridge University Press, 1997.

Mathews, Anne. *The Life and Correspondence of Charles Mathews, the Elder, Comedian*. Edited by Edmund Yates. London: Routledge, Warne, and Routledge, 1860.

Mathews, Anne. *Memoirs of Charles Mathews, Comedian*. 4 vols. London: Richard Bentley, New Burlington Street, Publisher in Ordinary to Her Majesty, 1838.

Mathews, Charles. "Manuscript letter to George Colman," London, July 10, 1807. Betty Wharton collection of theatrical autographs, 1707–1869. Harvard Theatre Collection, Houghton Library, Harvard University, MS Thr 357 (100).

Matthews, W. "The Piracies of Macklin's *Love À-La-Mode*." *Review of English Studies* 10, no. 39 (July 1934): 311–18.

McGill, Meredith. "Copyright and Intellectual Property: The State of the Discipline." *Book History* 16 (2013): 387–427.

Memoirs of the Life and Writings of Samuel Foote, Esq.; the English Aristophanes: to which are added the Bon Mots, Repartees, and Good Things said by that great Wit and Excentrical Genius. London: printed for J. Bew, Paternoster-Row, 1777.

Milhous, Judith, and Robert D. Hume. "Playwrights' Remuneration in Eighteenth-Century London." *Harvard Library Bulletin* 10, nos. 2–3 (1999): 3–90.

Milhous, Judith, and Robert D. Hume. *The Publication of Plays in London, 1660–1800: Playwrights, Publishers, and the Market*. London: British Library, 2015.

Milhous, Judith, and Robert D. Hume. *A Register of English Theatrical Documents, 1660–1737*. 2 vols. Carbondale: Southern Illinois University Press, 1991.

Milhous, Judith, and Robert D. Hume. "Theatrical Custom versus Rights: The Performers' Dispute with the Proprietors of Covent Garden in 1800." *Theatre Notebook* 63, no. 2 (2009): 92–125.

Miller, Derek. *Copyright and the Value of Performance, 1770–1911*. New York: Cambridge University Press, 2018.

Milling, Jane. "'Abominable, Impious, Prophane, Lewd, Immoral': Prosecuting the Actors in Early Eighteenth-Century London." *Theatre Notebook* 61, no. 3 (2007): 132–43.

Moody, Jane. *Illegitimate Theatre in London, 1770–1840*. New York: Cambridge University Press, 2000.

Moody, Jane. "Playbills under House Arrest: A Reply to Richard Schoch, Victorian Theatricalities Forum." *19: Interdisciplinary Studies in the Long Nineteenth Century* 8 (2009): 1–4.

Moody, Jane. "Stolen Identities: Character, Mimicry and the Invention of Samuel Foote." In *Theatre and Celebrity in Britain, 1660–2000*, edited by Mary Luckhurst and Jane Moody, 65–89. New York: Palgrave Macmillan, 2005.

Morash, Chris, and Shaun Richards. *Mapping Irish Theatre: Theories of Space and Place*. New York: Cambridge University Press, 2013.

Mowat, Barbara A. "The Theatre and Literary Culture." In *A New History of Early English Drama*, edited by John D. Cox and David Scott Kastan, 213–30. New York: Columbia University Press, 1997.

"Mr. Elliston for the Representation of Marino Faliero. Court of Chancery, April 27." *The Edinburgh Annual Register, for 1821*. Edinburgh: Printed by James Ballantyne and Co., 1823.

The Multigraph Collective. *Interacting with Print: Elements of Reading in the Era of Print Saturation*. Chicago: University of Chicago Press, 2018.

Murphy, Arthur. "Advertisement." In *Love à la Mode. A Farce. As Performed at the Theatres-Royal, Drury-Lane and Covent-Garden*. London: Printed by John Bell, 1793.

Nachumi, Nora. *Acting Like a Lady: British Women Novelists and the Eighteenth-Century Theatre*. New York: AMS Press, 2008.

Newey, Katherine. "The 1832 Select Committee." In *The Oxford Handbook of the Georgian Theatre, 1737–1832*, edited by Julia Swindells and David Francis Taylor, 140–55. New York: Oxford University Press, 2014.

Nicoll, Allardyce. *A History of Early Eighteenth Century Drama, 1700–1750*. Cambridge: Cambridge University Press, 1925.

Nussbaum, Felicity. *Rival Queens: Actresses, Performance, and the Eighteenth-Century British Theater*. Philadelphia: University of Pennsylvania Press, 2010.

O'Brien, John. *Harlequin Britain: Pantomime and Entertainment, 1690–1760*. Baltimore: Johns Hopkins University Press, 2004.

O'Brien, William. "Manuscript letter to David Garrick, 1767." David Garrick Papers from the Thomas Rackett Collection. James Marshall and Marie-Louise Osborn Collection, Beinecke Rare Book and Manuscript Library, Yale University.

O'Keeffe, John. *The Dramatic Works of John O'Keeffe, Esq. Published Under the Gracious Patronage of His Royal Highness the Prince of Wales. Prepared for the Press by the Author. In Four Volumes*. London: Printed for the Author, by T. Woodfall, 1798. Victoria and Albert Museum, National Art Library Dyce 8vo 7030.

O'Keeffe, John. *The Prisoner at Large: A Comedy. In Two Acts*. London: Printed for G.G.J. and J. Robinson, Paternoster-Row, 1788.

O'Keeffe, John. *Recollections of the Life of John O'Keeffe, Written by Himself*. 2 vols. London: Henry Colburn, New Burlington Street, 1826.

O'Keeffe, John. *Tony Lumpkin in Town*. London: Printed for T. Cadell in the Strand, 1780.

Oliar, Dotan, and Christopher Sprigman. "There's No Free Laugh (Anymore): The Emergence of Intellectual Property Norms and the Transformation of Stand-Up Comedy." *Virginia Law Review* 94, no. 8 (December 2008): 1787–867.

O'Quinn, Daniel. *Entertaining Crisis in the Atlantic Imperium, 1770–1790*. Baltimore: Johns Hopkins University Press, 2011.

Orgel, Stephen. "What Is a Text?" In *Staging the Renaissance: Reinterpretations of Elizabethan and Jacobean Drama*, edited by David Scott Kastan and Peter Stallybrass, 83–87. New York: Routledge, 1991.

O'Shaughnessy, David. "'Rip'ning Buds in Freedom's Field': Staging Irish Improvement in the 1780s." *Journal for Eighteenth-Century Studies* 38, no. 4 (2015): 541–54.

Peake, Richard Brinsley. *Memoirs of the Colman Family, Including their Correspondence with the Most Distinguished Personages of their Time*. 2 vols. London: Richard Bentley, 1841.

Peters, Julie Stone. *Theatre of the Book, 1480–1880: Print, Text, and Performance in Europe*. New York: Oxford University Press, 2000.

Phelan, Peggy. *Unmarked: The Politics of Performance*. New York: Routledge, 1993.

Phillips, Chelsea. "Bodies in Play: Maternity, Repertory, and the Rival *Romeo and Juliet*s, 1748–51." *Theatre Survey* 60, no. 2 (May 2019): 207–36.

Playbills: Drury Lane, Covent Garden, Dublin, Edinburgh, Glasgow, and others, 1748–1778. Lewis Walpole Library, Yale University, Folio 767 P69B W65.

Plumptre, Anne. *The Natural Son; a Play, in five Acts, by Augustus von Kotzebue, Poet Laureat and Director of the Imperial Theatre at Vienna. Being the Original of Lovers' Vows, now Performing, with Universal Applause, at the Theatre Royal, Covent Garden. Translated from the German by Anne Plumptre, (Author of the Rector's Son, Antoinette, &c.) who has prefixed a Preface, Explaining the Alterations in the Representation; and has also annexed A Life of Kotzebue*. London: Printed for R. Phillips, 1798.

Porter, Stephen. *Lovers' Vows, or, the Child of Love. A Play, in Five Acts. Translated from the German of Augustus von Kotzebue: with a Brief Biography of the Author*. London: Printed for J. Parsons, Paternoster-Row, and sold by J. Hatchard, Piccadilly; R.H. Westley, Strand, and may also be had of all booksellers, 1798.

The Present State of the Stage in Great-Britain and Ireland. And the Theatrical Characters of the Principal Performers, in both Kingdoms, Impartially Considered. London: Printed for Paul Vaillant, 1753.

Ragussis, Michael. *Theatrical Nation: Jews and Other Outlandish Englishmen in Georgian Britain*. Philadelphia: University of Pennsylvania Press, 2010.

Report from the Select Committee on Dramatic Literature: with the Minutes of Evidence. London: Ordered, by The House of Commons, to be Printed, 1832.

Ritchie, Leslie. "Pox on Both Your Houses: The Battle of the Romeos." *Eighteenth-Century Fiction* 27, nos. 3–4 (Spring–Summer 2015): 373–93.

Ritchie, Leslie. "The Spouters' Revenge: Apprentice Actors and the Imitation of London's Theatrical Celebrities." *Eighteenth Century: Theory and Interpretation* 53, no. 1 (Spring 2012): 41–71.

Roach, Joseph. *Cities of the Dead: Circum-Atlantic Performance*. New York: Columbia University Press, 1996.

Roach, Joseph. "Public Intimacy: The Prior History of 'It.'" In *Theatre and Celebrity in Britain, 1660–2000*, edited by Mary Luckhurst and Jane Moody, 15–30. New York: Palgrave Macmillan, 2005.

Robertson, Ben P. *Elizabeth Inchbald's Reputation: A Publishing and Reception History*. London: Pickering & Chatto, 2013.

Rogers, C. S., and Betty Rizzo. "Kenrick, William (1729/30–1779)." In *Oxford Dictionary of National Biography*. Oxford University Press, 2004; online edition, January 2008.

Rose, Mark. "The Author as Proprietor: Donaldson v. Becket and the Genealogy of Modern Authorship." *Representations* 23 (Summer 1988): 51–85.

Rose, Mark. *Authors and Owners: The Invention of Copyright*. Cambridge, MA: Harvard University Press, 1993.

Rosenfeld, Sybil. *The York Theatre*. London: Society for Theatre Research, 2001.

Rowe, Nicholas. *The Works of Mr. William Shakespear*. 6 vols. London: Printed for Jacob Tonson, 1709.

Sableman, Mark. "Copyright and Performance Rights in an Online Video World." *Licensing Journal* 35, no. 1 (January 2015): 22–25.

Saunders, J. W. *The Profession of English Letters*. New York: Routledge, 1964.

Schneider, Rebecca. *Performing Remains: Art and War in Times of Theatrical Reenactment*. New York: Routledge, 2011.

Schoch, Richard. "'A Supplement to Public Laws': Arthur Murphy, David Garrick, and Hamlet, with Alterations." *Theatre Journal* 57, no. 1 (March 2005): 21–32.

Schoch, Richard. *Writing the History of the British Stage, 1660–1900*. New York: Cambridge University Press, 2016.

Scrapbook of David Garrick [manuscript], bound ca. 1890. W.b.472, Folger Shakespeare Library.

Shakespeare, William. *The Merchant of Venice*. Edited by Jay Halio. New York: Oxford University Press, 2008.

Sheridan, Richard Brinsley. *The Dramatic Works of Richard Brinsley Sheridan*. Edited by Cecil Price. 2 vols. Oxford: At the Clarendon Press, 1973.

"Sketch of Mr. Foote's Lectures on Oratory, delivering at the Little Theatre in the Haymarket." *London Magazine, or, Gentleman's Monthly Intelligencer* 31 (May 1762): 258–59.

Sketches of Mr. Mathews' Celebrated Lecture on Character, Manners, and Peculiarities, Entitled the Home Circuit; or, Cockney Gleanings. London: published by J. Limbird, 1827.

Stanhope, Philip Dormer, Fourth Earl of Chesterfield. *Miscellaneous Works of the Late Philip Dormer Stanhope, Earl of Chesterfield: Consisting of Letters to his Friends, never before printed, and Various other Articles*. 3 vols. Dublin: printed for Messrs. W. Watson, Whitestone, Sleater, Chamberlaine, Potts . . . , 1777.

Stephens, John Russell. *The Profession of the Playwright: British Theatre, 1800–1900*. New York: Cambridge University Press, 1992.

Stern, Simon. "Copyright, Originality, and the Public Domain in Eighteenth-Century England." In *Originality and Intellectual Property in the French and English Enlightenment*, edited by Reginald McGinnis, 69–101. New York: Routledge, 2009.

Stern, Tiffany. *Rehearsal from Shakespeare to Sheridan*. Oxford: Clarendon Press, 2000.

Straub, Kristina. "The Newspaper 'Trial' of Charles Macklin's Macbeth and the Theatre as Juridical Public Sphere." *Eighteenth-Century Fiction* 27, nos. 3–4 (Spring–Summer 2015): 395–418.

Taylor, David Francis. "Introduction." In *The Oxford Handbook of the Georgian The-*

atre, 1737–1832, edited by Julia Swindells and David Francis Taylor, 1–7. New York: Oxford University Press, 2014.

Taylor, Diana. *The Archive and the Repertoire: Performing Cultural Memory in the Americas.* Durham, NC: Duke University Press, 2003.

Taylor, Diana. "Performance and Intangible Cultural Heritage." In *The Cambridge Companion to Performance Studies,* edited by Tracy C. Davis, 91–106. New York: Cambridge University Press, 2008.

The Theatrical Register containing Candid and Impartial Strictures on the Various Performances at the Theatre-Royal, York. York: Printed by Lucas Lund, in Low-Ousegate, 1788.

Thomas, David. *Restoration and Georgian England, 1660–1788.* New York: Cambridge University Press, 1989.

Tillyard, Stella. "Celebrity in 18th-Century London." *History Today* 55 (June 2005): 20–27.

Trefman, Simon. *Sam. Foote, Comedian, 1720–1777.* New York: New York University Press, 1971.

Vareschi, Mark, and Mattie Burkert. "Archives, Numbers, Meaning: The Eighteenth-Century Playbill at Scale." *Theatre Journal* 68, no. 4 (December 2016): 597–613.

Victor, Benjamin. *The History of the Theatres of London, from the Year 1760 to the Present Time.* London: printed for T. Becket, in the Strand, 1771.

Wessel, Jane. "'My Other Folks' Heads': Reproducible Identities and Literary Property on the Eighteenth-Century Stage." *Eighteenth-Century Studies* 53, no. 2 (Winter 2020): 279–97.

West, William W. "Intertheatricality." In *Early Modern Theatricality,* edited by Henry S. Turner, 151–72. New York: Oxford University Press, 2013.

Wilkinson, Tate. "Manuscript Letter to Charles Macklin," September 30, 1772. Lewis Walpole Library, Yale University.

Wilkinson, Tate. *Memoirs of his Own Life, by Tate Wilkinson, Patentee of the Theatres-Royal, York & Hull.* 4 vols. York: Printed for the Author, by Wilson, Spence, and Mawman, 1790.

Wilkinson, Tate. *The Wandering Patentee; or, a History of the Yorkshire Theatres, from 1770 to the Present Time: Interspersed with Anecdotes Respecting Most of the Performers in the Three Kingdoms, from 1765 to 1795.* 4 vols. York: printed for the author, by Wilson, Spence, and Mawman, 1795.

Worthen, W. B. "Intoxicating Rhythms: Or, Shakespeare, Literary Drama, and Performance (Studies)." *Shakespeare Quarterly* 62, no. 3 (2011): 309–39.

Young, Edward. *Conjectures on Original Composition. In a Letter to the Author of Sir Charles Grandison.* London: Printed for A. Millar, in The Strand; and R. and J. Dodsley, in Pall-Mall, 1759.

NEWSPAPERS AND PERIODICALS CITED AND CONSULTED

Courier and Evening Gazette
Daily Gazetteer
English review, or, An abstract of English and Foreign Literature
Gazetteer and New Daily Advertiser
General Advertiser

Hibernian Journal
Literary Chronicle and Weekly Review
Lloyd's Evening Post
London Chronicle and Universal Evening Post
London Daily Advertiser
London Daily Post and General Advertiser
London Evening Post
Middlesex Journal or Universal Evening Post
Morning Chronicle and London Advertiser
Morning Herald
Morning Post and Daily Advertiser
Morning Post and Gazetteer
New Monthly Magazine and Literary Journal
Oracle and Public Advertiser
Read's Weekly Journal
True Briton
Whitehall Evening Post
World and Fashionable Advertiser

Index

Italics indicate photographs or figures.

O'Keefe, John, works by:
  The Agreeable Surprise, 82, 84, 101,
    116, *118*, 138, 140, 141, 142, 144, 145,
    147, 154, 188n87, 189n102
  The Banditti, 141
  The Birthday, 189n100
  The Castle of Andalusia, 188n90,
    189n92, 189n96
  The Dead Alive, 116, 140, 144, 147,
    188n87
  The Dramatic Works, 11, 19, 82, 116–17,
    118, 143–48, 185n6, 188n90
  The Farmer, 138, 189n96
  Fontainebleau, 188n90, 189n92
  The Highland Reel, 188n90
  The Lie of the Day, 147
  The Little Hunchback, 143
  The London Hermit, 143
  Love in a Camp, 140, 188n90
  Modern Antiques, 188n90
  Omai, 189n100
  Peeping Tom, 116, 138, 140, 144, 147,
    188n90
  The Poor Soldier, 138, 188n90, 189n92,
    189n96
  The Positive Man, 188n90
  The Prisoner at Large, 142–43, 188n89
  *Recollections of the Life of John
    O'Keeffe*, 2–3, 19, 82, 117, 139, 144–
    46, 189n94, 189n96, 189n99
  The Son-in-Law, 82, 116, 138–42, 144,
    145, 147, 188n84
  Sprigs of Laurel, 143, 188n90
  Tony Lumpkin in Town, 137–39,
    188n72, 188n84, 189n100
  The Toy, 189n92
  The Wicklow Mountains, 146
  Wild Oats, 138, 189n92
  The World in a Village, 143
  The Young Quaker, 116, 140, 141, 144,
    145, 147, 188n90, 189n96
Oliar, Dotan, 62, 173n101
O'Quinn, Daniel, 174n18
orality:
  and literary property, 85
  oral publication, 37
  and print, 38

repetition from memory, 85–86
  transitory performance vs. print, 52
Orgel, Stephen, 176n74
originality:
  and authorship, 1, 30, 124, 165n21
  and interpretation in acting, 30, 32,
    36–37
  and mimicry, 64, 68, 69, 96
O'Shaughnessy, David, 138
Owenson, Robert, 39–40, 43

Palmer, John (actor), 186n36
Palmer, John (manager, Bath), 128, 131,
    186n36
part possession, 11–13, 16, 22, 23, 25–30,
    35–37
  and continuity of performance, 25
  and dramatic literary property, 24, 37
  criticism of, 27, 28
  end of practice, 27–28
  and repertory, 25
  See also Garrick, David; Macklin,
    Charles
patents, royal:
  Charles II grants, 10
  division of the repertory, 11, 12, 15,
    25, 39
  duopoly (Covent Garden and Drury
    Lane Theatres), 50, 51, 55, 157, 159,
    164n13
  and Foote, 50–55, 70, 79, 104, 149
  and legitimate drama, 46–47, 50,
    191n20
  and the Little Theatre in the Haymar-
    ket, 70–71, 79, 104, 149
  provincial theaters with, 12, 97
  Wilkinson's theaters in Hull and
    York, 97–98
Peake, Richard Brinsley, 137, 145, 148
performance, 3, 11, 74, 157, 163n7
  continuity of performance, 25, 92
  as creative labor, 151
  difficult to regulate, 48
  dramatists perform ownership, 4–5,
    16, 19, 20, 23, 48, 120, 159
  incorporated into literary criticism,
    110